ILLINOIS POLITICS AND GOVERNMENT

Politics and Governments
of the American States

General Editor

John Kincaid
Robert B. & Helen S. Meyner Center
for the Study of State and Local
Government, Lafayette College

Founding Editor

Daniel J. Elazar
Temple University

Editorial Advisory Board

Thad L. Beyle
University of North Carolina
at Chapel Hill

Diane D. Blair
University of Arkansas

Ellis Katz
Temple University

Charles Press
Michigan State University

Stephen L. Schechter
Russell Sage College

Published by the University of
Nebraska Press in association
with the Center for the Study
of Federalism and the
Robert B. and Helen S. Meyner Center
for the Study of State and Local
Government, Lafayette College

SAMUEL K. GOVE AND JAMES D. NOWLAN

Illinois Politics & Government

THE EXPANDING METROPOLITAN FRONTIER

UNIVERSITY OF NEBRASKA PRESS

LINCOLN AND LONDON

⊛ The paper in this book
meets the minimum requirements of
American National Standard
for Information Sciences–Permanence of
Paper for Printed Library Materials,
ANSI Z39.48-1984.

Library of Congress
Cataloging-in-Publication Data
Gove, Samuel Kimball.
Illinois politics and government :
the expanding metropolitan frontier /
Samuel K. Gove and James D. Nowlan.
p.   cm.—(Politics and governments
of the American states)
Includes bibliographical references and index.
ISBN 0-8032-2120-7 (cloth : alk. paper).–
ISBN 0-8032-7014-3 (pbk : alk. paper)
1. Illinois–Politics and government–1951–
I. Nowlan, James Dunlap, 1941–
II. Title.   III. Series.
JK5716.G66   1996
320.9773'09'045.DC20
95-46017
CIP

CONTENTS

TABLES, MAPS, AND FIGURES

JOHN KINCAID

Series Preface

The purpose of this series is to provide information and interesting books on the politics and governments of the fifty American states, books that are of value not only to the student of government but also to the general citizens who want greater insight into the past and present civic life of their own states and of other states in the federal union. The role of the states in governing America is among the least well known of all the 85,006 governments in the United States. The national media focus attention on the federal government in Washington DC and local media focus attention on local government. Meanwhile, except when there is a scandal or a proposed tax increase, the workings of state government remain something of a mystery to many citizens—out of sight, out of mind.

In many respects, however, the states have been, and continue to be, the most important governments in the American political system. They are the main building blocks and chief organizing governments of the whole system. The states are the constituent governments of the federal union, and it is through the states that citizens gain representation in the national government. The national government is one of limited, delegated powers; all other powers are possessed by the states and their citizens. At the same time, the states are the empowering governments for the nation's 84,955 local governments—counties, municipalities, townships, school districts, and special districts. As such, states provide for one of the most essential and ancient elements of freedom and democracy, the right of local self-government.

Although, for many citizens, the most visible aspects of state government are state universities, some of which are the most prestigious in the world, and state highway patrol officers, with their radar guns and handy ticket books, state governments provide for nearly all domestic public services.

Whether elements of those services are enacted or partly funded by the federal government and actually carried out by local governments, it is state government that has the ultimate responsibility for ensuring that Americans are well served by all their governments. In so doing, all of the American states are more democratic, more prosperous, and better governed than most of the world's nation-states.

This is a particularly timely period in which to publish a series of books on the governments and politics of each of the fifty states. Once viewed as the "fallen arches" of the federal system, states today are increasingly seen as energetic, innovative, and fiscally responsible. Some states, of course, perform better than others, but that is to be expected in a federal system. Each state is unique in its own right. It is our hope that this series will shed light on the public life of each state and that, taken together, the books will contribute to a better, more informed understanding of the states themselves and of their often pivotal roles in the world's first and oldest continental-sized federal democracy.

DANIEL J. ELAZAR

Series Introduction

The American domain is given form and character as a federal union of fifty different states whose institutions order the American landscape. The existence of these states made possible the emergence of a nation where liberty, not despotism, reigns and self-government is the first principle of order. The great American republic was born in its states, as its very name signifies. America's first founding was repeated on thirteen separate occasions over 125 years, from Virginia in 1607 to Georgia in 1732. Each colony became a self-governing commonwealth. Its revolution and second founding was made by those commonwealths, now states, acting in congress, and its constitution was written together and adopted separately. As the American tide rolled westward from the Atlantic coast, it absorbed new territories by organizing thirty-seven more states over the next 169 years.

Most of the American states are larger and better developed than most of the world's nations. Territorially, Illinois is a medium-sized state, but in population and gross domestic product it ranks with the larger nations of the world and is a small power in its own right.

Illinois stands at the geohistorical center of the United States, crossed by the great waves of migration that spread settlements across the country in the late eighteenth and nineteenth centuries from the middle states, the South, and New England, reinforced by the great migrational streams from Europe in the nineteenth century and of African Americans, Hispanics, and Asians in the twentieth. Its north was settled as part of greater New England, its central area marks the end of the eastern big woods and the eastern beginning of the western prairie plains, and its southern third, which stretches as far south as Virginia and North Carolina, attracted southern settlers accordingly. Although Illinois is part of the Old Northwest or, if one prefers, the Near West, the three great spheres into which the United States is divided, the Greater Northeast, the Greater South, and the Greater West, came together in the state.

The American states exist because each is a unique civil society within their common American culture. First given political form, they then acquired their other characteristics. Each has its own constitution and laws, its own political culture and history, its own relationship to the federal union.

It is in and through the states, no less than the nation, that the great themes of American life play themselves out. The advancing frontier and the continuing experience of Americans as a frontier people, the drama of American ethnic blending, the tragedy of slavery and racial discrimination, all have found their expression in the states.

Some states began as commonwealths devoted to establishing model societies based on a religiously informed vision (Massachusetts, Connecticut, Rhode Island). At the other end of the spectrum, Hawaii is a transformed pagan monarchy. At least three were independent for a significant period of time (Hawaii, Texas, and Vermont). Others were created from nothing by hardly more than a stroke of the pen (the Dakotas, Idaho, Nevada). Several are permanently bilingual (California, Louisiana, New Mexico). Each has its own landscape and geographic configuration, which time and history transform into a specific geohistorical location. In short, the diversity of the American people is expressed in no small measure through their states, the politics and government of each of which have their own fascination.

Illinois Politics and Government is the fifteenth book in the Center for the Study of Federalism and University of Nebraska Press series Politics and Governments of the American States. The aim of the series is to provide books on the politics and government of the individual states of the United States that will appeal to three audiences: political scientists, their students, and the wider public in each state. Each volume in the series examines the specific character of one of them, looking at the state as a polity—its political culture, traditions and practices, constituencies and interest groups, constitutional and institutional frameworks.

Each book in the series reviews the political development of the state to demonstrate how its political institutions and characteristics have evolved from the first settlement to the present, presenting the state in the context of the nation and section of which it is a part, and reviewing the roles and relations of the state vis-à-vis its sister states and the federal government. The state's constitutional history, its traditions of constitution making and constitutional change, is examined and related to the workings of the state's political institutions and processes. State-local relations, local government, and community politics are examined. Finally, each volume reviews the state's policy concerns and their implementation from the budgetary process to particular substantive policies. Each book concludes by summarizing the principal themes and findings to draw conclusions about the current state of the state, its continuing traditions, and emerging issues. Each volume also contains a bibliographic survey of the existing literature on the state and a guide to the use of that literature and state government documents in learning more about the state and political system. Although the books in the series are not expected to be uniform, all focus on the common themes of federalism, constitutionalism, political culture, and the continuing American frontier, to provide a framework within which to consider the institutions, routines, and processes of state government and politics.

FEDERALISM

Both the greatest conflicts of American history and the most prosaic day-to-day operations of American government are closely intertwined with American federalism—the form of American government (in the eighteenth-century sense of the term, which includes both structure and process). American federalism has been characterized by several basic tensions. One is between state sovereignty—the view that in a proper federal system, authority and power over most domestic affairs should be in the hands of the states—and national supremacy—the view that the federal government has a significant role to play in domestic matters affecting the national interest. The other tension is between dual federalism—the idea that a federal system functions best when the federal government and the states function as separately as possible, each in its own sphere—and cooperative federalism—the view that federalism works best when the federal government and the states, while preserving their own institutions, cooperate closely on the implementation of joint or shared programs.

Politically, Illinois has long been one of the key states in the federal system. In many respects its voting in federal elections most closely approximates that of the nation as a whole, a reflection of its geohistorical and cultural location. Carved out of the public domain of the Old Northwest and shaped by the Northwest Ordinance of 1787, Illinois was one of the cornerstones of the then new doctrine of federal liberty through a new nationalism.

Although divided internally by the slavery controversy, once the Civil

War broke out Illinois was a bulwark of the Union, and furnished so many of the leaders of the struggle to preserve what Abraham Lincoln felicitously referred to as "the constitution, the Union, and the liberties of the people." In the forefront of national development in the nineteenth century, Illinois remained a major political power within the Union at least through the 1960s and still carries considerable weight. As a midwestern state, however, it has received proportionately little in the way of federal benefits since the land grant era.

In sum, Illinois has been more of a giver than a taker and has benefited politically and economically in other ways from its influence in Washington. Its location gave it major transportation advantages, both in the days of the railroads and in the airways of our time. The railroads brought federal grants-in-aid and contracts, while aviation has brought different forms of federal assistance. But Illinois remains relatively less dependent on the federal government than many other states.

CONSTITUTIONALISM

The American constitutional tradition grows out of the Whig understanding that civil societies are founded by political covenant, entered into by the first founders and reaffirmed by subsequent generations, through which the powers of government are delineated and limited and the rights of the constituting members clearly proclaimed in such a way as to provide moral and practical restraints on governmental institutions. That constitutional tradition was modified by the federalists, who accepted its fundamental principals but strengthened the institutional framework designed to provide energy in government while maintaining the checks and balances they saw as needed to preserve liberty and republican government. At the same time, they turned nonbinding declarations of rights into enforceable constitutional articles.

American state constitutions reflect a melding of these two traditions. Under the U.S. Constitution, each state is free to adopt its own constitution, provided that it establishes a republican form of government. Some states have adopted highly succinct constitutions, as did the Vermont Constitution of 1793 with 6,600 words that is still in effect with only fifty-two amendments. Others are just the opposite, for example, Georgia's Ninth Constitution, adopted in 1976, which has 583,000 words.

State constitutions are potentially far more comprehensive than the federal Constitution, which is one of limited, delegated powers. Because states are plenary governments, they automatically possess all powers not specifically denied them by the U.S. Constitution or their citizens. Consequently, a state constitution must be explicit about limiting and defining the scope of governmental powers, especially on behalf of individual liberty. So state constitutions normally include an explicit declaration of rights, almost invariably broader than the first ten amendments to the U.S. Constitution.

The detailed specificity of state constitutions affects the way they shape each state's governmental system and patterns of political behavior. Unlike the open-endedness and ambiguity of many portions of the U.S. Constitution, which allow for considerable interpretative development, state organs, including state supreme courts, generally hew closely to the letter of their constitutions because they must. This means that formal change of the constitutional document occurs more frequently through constitutional amendment whether initiated by the legislature, special constitutional commissions, constitutional conventions, or direct action by the voters, and, in a number of states, the periodic writing of new constitutions. As a result, state constitutions have come to reflect quite explicitly the changing conceptions of government which have developed over the course of American history.

Overall, six different state constitutional patterns have developed. One is the commonwealth pattern, developed in New England, which emphasizes Whig ideas of the constitution as a philosophic document designed first and foremost to set a direction for civil society and to express and institutionalize a theory of republican government. A second is the constitutional pattern of the commercial republic. The constitutions fitting this pattern reflect a series of compromises required by the conflict of many strong ethnic groups and commercial interests generated by the flow of heterogeneous streams of migrants into particular states and the early development of large commercial and industrial cities in those states.

The third is that found in the South and which can be described as the southern contractual pattern. Southern state constitutions are used as instruments to set explicit terms governing the relationship between polity and society, such as those which protected slavery or racial segregation, or those which sought to diffuse the formal allocation of authority to accommodate the swings between oligarchy and factionalism characteristic of southern state politics. Of all the southern states, only Louisiana stands somewhat outside this pattern because its legal system was founded on the French civil code. Its constitutions have been codes—long, highly explicit documents that form a pattern in and of themselves.

A fifth pattern is that found frequently in the states of the Far West, where the state constitution is first and foremost a frame of government explicitly reflecting the republican and democratic principles dominant in the nation in the late nineteenth century but emphasizing the structure of state government and the distribution of powers within that structure in a direct, businesslike manner. Finally, the two newest states, Alaska and Hawaii, have adopted constitutions following the managerial pattern developed and promoted by twentieth-century constitutional reform movements in the United States. Those constitutions are characterized by conciseness, broad grants of power to the executive branch, and relatively few structural restrictions on the legislature. They emphasize natural resource conservation and social legislation.

Illinois's constitutions have been of the second pattern because Illinois seems to have been destined to be a commercial republic from the first. From its 1818 constitution onward, which was drafted by its initial settlers, principally from the South, the Illinois constitution kept that frame of government basis and added to it the necessary compromises that came with acquiring a very mixed population with strong commercial goals. Illinois's 1848 constitution implicitly rested on the new party system and its politics as well as a series of political compromises between New Englanders who settled in the north and west of the state and southerners who had settled in its southern third and the Illinois River valley. The 1870 constitution represented the apogee of the state's north-south compromises and its commitment to commercial interests.

Although the 1970 constitutional reformers were strongly pulled by the managerial models then in vogue in the United States, the state's strong and highly party-oriented political culture, so well described in this volume, functioned as a corrective to that tendency. This led to a compromise between the political and managerial approach in the document. Prior and subsequent constitutional reforms in the post–World War II period have also followed along these lines.

THE CONTINUING AMERICAN FRONTIER

For Americans, the very word *frontier* conjures up the images of the rural-land frontier of yesteryear—of explorers and mountain men, of cowboys and Indians, of brave pioneers pushing their way west in the face of natural obstacles. Later, Americans' picture of the frontier was expanded to include the inventors, the railroad builders, and the captains of industry who created the urban-industrial frontier. Recently television has begun to celebrate the entrepreneurial ventures of the automobile and oil industries, portraying the magnates of those industries and their families in the same larger-than-life frame as once was done for the heroes of that first frontier.

As is so often the case, the media responsible for determining and catering to popular taste tell us a great deal about ourselves. The United States was founded with a rural-land frontier that persisted until World War I, more or less, spreading farms, ranches, mines, and towns across the land. Early in the nineteenth century, the rural-land frontier generated the urban frontier based on industrial development. The generation of new wealth through industrialization transformed cities from mere regional service centers into generators of wealth in their own right. That frontier persisted for more than one hundred years as a major force in American society as a whole and perhaps another sixty years as a major force in various parts of the country. The population movements and attendant growth on the urban-industrial frontier brought about the effective settlement of the United States in freestanding cities from coast to coast.

Between the world wars, the urban-industrial frontier gave birth in turn to a third frontier stage, one based on the new technologies of electronic communication, the internal combustion engine, the airplane, synthetics, and petrochemicals. These new technologies transformed every aspect of life and turned urbanization into metropolitanization. This third frontier stage generated a third settlement of the United States, this time in metropolitan regions from coast to coast, involving a mass migration of tens of millions of Americans in search of opportunity on the suburban frontier.

In the 1970s, despite the widespread "limits of growth" rhetoric, a fourth frontier stage was opened in the form of the rurban, or citybelt-cybernetic, frontier generated by the metropolitan-technological frontier just as the latter had been generated by its predecessor.

The rurban-cybernetic frontier first emerged in the Northeast, as did its predecessors, as the Atlantic Coast metropolitan regions merged into one another to form a six-hundred-mile-long megalopolis—a matrix of urban and suburban settlements in which the older central cities yielded importance if not prominence to smaller ones. It was a sign of the times that the computer was conceived at MIT in Cambridge, first built at the University of Illinois in Urbana, and developed at IBM in White Plains, three medium-sized cities that have become special centers in their own right. This in itself is a reflection of the two primary characteristics of the new frontier. The new loci of settlement are in medium-sized and small cities and in the rural interstices of the megalopolis.

The spreading use of computer technology is the most direct manifestation of the cybernetic tools that make such citybelts possible. Both the revival of small cities and the shifting of population growth into rural areas are as much a product of long-distance direct dialing, the fax, and the Internet as they are of the continued American longing for small town or country living. The new rurban-cybernetic frontier is finding its true form in the South and West, where these citybelt matrices are not being built on the collapse of earlier forms but are developing as an original form. The present sunbelt frontier—strung out along the Gulf Coast, the southwestern desert, and the fringes of the California mountains—is classically megalopolitan in citybelt form and cybernetic with its aerospace-related industries and sunbelt living made possible by air conditioning and the new telecommunications.

The continuing American frontier has all the characteristics of a chain reaction. In a land of great opportunity, each frontier, once opened, has generated its successor and, in turn, has been replaced by it. Each frontier has created a new America with new opportunities, new patterns of settlement, new occupations, new challenges, and new problems. As a result, the central political problem of growth is not simply how to handle the physical changes brought by each frontier, real as they are. It is how to accommodate newness, population turnover, and transience as a way of life. That is the American frontier situation.

Illinois, located as it has been in the mainstream of American life since it was settled, has passed through or entered each of the four frontier stages in proper time, has capitalized on each in turn, and has developed accordingly. Indeed, the history of Illinois is exemplary of each of the four stages, and Illinois has been a pioneer on all of them. On the rural-land frontier it initiated settlement of the western prairie-plains, and its settlers and entrepreneurs were responsible for many of the major inventions that made that settlement possible. Illinois became one of the great centers of the urban-industrial frontier, in industrial development and in commercial techniques to maximize the benefits of that development. Illinois then became one of the great centers of the metropolitan-technological frontier, both in Chicago and the collar counties surrounding it, representing from one-half to two-thirds of the state's population at different times, and in its medium-sized and smaller metropolitan areas. Much of the technology of the rurban-cybernetic frontier was initially developed in Illinois, often at its universities. In all of these Illinois has been a major pioneer and entrepreneur and each in turn has reshaped the state.

THE PERSISTENCE OF SECTIONALISM

Sectionalism—the expression of social, economic, and especially political differences along geographic lines—is part and parcel of American political life. The more or less permanent political ties that link groups of contiguous states together as sections reflect the ways in which local conditions and differences in political culture modify the impact of the frontier. This overall sectional pattern reflects the interaction of the three basic factors. The original sections were produced by the variations in the impact of the rural-land frontier on different geographic segments of the country. They, in turn, have been modified by the pressures generated by the various frontier stages. As a result, sectionalism is not the same as regionalism. The latter is essentially a phenomenon—often transient—that brings adjacent state, substate, or interstate areas together because of immediate and specific common interests. The sections are not homogeneous socioeconomic units sharing a common character across state lines but complex entities combining highly diverse states and communities with common political interests that generally complement one another socially and economically.

Illinois, given first form by the Northwest Ordinances of 1785 and 1787, has from the first been part of the Old Northwest. Although its narrower sectional position has remained as it began, because of the state's geohistorical location and in particular the growth of Chicago, Illinois, became the cornerstone of the greater West, stretching westward at least to the Rocky Mountains if not to the Pacific Ocean and, more narrowly, what has become known as the Middle West. Throughout much of the nineteenth century Chicago was the entrepôt of the greater West and to this day remains its greatest city.

Intrasectional conflicts often exist, but they do not detract from the long-term sectional community of interest. More important for our purposes, certain common sectional bonds give the states of each section a special relationship to national politics. This is particularly true in connection with those specific political issues that are of sectional importance, such as the race issue in the South, the problems of the megalopolis in the Northeast, and the problems of agriculture and agribusiness in the West.

The nation's sectional alignments are rooted in the three great historical, cultural, and economic spheres into which the country is divided. The greater Northeast includes all those states north of the Ohio and Potomac rivers and east of Lake Michigan gathered in these sections, New England, Middle Atlantic, and Near West. The greater South includes the states below that line but east of the Mississippi—the Upper and Lower South plus Missouri, Arkansas, Louisiana, Maine, and Texas. All the rest of the states compose the greater West, both Northwest and Far West.

From the New Deal years through the 1960s, Americans' understanding of sectionalism was submerged by their concern with urban-oriented socioeconomic categories such as the struggle between labor and management or between the haves and have-nots in the big cities. Even the racial issue, once the hallmark of the greater South, began to be perceived in nonsectional terms as a result of black immigration northward. This is not to say that sectionalism ceased to exist as a vital force, only that it was little noted in those years.

Beginning in the 1970s, however, there was a resurgence of sectional feeling as economic social cleavages increasingly came to follow sectional lines. The sunbelt-frostbelt division is the prime example of this new sectionalism. "Sunbelt" is the new code word for the Lower South, western South, and Far West; "frostbelt," later replaced by "rust belt," is the code word for the New England, Middle Atlantic, and Great Lakes (near western) states. Illinois is not only part of the frostbelt but very much a part of the rust belt with the economy of Chicago and its medium-sized cities badly hit by obsolescence as the successes of the urban-industrial frontier receded into history, forcing Illinois to face up to new problems of economic development and the political conflicts that flow from them.

THE VITAL ROLE OF POLITICAL CULTURE

The United States as a whole shares a general political culture that is rooted in two contrasting conceptions of the American polity that can be traced back to the earliest settlement of the country. In the first, the polity is conceived as a marketplace in which the primary public relationships are products of bargaining among individuals and groups acting primarily out of self-interest. In the second, the polity is conceived to be a commonwealth, in which the whole people have an undivided interest and the citizens cooperate in an effort to create and maintain the best government in order to implement certain shared moral principles. The influence of these two conceptions can be felt through that American political history, sometimes in conflict and sometimes complementing each other.

This general political culture is a synthesis of three major political subcultures—individualistic, moralistic, and traditionalistic. Each of the three reflects its own particular synthesis of the marketplace and the commonwealth. All three are of nationwide proportions, having spread, in the course of time, from coast to coast. At the same time each subculture is strongly tied to specific sections of the country, reflecting the streams and currents of migration that have carried people of different origins and backgrounds across the continent in more or less orderly patterns. Considering their central characteristics, the three may be called *individualistic, moralistic,* and *traditionalistic.* Each of the three reflects its own particular synthesis of the marketplace and the commonwealth.

The individualistic political culture emphasizes the democratic order as a marketplace in which government is instituted for strictly utilitarian reasons to handle those functions demanded by the people it is established to serve. Beyond the commitment to an open market, a government need not have any direct concern with questions of the good society, except insofar as it may be used to advance some common view formulated outside the political arena just as it serves other functions. Since the individualistic political culture emphasizes the centrality of private concerns, it places a premium on limiting community intervention—whether governmental or nongovernmental —into private activities to the minimum necessary to keep the marketplace in proper working order.

The character of political participation in the individualistic political culture reflects this. Politics is just another means by which individuals may improve themselves socially and economically, a business like any other, competing for talent and offering rewards to those who take it up as a career. Those individuals who choose political careers may rise by providing the governmental services demanded of them and, in return, may expect to be adequately compensated for their efforts. Interpretations of officeholders' obligations under this arrangement vary. Where the norms are high, such people are expected to provide high-quality public services in return for appropriate rewards. In other cases, an officeholder's primary responsibility is to serve himself and those who have supported him directly, favoring them even at the expense of the public.

Political life within the individualistic political culture is based on a system of mutual obligations rooted in personal relationships. Political parties serve as the major vehicles for maintaining the obligational network, and party regularity is the means for coordinating individual enterprise in the political arena and is the one way of preventing individualism in politics from running wild.

Since the individualistic political culture eschews ideological concerns in its businesslike conception of politics, both politicians and citizens consider political activity to be specialized, essentially the province of professionals, of minimum and passing concern to the public, and with no place for amateurs to play an active role. Furthermore, there is a strong tendency among the public to believe that politics is a dirty—if necessary—business, better left to those who are willing to soil themselves by engaging in it. In practice, then, where the individualistic political culture is dominant, there is likely to be an easy attitude toward the limits of the professionals' perquisites. Because a fair amount of corruption is expected in the normal course of events, there is relatively little popular excitement when any is found, unless it is of an extraordinary character. It is as if the public is willing to pay a surcharge for services rendered and rebels only when it feels the surcharge has become too heavy. (Of course, the judgments as to what is normal and what is extraordinary are themselves subjective and culturally conditioned.)

Public officials, committed to giving the public what it wants, normally will initiate new programs only when they perceive an overwhelming public demand for them to act. The individualistic political culture is ambivalent about the place of bureaucracy in the political order. Bureaucratic methods of operation fly in the face of the favor system, yet organizational efficiency can be used by those seeking to master the market.

To the extent that the marketplace provides the model for public relationships in American civil society, all Americans share some of the attitudes that are of first importance in the individualistic political culture. At the same time, substantial segments of the American people operate politically within the framework of two political cultures.

The moralistic political culture emphasizes the commonwealth as the basis for democratic government. Politics is considered one of the great activities of humanity in its search for the good society—a struggle for power, it is true, but also an effort to exercise power for the betterment of the commonwealth. Consequently, both the general public and the politicians conceive of politics as a public activity centered on some notion of the public good and properly devoted to the advancement of the public interest.

There is a general commitment to using communal—preferably nongovernmental, but governmental if necessary—power to intervene in the sphere of private activities when it is considered necessary to do so for the public good or the well-being of the community. Accordingly, issues have an important place in the moralistic style of politics, functioning to set the tone for political concern. Government is considered a positive instrument with a responsibility to promote the general welfare, though definitions of what its positive role should be may vary considerably from era to era.

Politics is ideally a matter of concern for every citizen. Government service is public service, placing moral obligations on those who serve in government more demanding than those of the marketplace. Politics is not considered a legitimate realm for private economic enrichment. A politician is not expected to profit from political activity and in fact is held suspect if he or she does.

The concept of serving the commonwealth is at the core of all political relationships, and politicians are expected to adhere to it even at the expense of individual loyalties and political friendships. Political parties are considered useful political devices but are not valued for their own sakes. Regular party ties can be abandoned with relative impunity for third parties, special local parties, nonpartisan systems, or the opposition party if such changes are believed helpful in gaining larger political goals.

In practice, where the moralistic political culture is dominant today, there is considerably more amateur participation in politics. There is also much less of what Americans consider corruption in government and less tolerance of actions that are considered corrupt, so politics does not have the taint it so often bears in the individualistic environment.

By virtue of its fundamental outlook, the moralistic political culture creates a greater commitment to active government intervention in the economic and social life of the community. At the same time, its strong commitment to communitarianism tends to keep government intervention local wherever possible. Public officials will themselves initiate new government activities in an effort to come to grips with problems as yet unperceived by a majority of the citizenry.

The moralistic political culture's major difficulty with bureaucracy lies in the potential conflict between communitarian principles and large-scale organization. Otherwise, the notion of a politically neutral administrative system is attractive. Where merit systems are instituted, they tend to be rigidly maintained.

The traditionalistic political culture is rooted in an ambivalent attitude toward the marketplace, coupled with a paternalistic and elitist conception of the commonwealth. It reflects an older attitude that accepts a substantially hierarchical society as part of the ordered nature of things, authorizing and expecting those at the top of the social structure to take a special and dominant role in government. The traditionalistic political culture accepts government as an actor with a positive role in the community, but it tries to limit that role to securing the continued maintenance of the existing social order. To do so, it functions to confine real political power to a relatively small and self-perpetuating group drawn from an established elite who often inherit their right to govern through family ties or social position. Those who do not have a definite role to play in politics are not expected to be even minimally active as citizens. In many cases, they are not even expected to vote. Those active in politics are expected to benefit personally from their activity, although not necessarily by direct pecuniary gain.

Political parties are not important in traditionalistic political cultures because they encourage a degree of openness that goes against the grain of an elitist political order. Political competition is expressed through factions, an extension of the personal politics characteristic of the system. Hence political systems within the culture tend to have loose one-party systems if they have political parties at all. Political leaders play conservative and custodial rather than initiatory roles unless pressed strongly from the outside.

Traditionalistic political cultures tend to be antibureaucratic. Bureaucracy by its very nature interferes with the fine web of social relationships that lies at the root of the political system. Where bureaucracy is introduced, it is generally confined to ministerial functions under the aegis of the established powerholders.

Because of its geohistorical location, Illinois has received infusions of all three political subcultures since its earliest days. Southern Illinois became a stronghold of the traditionalistic political culture, northern Illinois a stronghold of the moralistic, while the middle and northeastern parts of the state were settled by the individualistic. The political culture of the state as a whole became clearly individualistic and, as the authors of this volume indicate, has remained so. This volume portrays the continuing consequences of that political culture on Illinois state politics most effectively.

ILLINOIS AS AMERICA'S GEOHISTORICAL CENTER

Both at the beginning and at the end of this book, the authors refer to this writer's references to Illinois's vital positioning at the geohistorical center of the continental United States and all that has flowed from it. As one who has known Illinois from childhood, I first felt that and then discovered it empirically in the late 1950s and 1960s through extensive, systematic research on the ground. Indeed, much of what I learned about the United States at that time grew out of learning about Illinois. The world has turned many times since those days, but Illinois's position has remained the same. Only its expressions may be different.

One has to be very attentive when one approaches Illinois in any way.

Geographically, at first glance it looks plain. Only when one gets to know the state does one see its physical beauty and geographic complexity. Politically it varies from appearing corrupt to problematic. Here, too, one has to look closer to see how well it has served its highly diverse people in various ways, not the least in enabling them to live together with a minimum of conflict and a maximum of opportunity relative to the possibilities at their disposal.

Illinois, then, has been a successful polity, once we recognize human weaknesses and how hard it is to be successful in the face of those weaknesses. If, for some, this flawed success is offputting, for many it has a certain relaxed and human quality that is lacking in more straitlaced civil societies. Certainly Illinois has its own compelling attractions.

Preface

This book was written in appreciation of the scores of our former students who have served Illinois as governor, lieutenant governor, members of the legislature, directors of state agencies, civic and community leaders, and in other capacities that have benefited this state. These students, now our friends as well as public servants, have in turn taught us much about Illinois. We hope their lessons are faithfully reflected in the following pages.

Our greatest single debt is to Patrick Barry, a talented writer, editor, and student of Illinois, whose numerous comments and suggestions across all the chapters have richly enhanced the readability and substance of the book.

Professor Jack Van Der Slik provided a pointed critique of an earlier draft that proved valuable in sharpening our focus and observations.

Special thanks go to John Kincaid, general editor of this series, for his thoughtful comments and suggestions throughout several drafts of the manuscript. Thanks also to Daniel Elazar, a former colleague at the University of Illinois, for founding the series and for his fine introduction.

Lorena McClain of the Institute of Government and Public Affairs staff has done yeoman work in preparing the manuscript for publication. She performed beyond the call of duty. Upon Lorena's retirement, Shirley Burnette took over this responsibility in a most competent manner. She was ably assisted by Jean Baker. Christopher Romans, Kraig Lounsberry, Laura Staley, Kelly Shaw-Barnes, and Betsy Mitchell provided valuable research assistance for earlier drafts of the manuscript.

Joan Agrella Parker, vice-president of the Taxpayers' Federation of Illinois, read the chapter on the legislature. Robert Mandeville, former director of the Illinois Bureau of the Budget, read an early draft of the chapter on taxing and spending. As expected, both offered valuable clarifications and improvements.

We asked several persons to comment on other individual chapters. These included William Boys, former director of the Illinois Department of Personnel; Ken Bruce, former chief lobbyist for the Illinois Education Association; Dr. Edwin E. Dale, former state representative; Gerald Glaub, Illinois Association of School Boards; Professor Gordon Hoke, University of Illinois; Professor Ann Lousin, John Marshall College of Law; Michael Pollak, House of Representatives, parliamentarian; Professor James Ward, University of Illinois; Peter Weber, Illinois Association of School Boards; and Douglas Whitley, president of Ameritech Illinois.

Having said all these thanks, we take full responsibility for the final publication.

ILLINOIS POLITICS AND GOVERNMENT

CHAPTER ONE

For Better or Worse, Individualism Reigns

Norma Wirth had seen it all before: the relentless advance of the frontier. Her hometown of Crystal Lake, a onetime summer retreat for Chicagoans, had long ago been absorbed by suburban sprawl. So in 1988, she and her husband moved to Harvard (population 6,361), the "Milk Capital of Illinois," seventy miles northwest of Chicago. Only six years later, the electronics giant Motorola announced its plan to build a $100 million cellular phone manufacturing facility just across the road from the barn the Wirths were constructing on their twelve-acre plot.[1]

Since World War II the defining transformation of Illinois has been the continuing migration of Chicagoans, downstaters, and others into the suburban "collar counties" that surround the city. Thousands like the Wirths have been drawn to suburbia and beyond by the unwritten but seemingly inalienable right of Americans to independence, space, and freedom of choice. Others have been pulled closer to jobs in the footloose industries that have built new business parks along the highways that radiate from Chicago. But instead of encountering open country and easy living, these new residents are meeting their neighbors—hundreds of thousands of them—in the traffic jams, at the strip shopping malls, and in the residential subdivisions that characterize the metropolitan fringe.

The urban exodus has not simply fallen short of its promise for those seeking rural splendor. It also has hurt many residents in the close-in suburbs and city, where dwindling populations, racial segregation, and shuttered businesses mean less money and other support to keep up the streets and schools. The small towns and cities of downstate Illinois have been affected as well: they now have to be doubly agile when the state's resources are being divided up because what powerful Chicago doesn't get might be grabbed by the suburbs.

This book shows that unchecked expansion of suburbia is but the latest example of the individualistic political and social culture that reigns in Illinois. It is a state where the power and initiative of the individual is not only cherished—even if it sometimes leads to trouble—but even protected and nurtured for its contribution to the state's vitality.

Who can argue, after all, that Illinois is not a powerhouse? The state has produced, in less than two hundred years of modern history, an enviable accumulation of riches. Its tough and hardworking early settlers took maximum advantage of fertile soil and excellent access to water, building dozens of towns by 1830 along the Ohio, Mississippi, and Wabash rivers. Soon after, a separate band of business-savvy immigrants began transforming the northeastern end of the state—at a swamp called Chikagou—into an astounding if smoky center of railroads, manufacturing plants, trading rooms, and skyscrapers. There has been no lack of political leadership in Illinois. A lean downstate lawyer, Abraham Lincoln, led the entire country on a successful moral crusade against slavery, and though his political descendants have taken up some less noble causes, no one questioned the clout of Chicago mayor Richard J. Daley or U.S. representative Dan Rostenkowski.

Like many of its best politicians, Illinois has staying power. Through the Great Depression and more recent recessions, against the tide of traffic to California and the sunbelt, Illinois has remained a prominent player on the national and international scenes. With support from various state, local, and federal government agencies, manufacturers have retooled and gone global, farmers have convinced the federal bureaucracy that corn-based ethanol should be added to gasoline, and the money men behind downtown Chicago laughed at the softer rust belt cities as they pumped billions into renewing Chicago's spectacular skyline.

To its boosters, these achievements are argument enough that the dominant political culture of Illinois is robust and versatile, more than equal to the challenges of our times. That view, alas, is sometimes difficult to defend. For the same culture that helped Swift and Armour build up Chicago's fabled meatpacking industry is also the one that winked at horrendous working conditions in the slaughterhouses and steel mills. The governmental culture that helped the railroads bring prosperity to so many downstate communities is the same one that lets those towns suffer now that the action has shifted to rubber-tired suburbia. And as Norma Wirth and her exurban neighbors are finding on the green fringes of metro Chicago, the same system that encouraged them to do whatever they wanted is not always so adept at helping them solve the problems they create.

There are states in the Union where politics is seen as a clear path to moral and social improvement, where government provides a civic mechanism for those who want to make things better. Minnesota is one of them, and Wisconsin is another. Illinois is not. But it is resilient, dynamic, and even, now and again, proficient at responding to its weaknesses. It is also changing, inexorably, as the collar counties take their place on the political chessboard alongside the city and the downstate interests.

This book is about the political culture of Illinois and how it has shaped the state. It traces the evolution of this culture across the full spectrum of government life, from the brass rail at the Capitol rotunda where lobbyists "educate" Illinois legislators through the ward offices of Chicago and the corruption-stained courtrooms of Cook County. The cast of characters has changed dramatically over the years, from the early population of American Indians (who held no political power whatsoever and were driven from the state) through a succession of migrations that brought the Germans, Poles, Irish, southern blacks, Italians, and more recently the Asian Indians, Koreans, Mexicans, Arabs, Africans, and Central Americans. Despite this shifting population, the underlying values and attitudes that shape the state's culture have a long and consistent, though evolving, history. In Chicago parlance, the culture is best described as "Where's mine?" but in more genteel circles, the Illinois system might be termed a government-as-marketplace, where a give-and-take process allocates "fair shares" of the pie to those who have earned a place at the table.

FROM THE START, A PLACE OF OPPORTUNITY

With a gross state product of more than $339 billion in 1995, the Illinois economy is a big pie to cut into and a juicy one at that, filled with opportunities across a broad range of business sectors, geographies, and social settings. As the Roman philosopher Seneca observed, "All that is past is prologue," and that is certainly true in Illinois, where the early settlers found almost as wide a variety of opportunities as their modern-day equivalents. One of the earliest business endeavors was exploitation of the salt springs near Shawneetown, where slave labor dried and bagged the salt and river transportation brought it to markets. There was wood to be cut, bottomland to be planted, shipping companies to manage, coal and lead to be dug from the ground. Then came the railroads and the land grants that opened up the prairie, while Chicago was still getting on its feet. Work was not always steady, but the people came, hustled, found ways to survive and, sometimes, thrive beyond their wildest dreams. In the process, of course, governments were created, leaders chosen, and bureaucracies built.

The "Tall State," as it was called in a 1960s tourism campaign, stretches almost four hundred miles from the Wisconsin line to its southern tip at Cairo (pronounced "kay-ro"), nestled between Kentucky and Missouri (see map 1). The northernmost latitude is on line with Portsmouth, New Hampshire, and at Cairo, close to that of Portsmouth, Virginia.

The state's diversity is owing in great measure to U.S. territorial delegate Nathaniel Pope, who, in 1818, succeeded in passing an amendment to the Illinois Enabling Act that moved the new state's northern boundary forty-one miles to the north. This addition of eight thousand square miles—mostly empty at the time—today encompasses metropolitan Chicago and almost 80 percent of the state's population;[2] without it, Illinois would never have become the powerhouse that it is.

Settlement of the state was facilitated by natural factors, ingenuity, and human achievements. The Ohio River offered a convenient super-waterway, while the state's generally level topography made the prairie relatively easy to traverse on foot. Opening of the Erie Canal in New York in 1825 facilitated the flow of Yankees and European immigrants via the Great Lakes. The early development of Illinois as a railroad center helped disperse throughout the state those newly arrived; later, the main line of the Illinois Central Railroad, running from New Orleans, would bring tens of thousands of blacks to jobs in Chicago.

The platting, or dividing, of Illinois into uniform square townships of thirty-six square miles, as decreed by Congress in 1785, was designed to transfer public lands efficiently into private hands.[3] This it did. Each of the thousands of "congressional townships" was divided into thirty-six one-mile-square sections of 640 acres. Township roads were laid out along the sections. The township plats made it simple to survey and sell virgin land with a minimum of confusion and dispute. Even today, for the air traveler crossing Illinois, a geometric checkerboard pattern unfolds below.

There was a hunger to develop this rich flatland, but transportation infrastructure was needed first to get the settlers in and the bounty of the fields to market. When Abraham Lincoln and Stephen A. Douglas were state lawmakers in the 1830s, the legislature embarked on an ambitious scheme of "internal improvements," but the dreamed-of network of wood-plank roads, canals, and railroads collapsed under the weight of poor planning, a

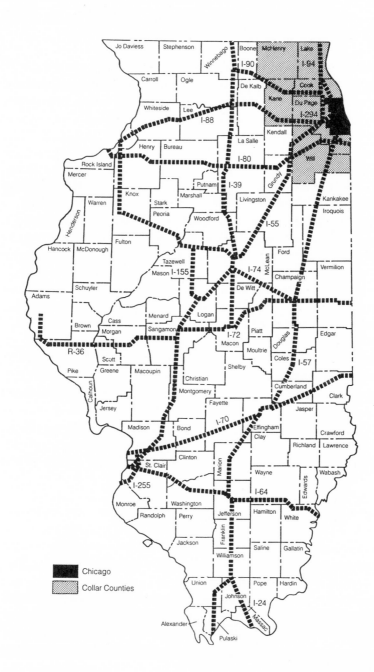

Map 1. Map of Illinois

weak national economy, and a lack of capital and engineering capacity.[4] Lincoln and Douglas later became U.S. congressmen and revived the idea, this time convincing the U.S. government to assist with huge land grants for private investors (Chicago mayor Richard J. Daley would later show similar skill with federal transportation funds). In 1851 the federal government offered 3.75 million acres of railroad right-of-way and adjoining land to investors in the Illinois Central Railroad (IC). Within five years, 705 miles of track had been laid from Cairo to Galena, with a spur to Chicago. The IC became the longest railway in the world and the nation's largest private venture to date, foreshadowing similar growth by Illinois companies such as International Harvester, Caterpillar, and Sears, Roebuck.

Railroads were the interstate highways of the nineteenth century. If a town was on a rail line, it generally prospered; if not, the town was often abandoned. Railroad trackage in Illinois increased from 111 miles in 1850 to 2,800 in 1860 and 7,000 by 1875. In part because of its railroad grid, Illinois was the fastest growing territory in the world by the middle of the nineteenth century.[5] The 36 million acres of land in Illinois were enough for about a quarter-million quarter section (160 acre) farms. One-fourth of those farms had been taken by 1850, nearly all by 1875. Three in four farms were within five miles of a railroad, and only 5 percent were more than ten miles distant.[6]

EARLY TRIUMPH FOR THE ''MODERNIZERS''

In the free-for-all environment of the state's early days, no one culture held sway. Southern Illinois had been settled first, primarily by poor, land-hungry Scots-Irish pioneers from Virginia and the Carolinas.[7] A second surge came in the 1830s, via the new Erie Canal, primarily from New England and the Middle Atlantic states. These Yankees, who mostly settled in the central and northern parts of Illinois, generally brought more assets with them and put down roots into richer farmland than did those further south.

These demographics set the stage for a struggle between the ''traditionalists'' in southern Illinois and the ''modernizers,'' primarily Yankees, in the north.[8] The genius of the modernizers, according to Richard Jensen, lay in a combination of values: faith in reason, a drive for middle-class status, equal rights, and a sense of mission to transform the world in their image. Education was their remedy; efficiency their ideal.

Everyone in Illinois recognized the difference between modernizers and traditionalists, although nobody used those words. Each group thought the other peculiar. Fast-talking Yankee peddlers were distrusted—one county even set a prohibitive fifty-dollars-per-quarter license for clock peddlers. A Yankee woman was amused by the drinking, horse trading, and quaint, slow drawl of the southerners. She talked with one who allowed that "it's a right smart thing to be able to read when you want to" but who didn't figure that books and the sciences would "do a man as much good as handy use of the rifle."

Strong commitment to education was the hallmark of the modernizers. By 1883, the northern part of the state provided its children a third more days of schooling than did the schools in "Egypt," the nickname for deep southern Illinois, with its towns of Cairo, Carnak, and Thebes.[9] Jensen quotes a nineteenth-century governor on the values in northern Illinois: "Is a school house, a bridge, or a church to be built, a road to be made, a school or minister to be maintained, or taxes to be paid? The northern man is never to be found wanting."[10]

By 1860, the Yankee modernizers dominated northern Illinois politics, while traditionalists held sway in the south. Central Illinois became the uncertain political battleground. With Lincoln's election and the ensuing Civil War, the modernists triumphed and, through the Republican party, controlled Illinois politics almost continuously for the following seventy years. (To emphasize that generalizations about traditionalists and modernizers are just that, note that Lincoln the modernizer came from southern, traditionalist roots while Stephen A. Douglas, who represented the traditionalist viewpoint in the 1860 presidential election, came from upper New York.)

CHICAGO AND THE GREAT MIDWEST

Another emerging culture would mark Illinois forever, and it had its roots in commerce. In a compelling synthesis of the organic relationship between a great city and the vast prairie that envelops it, William Cronon explains that neither Chicago nor the rich countryside of the Midwest would have developed their great wealth if not for the symbiosis between the two: the urban center contributing creativity, energy, and capital while the farmers and small towns provided ambition, intelligence, and the harvest from incredibly fecund soils.[11] Plentiful water and easy waterborne transportation provided further economic irrigation. The Wabash, Ohio, and Mississippi rivers carved Illinois's natural boundaries, while the Illinois River traversed the middle, positioning the state at the heart of the young nation's economic expansion.[12]

At the southern tip of Lake Michigan, Chicago sat astride the boundary between East and West. Chicago's meatpackers, grain merchants, and manufacturers showed extraordinary drive and creativity, not to mention a knack for attracting capital. The railroads were eager to carry their goods, and these capitalists put the Midwest's natural resources to use to create an unprecedented hive of economic development by the end of the 1800s.

Almost all the Chicago capitalists were Yankees, such as meatpackers Philip Swift and Gustavus Armour. These two men and their collaborators systematized the market in animal flesh. Building on the adage that "the hog is regarded as the most compact form in which the Indian corn crop . . . can be transported to market," they created hog slaughtering lines that were the forerunners of the assembly line.[13] Cattle were standardized as Grades No. 1, 2, or 3. Rail cars were refrigerated so that dressed beef from Chicago could be marketed in the East.

According to Cronon, the overarching genius of Swift and Armour lay in the immense impersonal, hierarchical organizations they created, operated by an army of managers and workers who would outlive and carry on after the founders (not coincidentally, using the same basic structure as would the Chicago Democratic machine). By 1880 Chicago had more than seventy-five thousand industrial workers, the largest such labor force west of the Appalachians.[14] To quote muckraker Frank Norris: "The Great Grey City, brooking no rival, imposed its dominion upon a reach of country larger than many a kingdom of the Old World."[15]

By 1890, with more than a million residents, Chicago was the nation's second largest city. It bragged of itself in 1893 by presenting the World's Columbian Exposition to twenty-seven million visitors. From a square-mile tract of marshes and scrub pines on the south side of Chicago arose a fairy city that hosted the exhibits of forty-six nations, a single exposition building said to seat three hundred thousand persons, and an amusement park ride by George Ferris of downstate Galesburg that could carry forty persons in each of thirty-six cars on a 250-foot-high revolving wheel.[16] Visitors were equally impressed with the real-world development a few miles up the lakefront in the city center. At twenty-one stories, the Masonic Temple was the world's tallest building, a so-called skyscraper.

There was a tension between the fairy city of the exposition and the real city that enveloped it, a tension that persists to this day. Rural visitors from downstate were agog at the artificial White City but "afeared" of the perceived dangers and tumult of Chicago. Many Chicagoans, in fact, had already become eager for the tranquillity of the country. In 1868, urban planner Frederick Law Olmsted designed Riverside, west of Chicago, as a new community where families could enjoy the country while the breadwinner could take the train to his job downtown. Skyscraper and suburb created each other, said Cronon, and the railroad made both possible.[17]

By 1930 Chicago had reached 3.4 million inhabitants—almost half the state's total—and was the fourth largest city in the world, second only to New York in the United States. By 1945 Chicago peaked at 3.6 million, as the suburban era began in earnest. Auto ownership doubled between 1945 and the early 1950s, and expressways were being built, foreshadowing suburban growth. According to historian Jensen, "Comfort, security, and the promise of continued progress . . . made the suburban era a time of placid complacency."[18]

COMPETITION FOR RICHES

With Chicago leading the way and many downstate communities still thriving under mixed industrial and agricultural economies, Illinois was a relatively strong state through most of the twentieth century. But driven as it was by commercial success and with a succession of both local and statewide leaders who worked closely with and profited from business interests, Illinois became a place where the wealth of opportunity was matched only by the ruthlessness of those pursuing it. The grizzled writer Nelson Algren, in his prose-poem *Chicago: City on the Make,* identified two key characteristics of the culture that came to dominate Illinois. First, leadership and success were highly prized, and second if the success involved a bit of shady dealing, so be it. "If he can get away with it I give the man credit," Algren said of a safe-blower. The same culture has always looked askance at weakness, brooking no sympathy for a woman reduced to prostitution or a jobless man numbing himself with beer. Warned Algren: "Wise up, Jim: it's a joint where the bulls and the foxes live well and the lambs wind up head-down from the hook."[19]

Truth be told, Illinois is not so different from other states as it is representative of them and of the nation as a whole. Daniel J. Elazar writes:

Illinois . . . is one the most heterogeneous states in the union. In its social structure and patterns of political response it is very likely the nation's most representative state. . . . Illinois is simultaneously the western anchor of the industrial and megapolitan greater Northeast and the gateway and chief trading center for the greater West. In its southern reaches it also includes a substantial extension of the physiographic and demographic elements which combine to form the distinctive character of the greater South.[20]

Political pollster Peter Hart calls Illinois "the best bellwether state in America. It is a state that has it all: north, south, urban, rural, black, white, Hispanic. What usually plays well nationally plays pretty well in Illinois."[21] By extension, what plays out in Illinois very often has national parallels.

Elazar has identified three primary strains of political culture among the groups that settled the American states—traditionalistic, moralistic, and individualistic.[22] For the traditionalistic culture, government's function is positive but limited to securing the continued maintenance of the existing social order and its dominating elites. The moralistic orientation tends to view government as a positive instrument for promoting public good, with honesty and commitment to public service as strong values. The individualistic strain sees the democratic order as just another marketplace, where individuals and groups may improve themselves socially and economically; ideology is of little concern, and because of the government-as-market orientation, profiting from government activity is tolerated.[23]

All three cultures still exist in Illinois, but the values of individualism are dominant, according to Elazar. "Politics in Illinois came early to be centered on personal influence, patronage, distribution of federal and later state benefits, and the availability of economic gain of those who were professionally committed to politics as their 'business.'"[24]

DIVISION BY DEMOGRAPHICS

If politics is a business, votes are the currency, and since its earliest days Illinois politics has been shaped by the demographics of the voting public. In 1858 senatorial candidate Abraham Lincoln gave most of his campaign speeches in central Illinois (and only one in Chicago), from Danville on the east to Carthage and Dallas City on the west. This made sense because nearly half the state's population lived in the central third of the state.[25] Sympathies in northern Illinois were clearly with the new Republican party, and those in southern Illinois were strongly with the Democrats, while central Illinois was mixed; it was divided and competitive politically. In contrast, statewide candidates in 1992 devoted great effort to garnering coverage by the television stations based in Chicago, which reach two-thirds of all the households in Illinois. Candidates spent little, if any, time in Danville, Carthage, or Dallas City.

The demographics of Illinois have been shifting, often dramatically, since the 1840s, when immigrants fleeing famine or turmoil in Ireland, Germany, and the Scandinavian countries began to reach the state. For the whole of the nineteenth century, Germans were the largest immigrant group in St. Louis, Chicago, and Illinois as a whole. By 1860 nearly half of Chicago's burgeoning population was foreign-born.

A decade later, the sources of immigration had shifted to Italy and eastern Europe; they came in great numbers until quotas went into effect in 1927. Poles began pouring into Chicago around the turn of the century, and by 1920 they numbered almost five hundred thousand.[26]

The first blacks were brought to the Illinois territory as slaves. The state's first six governors were all slave owners at one time, and several had registered black servants while in office.[27] The Northwest Ordinance of 1787 had banned slavery, but it failed to ban its surrogate, registered servitude, and the adoption in 1824 of a "black code" effectively prevented free blacks from settling in the state.[28] (Still, several thousand slaves from Kentucky and Tennessee were "leased" in the early 1800s to work in the salt springs near Shawneetown.[29])

Major black settlement did not begin until after the Civil War, and even then it grew slowly. Chicago's black neighborhood in 1871 was three blocks wide and fifteen blocks long, with some twenty-five hundred residents.[30] But when severe labor shortages during World War I hampered production in Chicago factories, a large-scale migration from the South began. Between 1910 and 1920, about fifty thousand blacks rode north on the Illinois Central Railroad and crowded into the expanding Black Belt, triggering the first of many waves of white flight. (Segregation was not limited to Chicago; even after World War II, black state legislators were denied access to restaurants and hotel rooms, including the Abraham Lincoln Hotel, in Lincoln's hometown of Springfield.) The expansion of the south-side Black Belt and, after another surge of migration during World War II, the growth of the west-side ghetto, proved politically important; the concentrated voting power resulted in the 1928 election of a black congressman, former Chicago alderman Oscar DePriest, and, by 1983, the election of Harold Washington as Chicago's first black mayor.

SLOWER GROWTH MASKS DIVERSITY

Steady in-migration propelled Illinois's population from 3.8 million residents in 1890 to 11.4 million by 1990. But the decade-by-decade growth leveled off in the 1970s, when population grew by just 2.7 percent, and became virtually flat, at 0.4 percent, in the 1980s. The national population, meanwhile, grew by about 10 percent in each of those decades.

The stable total population masks a continuation of major demographic change in race, ethnicity, age, and regional proportions.[31] There has been significant net out-migration of whites from Illinois to other states in recent decades. From 1970 to 1980, it is estimated there was a net outflow of from 700,000 to 900,000 whites and net in-migration of about 400,000 blacks and Hispanics.[32] In 1950, one in thirteen Illinois residents belonged to a minority group; in 1990, the proportion was one in four. It is projected that by 2010, one in three residents will be from a minority group, with most of the growth coming among Hispanics, whose population is expected to reach 1,674,000 in 2020.[33]

The Asian American population jumped by 287 percent in the 1980s, from 107,000 to 307,000. The number of persons of Spanish origin increased from 636,000 to 904,000, a 42 percent boost, and Chicago was home to more than half a million Hispanics. The state's African American population inched up by only 1.1 percent in the decade.

The collar counties continued to experience significant growth during the 1980s, while Chicago and downstate each suffered population losses (see figure 1). Each of the five collar counties outside Cook grew by more than 10 percent in the 1980s, while more mature suburban Cook increased by only 3 percent. Naperville in DuPage County has almost doubled in population in each recent decade, from 12,000 in 1960 to 85,000 in 1990 and to 102,000 in 1994, based on a special census done for the municipality.[34]

In contrast, Chicago's population declined by 221,000, or 7.4 percent, in the 1980s, more than any other city in the nation.[35] Many rural counties downstate suffered even greater percentage losses. Fulton, Mason, Stark, and Warren in central Illinois each lost more than 10 percent of their residents between 1980 and 1990. Of 853 incorporated Illinois communities of less than 2,500 residents, 556 lost more than 5 percent of their population during the 1980s. The manufacturing-based counties of Macon, Peoria, and Rock Island lost both industrial jobs and about 10 percent of their residents.

Map 2 identifies municipalities in Illinois that either gained or lost more than 5 percent of their population in the 1980s. Losses are evident throughout downstate, while growth is heavily concentrated in the suburban collar. Growth also came to communities that are beginning to form "a ring around the collar." Other pockets of growth were in the Metro-East area across from St. Louis, in the state capital of Springfield, and around the university communities in Urbana and Normal.

The population mix is also changing within the regions. In 1950 blacks made up 13.6 percent of the population of Chicago; in 1990 it was about 41.8 percent; for Hispanics the figure was 5.0 percent in 1950 and 21.4 percent in 1990. Chicago is today clearly a "majority minorities" city.[36]

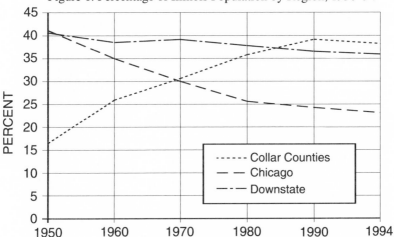

Figure 1. Percentage of Illinois Population by Region, 1950–94

Sources: County and City Data Book, Bureau of the Census, U.S. Department of Commerce, generally. *1994 Place Estimates* [population estimates branch of the census]: FTP: //ftp.census. gov/pub/population/estimates/place file: sc94flil.vip.

Nevertheless, Chicago lost 113,000 African Americans during the 1980s, while the black population in the collar counties increased by 103,000. The collar counties, though largely following the Chicago pattern of racial segregation, have become increasingly diverse overall. From only 2.8 percent of the collar county population in 1950, nonwhites constituted 11.7 percent by 1990.

White migrants tend to be younger, be better educated, and have higher incomes than whites who stay put.[37] Migrants also tend to flow toward strong economies. As economic fortunes downstate and in Chicago have generally trailed those in the suburbs, this may help explain why, between 1950 and 1980, the percentages of the population over age sixty-five grew significantly downstate and in Chicago but dropped in the collar counties. In 1980, for example, only 7.6 percent of the residents of the five suburban counties around Cook were age sixty-five or older, compared to 13.9 percent of residents in southern Illinois.[38]

Overall, the rates of demographic and social change have slowed across the state.[39] Growth is slowing in the suburbs, which are no longer as homogeneous as once thought. Robbins and Markham are two very poor, predominantly black communities; Flossmoor and Olympia Fields are almost all white and quite prosperous. All four are suburbs south of Chicago. The central city of Chicago has seen its population stabilize, with signs of net in-migration of young professional whites. During the 1980s, downstate Illinois experienced near-depression conditions caused by the double whammy

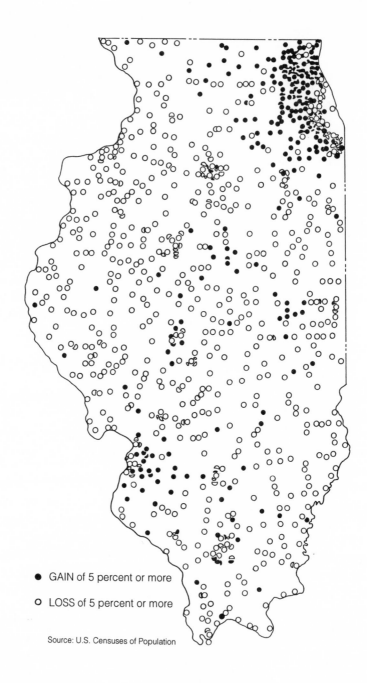

Map 2. Population Change in Incorporated Places, 1980–90

of industrial restructuring and hard times on the farm. The worst seems over, though rural counties may continue to lose population.

Generalizations and statistical trends tend to drain the color and texture from Illinois's rich mosaic of people from the world around. In the early 1970s coauthor Nowlan was a state representative for a rural district in northwestern Illinois. He recalls enjoying *bagna cauda* ("hot bath") stew and sumpanella (a flat, tortillalike bread) with the friendly Italian Americans in Dalzell and Ladd, watching preparations for pigeon races at the Flemish-American Club in Kewanee, and enjoying late night music at the Latino-Americano Club in Rock Falls.[40] Later, as a statewide candidate, this same politician helped celebrate the birthday of Santa Lucia (Swedish) in Galesburg in central Illinois; hoisted steins of beer with German descendants in Belleville and Millstadt, east of St. Louis; watched *bocce ball* played by Italian Americans on the green along the commuter rail tracks in suburban Highwood; and marched with blacks in the Bud Billiken Day parade on the south side of Chicago.[41]

The mosaic is at its most colorful in Chicago. On the Chicago Transit Authority train from the city's Loop to O'Hare Airport, a rider is likely to hear Spanish, Polish, and English in equal doses. A 1980 survey found that 122,000 Chicagoans speak Polish.[42] As of 1988 in the Chicago phone book, there were 437 O'Connors, 130 Wisniewskis, 355 Gomezes, and 201 Wongs. There were half a million Hispanics in Chicago in 1990, not including those *sin papeles,* that is, without immigration documentation. If the undocumented were included in the 1990 census, Hispanic numbers in the city could be over 750,000, according to one estimate.[43] In Chicago there are large communities of Filipinos, Asian Indians, Chinese, Koreans, Japanese, and Vietnamese.[44] Twenty-one languages are spoken in the homes of students at the Albany Park Multicultural Academy, a public school in a Chicago neighborhood that is an entry point for refugees and other migrants.[45]

For ethnic whites in metropolitan Chicago, the melting pot metaphor applies fairly well. There are now more Irish, Italians, Germans, and Poles in the Chicago suburbs than in the city. Within the city, however, a mosaic—with sharply etched lines separating the pieces—is more apt than a melting pot. According to Gregory Squires and his coauthors, "In the city, race has come to be a far more significant characteristic for defining group membership and neighborhood residence than ethnicity." In 1960, two-thirds of Chicago's blacks lived in census tracts that were over 90 percent black; by 1980 that index had increased to 91.9 percent in tracts over 90 percent black.[46]

THE POLITICS OF ETHNICITY

Although Hispanics face fewer barriers overall than blacks in the housing markets of metropolitan Chicago, Hispanic leaders are working to keep their communities together so they can build political influence and preserve cultural values. It is a difficult job in Chicago because unlike Los Angeles, New York, and Miami, where the Hispanics are predominantly either Mexican, Puerto Rican, or Cuban, Chicago's Hispanic population is highly diverse. Ten Latino nationalities each have more than 1,000 residents in Chicago.[47] Mexicans make up 69 percent and Puerto Ricans 16 percent of the city's 545,000 Latinos[48], and there are also communities of Guatemalans, Cubans, Colombians, Ecuadorians, Salvadorans, Peruvians, and others.

Hispanics can—and many do—live in Chicago without speaking English. There are Spanish-language television and radio stations and newspapers such as *La Raza, El Informador, Impacto,* and *El Imparcial.* In 1993, the *Chicago Tribune* recognized the advertising possibilities of the Latino market and launched a Spanish-language newspaper, *Exito* (Success), that circulates sixty thousand papers in Chicago and the suburbs. The *Chicago Sun-Times* responded by inserting more than one hundred thousand copies of *La Raza Domingo* in its Sunday editions.

Hispanics have been comparatively slow to develop their political skills and electoral strength, in part because many Mexicans and others come to Illinois with the dream—generally unfulfilled—of returning home someday with enough capital to buy a small farm or business. Thus many are here without a commitment to United States citizenship and political involvement. Nevertheless, as of 1994, there were 6 Hispanics among the 177 Illinois lawmakers and, on the strength of a congressional district that was drawn to ensure Hispanic representation, former Chicago alderman Luis Gutierrez was serving in the U.S. Congress.

Immigrant groups have brought different political needs and skills to Illinois. The Irish, Poles, and Italians brought less capital and education—and received less social acceptance—than the English and Germans who generally preceded them. The three ethnic groups found, however, that democratic institutions offered opportunities for success and acceptance that were often denied them in business and the professions.

The Irish have dominated Chicago politics since the Civil War and especially since the Kelly-Nash machine of the 1930s. Most recently, the mayors Richard J. Daley and his son Richard M. have been the most prominent representatives of Irish political power. Although they were always a distinct minority of the population in Illinois and Chicago, Irish political leaders have been skilled at building coalitions, especially with the Poles and Italians.[49]

Upon arriving in Chicago, the Poles seemed to find boss-directed patronage organizations attractive. The political bosses welcomed immigrants and helped them. "Seemingly anyone could become a boss in America," writes Edward Kantowicz, in contrast to a feudal nobility caste in Poland to which peasants had no access. "Thus American politics fulfilled economic, occupational and psychological functions in 'Polonia' (Poland in America)."[50]

The legendary skills of Chicago's politicians might give a false impression that strong political organizations have been the sole preserve of the urban Democrats. Not so. Getting out the vote is a result of cultural attitudes toward leadership and patrons, and here and there downstate Republicans learned the tricks as well. Coauthor Nowlan recalls his confrontation years ago with a rural Republican political boss:

> In my first try for office in 1966 I sought a Republican nomination for the Illinois house from a rural district. Heeding the abundant advice given by old-timers, I paid a call on Louis Falletti, owner of a popular tavern and precinct committeeman for the small community of Italian-Americans in and around the village of Dalzell in Bureau County, whose forebears had come to mine coal.
>
> Lou Falletti, a courtly gentleman, received me graciously. But he told me bluntly he already had two candidates and I wasn't one of them. Furthermore, I would not get a single vote in his precinct, Falletti said confidently. I left the Falletti home, adjacent to the tavern, vowing to prove him wrong. I spent more time and money in the precinct than planned, walking door-to-door to introduce myself, even hanging around the popular Italian bakery to say "Hi" to residents.
>
> I proved Lou Falletti wrong. Of 562 votes cast among six candidates for the two nominations, I received 10 votes. Falletti's candidates garnered 539 votes between them. Two years later I ran again. Falletti's candidates were not running this time, so he backed me in a four-way hotly contested race. I captured nearly all the votes in Dalzell this second time, and was elected. Whenever Lou wanted help finding a job or doing a favor for one of his constituents, I busted my tail trying to get what Lou wanted!

DOWNSHIFT IN THE ECONOMY

A strong economy is the best medicine for what ails a society because plentiful and well-paid jobs create robust tax revenues that help provide government services. A rich state, if it wishes, can provide more educational and social services than can a poor state, even if the latter taxes its citizens more heavily. Illinois has been and continues to be a rich state; its $327 billion gross state product in 1994 would make it the twelfth largest economy in the world, just below Spain or India and above Australia and Mexico.[51] But in the last thirty years, Illinois has experienced a gradual yet persistent slowing in its rate of growth, which creates problems for elected officials who would like to fulfill the high expectations of citizens but find their revenue stream can't always keep up.

Illinois still ranks first in the nation in railroad cars handled, moving 6.7 million cars in 1991 and accounting for almost 30 percent of the nation's total.[52] O'Hare Airport moves more passengers per year than any airport in the world. In part because of O'Hare, Illinois ranks second after California as home for Fortune 500 corporate headquarters.

Although the Illinois gross state product has been increasing, the state's product as a percentage of the national total has been declining, from 6.4 percent of the national total in 1972 to 5 percent in 1992.[53] The Illinois economy has also been growing more slowly than that of the nation. In 1949 average per capita personal income in Illinois was about 122 percent of the amount for the nation as a whole; in 1973 it had slipped to 114 percent and by 1992 had fallen to just 109 percent of the national average.[54]

Much of this decline can be attributed to rapid growth since World War II in the populations and economies of the southern and western states. If Illinois continues to maintain higher per capita income than the nation, it is partly because a larger share of the state's residents participate in the labor market. In 1989, 53 percent of eligible Illinois residents participated in the workforce, while only 50 percent did so nationally. Thus, though a report by the Illinois Department of Commerce and Community Affairs concludes that "working harder than the rest of the U.S. helps Illinois achieve a portion of its higher income,"[55] the same evidence might be used to say that Illinois residents are working harder and getting less than they used to.

This is certainly true for the many blue-collar workers who have been displaced from manufacturing jobs, often into lower-paying service occupations. Statewide employment in the production of machinery and other durable goods declined from more than 900,000 jobs in 1975 to 575,000 in

1992.[56] The painful contraction and retooling have probably been good for Illinois's long-term competitiveness. Downstate companies such as Caterpillar and John Deere are producing more heavy machines with fewer employees. According to the Federal Reserve Bank of Chicago, manufacturing productivity in Cook and the collar counties exceeded that for Japan in the eight years between 1984 and 1992.[57]

But prosperity continues to elude most of southern Illinois. During the 1980s jobs and wealth declined in rural western Illinois for the first time since the Great Depression. From 1980 to 1987, the average per acre value of farm property in Illinois declined about 50 percent, though it had stabilized by the early 1990s. The highest rate of public aid recipients is not in Chicago's Cook County but in Alexander County along the Ohio River, where 263 of every 1,000 residents were on welfare in 1990. Pulaski County had 225 per 1,000; Cook County, 212.[58]

One measure of the economic desperation in small communities is their willingness to pursue jobs that would have been shunned in better times. In the 1960s, a corrections department official would have been tarred, feathered, and run out of town if he had proposed building a prison in a community. By the 1980s, downstate communities were literally begging to be the sites for new prisons to hold Illinois's burgeoning inmate population. A similar phenomenon has occurred in the solid waste industry; although many communities still shun the idea of a landfill or garbage incinerator in their "backyard," others see the job possibilities as too rich to resist.

Extreme economic disparities, always present in both Chicago and downstate areas, have worsened considerably. Although Chicago boasts three of the nation's twelve most affluent communities, including the Gold Coast, where per capita income was $82,169 in 1989, the people in its poorest community, the Stateway Gardens public housing project, had a per capita income of only $1,650.[59] Ten of the nation's sixteen most concentrated areas of poverty are located in Chicago's housing projects, and as William Julius Wilson points out in devastating detail in his book *The Truly Disadvantaged,* the concentration of poverty in Chicago's neighborhoods increased dramatically when higher-income families fled for better neighborhoods or the suburbs. Sixteen of the city's seventy-seven community areas were classified as poverty areas in 1970, but only one of them was an "extreme poverty" area, where more than 40 percent of the households were poor. By 1980, there were twenty-six poverty areas, seven of them with extreme poverty levels and two more where more than 50 percent of the households lived in poverty.[60]

All the while many suburban areas have experienced sustained economic growth. Impressive research facilities and corporate offices for companies including AT&T, Amoco, Motorola, Baxter, and Ameritech have sprouted along highway corridors that reach from Cook County west to DeKalb, northwest almost to Rockford, and north into Lake County. The population increases in the suburbs have been accompanied by growth in income. The top seven counties in per capita income are all clustered around Chicago while the seven poorest are all in southern Illinois. Counties with the highest rates of unemployment are also concentrated in southern Illinois.[61]

TEST FOR THE INDIVIDUALIST APPROACH

The individualistic culture has made Illinois what it is: a state where ambition and hard work have often been rewarded and where the political system has done what it could to keep such opportunities alive. Many would argue that this system has worked well overall; although it has not solved the problems of poverty or racial and ethnic division, it has at least provided opportunities for some of the poor and some of the minorities to climb into prosperity.

What has changed in the last thirty years is that Illinois is no longer growing as it once was; its per capita income in relation to other states is falling; and the growth of suburbia has not only created some problems of its own but done little to alleviate the suffering in the cities and the poor rural areas.

This book does not attempt to predict whether the current political culture can overcome the challenges now facing Illinois. Instead, it provides an overview of the current culture so that the practitioners of politics, government, and public policy—and the voters of the state—can better understand the landscape on which they are standing.

The second and third chapters describe the evolution of the current three-way split of political power in Illinois and how that power is shared. The following six chapters describe the political culture in different areas of Illinois government, from the nonpartisan and successful 1970 Constitutional Convention to the often partisan workings of the executive branch, courts, and local governments. Chapters 10 and 11 illustrate how political forces collide around such touchy issues as budgeting and education, and Chapter 12 provides some modest predictions that the emergence of the suburbs will change Illinois but probably not the way politics "gets done."

CHAPTER TWO

Collar Counties Join Fight
for "Fair Share"

Huntley, a village in McHenry County, is evolving from farm town to boom town. Ground was broken in 1993 for a retail-housing complex whose planned 4,600 housing units would quintuple the village's 1992 population of 2,590.[1] Five miles south in Gilberts (population 1,130), builders announced plans in 1994 to put up 2,000 housing units. Farther south in Will County, the quiet, attractive town of Frankfort saw its population nearly double in the 1980s, to 7,844, with another doubling projected for the next fifteen years. And so it goes all along the frontier.

The hallmarks of the expanding metropolitan frontier are independence, space, a sense of security, lack of congestion, cleaner air, and a "back to the country" setting. For first-time home buyers, who make up half the suburban market, the largest and most affordable lots are found on the fringe of the region.[2] The outward trek generally moves along the Interstate highway corridors that radiate from Chicago almost as neatly as bicycle spokes: I-57, I-55, I-88, I-90 and I-94.

Jobs moved toward the frontier even faster than people during the 1980s. From 1980 to 1991, DuPage, Kane, Lake, and McHenry counties each registered job growth of more than 50 percent. Job opportunities in DuPage expanded by 83 percent, while population grew by 21 percent. With a job-to-population ratio of 67.8 percent, DuPage became a big importer of employees.[3] Joel Garreau has written about the growth of "edge cities" across the United States, which are booming single-end destinations for jobs, shopping, and entertainment and where population increases at 9 A.M. each weekday. He found four edge cities in the metro-Chicago region: Schaumburg-Woodfield-Hoffman Estates, the O-Hare area, the East-West Tollway, and the Lake Shore Corridor running north along the Edens and Tri-State expressways.[4]

Power has followed population growth in Illinois from its earliest days, and the trend did not stop with the growth of suburbia. As housing developments and business parks replaced cornfields and stables, suburban political muscle displaced rural interests and began to test its strength on the city. In an evolution spanning just thirty years, the state's traditional bi-polar political structure has been reshaped into a triad.

After World War II, Chicago held more than 40 percent of the state's population and often half its total vote; with Richard J. Daley in the mayor's office and a strong Democratic presence in the Illinois House of Representatives, Chicago protected its turf and negotiated skillfully with downstate interests for its share of government largesse. With the rapid development of the suburbs, five counties with mostly common needs joined the field (DuPage, Kane, Lake, McHenry and Will), throwing their lot in with the suburbs of Cook County outside Chicago.

This chapter profiles these three dominant political regions of Illinois. The collar county region is the newest player and perhaps the most powerful, but with more than twelve hundred independent units of government splayed across a huge, traffic-clogged landscape, it lacks the unity and political track record of its counterparts. Chicago is a somewhat battered but still formidable force; it has lost power to the suburbs but retains the dogged political will that made it a great city. Downstate is the weakest player but not without strengths; although its population and job shares have declined, downstate maintains a solid position in the legislature and held the governor's office in the early 1990s.

With the emergence of the suburbs and their demands for a fair share of resources, the politics of redistribution may dominate state politics in the coming years. As is detailed later, the collar counties have been contributing more than they have received back. This should be expected because there is more wealth per capita in the collar counties than in the other regions. Nevertheless, the questions of how state tax dollars are distributed for schools, highways, mass transit, and local governments—and how effectively the regions spend those dollars—are coming to dominate the political agenda. Now that the collar counties are the largest of the three regions not only in wealth but in population and political representation, the region has begun to flex its political muscle, primarily through the Republican-controlled state senate.

SUBURBS FROM WISCONSIN TO INDIANA

Metropolitan Chicago as defined by the U.S. Census Bureau in 1990 was an eight-million-person megalopolis stretching from the business parks and hamlets of southern Wisconsin to the steel mills of Gary, Indiana. The bulging center of this "consolidated metropolitan statistical area" remains Chicago and the collar counties, but as homes and businesses spiral outward, residents in both the Rockford and Kankakee regions (to the northwest and south of Chicago, respectively) have begun to wonder when their open spaces will be absorbed by the "frontier." Many Rockford-area residents already commute along the Interstate 290 corridor to jobs in the suburban collar, and their new neighbors are more frequently from the older suburban communities.

The metropolis has been expanding since the Civil War, when suburban villages began to punctuate the countryside as retreats from the bustle of the city and from cholera and other diseases. In 1856, Hyde Park House hotel became a stop on the Illinois Central Railroad and lots were sold to pioneering suburbanites whose homes would later become neighbors to the University of Chicago. By the 1890s, Riverside and Brookfield to the west of Chicago and Kenilworth and Lake Forest to the north were being developed along convenient rail lines from the city.[5]

Though still predominantly white and homogeneous, some suburban areas are showing more ethnic and racial diversity. Black and Hispanic population in the region covering five and half counties increased tenfold between 1950 and 1990, to half a million people, from just 2.8 percent of the population in 1950 to 11.7 percent in 1990.[6]

Suburban blacks and Hispanics tend, however, to be concentrated. As suburbanites with the means to do so reach farther out on the collar to fulfill their dream of a single-family home with spacious yard, increasing numbers of Hispanics move into the aging suburbs adjacent to Chicago and to older industrial cities farther out, such as Aurora and Elgin in Kane County. In 1990, Stone Park in west Cook County was 58 percent Hispanic; Cicero, abutting Chicago's west side, 37 percent Hispanic, while Aurora and Elgin had populations that were 23 percent and 19 percent Hispanic, respectively.

While Hispanics move west, blacks tend to go south. Low-income blacks are concentrated near Chicago in communities such as Chicago Heights and Ford Heights, while middle-class blacks bypass the poor suburbs for Hazel Crest and Country Club Hills farther south. In 1992, 90 percent of the 150 homes in the relatively new development of Butterfield Place in Matteson in south Cook County were owned by blacks; average household income in the community was $54,000.[7] "Blacks are moving for the same reasons as white families—better schools, less crime, more space," according to sub-urban observer Paul Green. The suburban settlement appears to be perpetu-ating the same patterns of segregation that separated poor blacks, middle-class blacks, and whites in Chicago. "The south suburbs will become an ex-tension of the old south side of Chicago," avers Green.[8]

The suburbs appear to be more diverse religiously than racially. One ma-jor survey found that Catholics outnumber Protestants in the collar region.[9] The telephone directory for north-central DuPage County listed five Catho-lic churches, five Baptist, three Methodist, and three Episcopal, as well as the Hindu Society, the Chinese Gospel Church, the Muslim Society, and the Korean Church of Western Chicagoland, among others.

During the 1980s, the wealthy suburbs generally got wealthier, and the poor ones, poorer. Most that slipped were older suburbs close to Chicago. Per capita income in 76 of the 263 suburbs in the collar region failed to keep pace with inflation. The communities that slipped included poor and pre-dominantly black Ford Heights as well as solidly middle-class Lincoln-wood. Mettawa, in Lake County, and Kenilworth, in north Cook County, had per capita incomes of about $70,000 each, while incomes in predomi-nantly black Phoenix and Robbins were only $8,000, and in neighboring Ford Heights, the poorest suburb in the nation, just $4,660.[10]

TROUBLE IN PARADISE

While the suburbs continue to attract new residents and indeed offer many perceived advantages over either rural or urban settings, the rapid and often unplanned development of the suburban landscape has, like a new house set-tling on its foundation, begun to show some cracks. The older, inner-ring suburbs are becoming more like the central city than the next ring of suburbs farther out. "The problems of the city have suburbanized," contends urban expert Louis Masotti.[11] The newer suburbs, meanwhile, face unanticipated problems of sprawl and fiscal strain.

The income disparities between neighboring communities, combined with a school financing system based largely on the property tax, have cre-ated a two-tiered education system. In wealthy Lake Forest, the high school district enjoyed $1.2 million in assessed property valuation to support each pupil, while three miles away in North Chicago, there was just $23,700 per pupil in assessed property valuation,[12] only one-fiftieth the tax base of its neighbor.

The constant building of new subdivisions and business parks has created more and more need to travel from one spot to another, almost always by car, and has led to frequent battles over the placement of new roads and highways. "Build the new road, and be quick about it, but not through my neighborhood, dammit," sums the plaint. Average daily vehicle-miles traveled in the six-county region increased 33 percent in the 1980s. New highways are not being developed fast enough to unclog bumper-to-bumper traffic.[13] Adding insult to injury, northeastern Illinois has been tagged by the U.S. Environmental Protection Agency as one of only seven "severe non-attainment areas" for ozone pollution. The region's major employers and governments are thus forced to reduce total auto travel per employee, further chipping away at suburbanites' sense of independence.[14]

Sprawl is becoming expensive, as well, because over two decades the region's population (including Chicago and the collar counties) increased by only 4.1 percent while residential land consumption jumped 45 percent.[15] The Northeastern Illinois Planning Commission (NIPC) looked at the problem from an engineer's perspective, figuring the costs of water pipes and sewers, roads and sidewalks, and answered the question suburbanites had been asking about their constantly increasing property taxes: "How can costs not rise if public services and infrastructures must be stretched over 45 percent more territory to serve virtually the same sized population?" The report goes on: These two forces—decentralizing activity and increasing land consumption—have produced the opposite of our vision: a region beset by traffic congestion, higher housing costs, polluted streams and contaminated soils, abandonment of older communities, and the loss of prime farmland and open space . . . decentralization has proven extremely costly to local governments, to taxpayers and to the environment."[16]

Nor are the suburbs any longer a refuge from concern about crime. A 1994 survey found crime the top concern of suburban residents, mentioned twice as often as taxes and three times more than education.[17] Gayle Franzen, president of the DuPage County Board, was startled to learn from focus groups during his 1994 campaign that gangs were their most important concern.[18]

Collar county residents, nevertheless, generally appear satisfied with the services they receive. A 1991 survey conducted by Northern Illinois University (NIU) found that 75 percent of collar county respondents gave A or B (excellent or good) grades to their police departments and 71 percent gave A or B marks to their local schoolteachers.[19] Respondents were less satisfied on issues of planning and development. Fifty-nine percent gave A or B grades for local officials' management of commercial and residential development, and a bare majority, 53 percent, gave high marks for officials' effectiveness in "planning for the future."

Still, collar county residents appear anxious about the challenges faced by the suburbs. Seventy-four percent of respondents considered crime a moderate or significant problem, and more than half characterized transportation and high-quality education as moderate or significant problems. The NIU survey indicates that suburban communities will continue to be magnets for families only as long as the local education is considered good and the communities are considered safe.

LACK OF SUBURBAN COHESION

The principal barrier to solving suburban problems is that there is no core, heart, or soul to the sprawling collar region, with its twelve hundred local governments and even broader division by subdivision and neighborhood. Like the geography, leadership and influence in the collar counties are highly fragmented. According to suburban writer Tom Andreoli, business leaders who reside and work in the suburbs often stake their claim to civic involvement in prestigious "downtown" organizations such as the Chicago Symphony Orchestra, the Lyric Opera, or the Commercial Club of Chicago (a civic organization limited to CEOs).[20] Adds Paul Green: "I bet if you asked 100 people, 'Who are the top suburban business leaders?' you wouldn't get 10 names, much less the same 10 names."[21]

A degree of cohesion is provided for collar county municipalities by four groups: the Northwest Municipal Conference, the DuPage Mayors and Managers Conference, the South Suburban Mayors and Managers Association, and the West Central Municipal Conference. Each group represents between thirty and forty municipalities and townships, and they lobby effectively in the state capital, build networks among communities, and provide professional training for new trustees and city council members. Suburban business leaders have begun to organize as well. The East-West Corporate Corridor Association, whose members bestride I-88 in west suburban DuPage County, includes representation from many high-technology companies and places a strong emphasis on such issues as education and quality of the workforce.

The collar counties have their greatest cohesion and political clout in the state legislature. In 1992, Republicans gained a thirty-two-to-twenty-seven majority in the Illinois Senate. Twenty of the GOP senators were from the collar counties. The senate president, James "Pate" Philip of DuPage County, is a lifelong basher of the city and booster of the collar counties; he complains loudly and effectively that the suburbs have not been getting their fair share of state government services and funding.

In 1994, the GOP also garnered a majority in the house, sixty-four to fifty-four, and elected Lee Daniels, also from DuPage County, as Speaker of the house. Daniels then named Robert Churchill of Lake County, second after DuPage in population among the counties that surround Cook, to the Number 2 post of majority leader. But just as the collar counties are no longer all-white enclaves, neither is elected representation wholly Republican. After the 1994 election, Democrats occupied three of twenty-four state senate seats from the collar counties and six of forty-six state representative seats.

The collar county bloc, therefore, is not so much a unified political force as a loosely knit and somewhat immature collection of leaders who are only beginning to learn how to work together on common problems. This situation contrasts sharply with the old-line system that had been in place in Chicago before the Democratic machine began its decline.

SUBURBS GAIN, CHICAGO LOSES

Chicago lost 837,000 people between 1950 and 1990, about one-fourth of its peak population. When the *Chicago Tribune* polled 3,000 residents who had moved out, it found that nearly two-thirds had settled in the suburbs.[22] Generally, Chicagoans have moved to the suburban areas closest to their old neighborhoods. South siders tend to go south; southwest siders, southwest, often to where friends have moved. It's as if the old neighborhood picks up and moves, over time, regrouping not too far away.

This movement has hurt Chicago overall and nearly destroyed some neighborhoods, where white flight prompted by black in-migration set off a decades-long spiral of depopulation that has left some west-side neighborhoods with just one-fourth of their peak populations.

Those who have been leaving are often affluent, young, well educated, longtime Chicagoans. Partly as a result, per capita income in Chicago is 50 percent lower than in the collar region and poverty rates are four times higher.[23] In 1994, Chicago had only about half as many people as the collar region and only one-third as many factories.

Seventy-seven percent of those who left Chicago for the suburbs in 1992 cited the desire for a safer place to live as an "extremely" or "very" important reason for moving out, according to the *Chicago Tribune* survey.[24] Chicago's violent crime rate is nine times higher than the rate for the rest of the six-county area—30.3 violent crimes per 1,000 in Chicago versus 3.2 in the suburban collar.

Many black Chicagoans who can afford to are among those moving out. In the 1980s the black population fell by 113,444 in the city and grew by 103,453 in the suburbs. More than half the blacks who moved in 1992 relocated in south suburbs such as Country Club Hills, Matteson, Hazel Crest, and Bellwood, all of which in 1994 had populations that were 50 percent or more black.

In the Chicago that remains behind, poverty has become more concentrated in neighborhoods that were already poor twenty years ago. The near south side and the near west side, which border the vibrant downtown Loop, registered 1990 poverty rates of 62.5 percent and 54.5 percent, respectively.[25] More than one-third of all Chicago children (and nearly half of black children) lived in poverty in 1990. At 16 percent, the poverty rate for the elderly was higher than the national average.

If this were the whole story about Chicago, the political balance would have long since shifted to suburbia, but there is another side of the city that is healthy, wealthy, highly influential, young, politically powerful, and still a significant contender in both the state and national arenas. The power of Chicago is squarely centered in the downtown area, which has quadrupled in land area over the past two decades as rail yards, warehouse districts, and the former Skid Row have been redeveloped into townhouse complexes, loft districts, and business towers. The first Mayor Daley set the stage for the downtown's rebirth by using city, state, and federal funds to create a base for future development; he built highways and rapid transit lines, O'Hare Airport, the McCormick Place convention center, and new civic buildings. Daley and subsequent mayors, including reform-minded Harold Washington, then created a rich environment for developers of office buildings and residential areas. The city bought up deteriorated buildings, tore them down, and resold the property at a discount. It relaxed already liberal zoning codes to convince developers to build higher and wider and leveraged subsidies or low-interest mortgage assistance from all levels of government. All this triggered a building boom that peaked in the 1980s, when more than 350 building projects accounted for $7 billion worth of investment, including seventeen thousand new or rehabilitated living units in the downtown area.[26]

As the Loop was reborn, Chicago's near-north and lakefront communities enjoyed a sustained period of residential and commercial redevelopment that provided comfortable and attractive environments for the young urban professionals—the yuppies—who occupied the desks downtown and rode the elevated trains back and forth to work. All along the north lakefront, apartments were rehabilitated and new townhouses squeezed onto any lot available. When Lincoln Park became too expensive (town homes with three baths cost $300,000 and up), the action shifted west into older neighborhoods like Bucktown and north into Lakeview surrounding the Chicago Cubs baseball park, Wrigley Field. To the south, vitality took root in several middle-class black neighborhoods, including the Gap area with its Frank Lloyd Wright buildings. On the far north lakefront, the working-class neighborhoods of Uptown, Edgewater, and Rogers Park became economically and racially integrated, so popular with whites, blacks, Asians, and Hispanics that they broke the Chicago pattern of segregated housing.

The other strength of the city is not new at all. Chicago's vast bungalow areas, though some have been ravaged by racial change and nearby industrial decline, remain for the most part what they have always been: mile after mile of neat residential enclaves. Unlike most of suburbia, Chicago's neighborhoods are well served by public transportation such as the new elevated line through the southwest side to Midway Airport. New shopping centers have also appeared, helping many bungalow-belt neighborhoods retain their value. Still, the continued weakness of the public school system, despite reform efforts, and the rise in crime throughout the city result in many families moving out when their children approach kindergarten or their first year in high school.

CHICAGO HANGS ON

It is this Chicago, strong and yet weak, that must fight to retain its share of resources against the emerging suburban power bloc and the needy downstate interests. Fighting for a fair share and then some has a colorful history in Chicago, where power has traditionally brought with it personal aggrandizement, jobs, and the ability to reward friends and punish foes.

For most participants, Chicago politics has been a full-time profession rather than a part-time civic activity. During the years of machine politics, many hundreds of people did strictly political work (or no city work at all) even though their city paycheck might have been for street-cleaning or an obscure desk job. Former U.S. judge Abner Mikva found this out when, as a college student, he called on the local Democratic ward committeeman: "I came in and said I wanted to help. Dead silence. 'Who sent you?' the committeeman said. I said, 'Nobody.' He said, 'We don't want nobody nobody sent.' Then he said, 'We ain't got no jobs.' I said, 'I don't want a job.' He said, 'We don't want nobody that don't want a job. Where are you from, anyway?' I said, 'University of Chicago.' He said, 'We don't want nobody from the University of Chicago.' "[27]

Mikva would later learn that patronage and insider contracts were frequently used tools that created webs of fierce political loyalty and rigid hierarchical management. Richard J. Daley is most famous for this style of politics, but he learned the game from predecessors such as William Hale "Big Bill" Thompson, Republican mayor of Chicago from 1915 to 1923 and 1927 to 1931. Thompson's patronage army, including the police department and the courts, shared in the proceeds of Prohibition by providing "a policy of noninterference with the illegal activities of gangsters," including Al Capone. Historian Robert P. Howard writes of a time when twenty thousand speakeasies served illegal beer and liquor in Chicago, when policemen, bailiffs, court clerks, and Prohibition agents all required bribes, "to say nothing of big payments to the higher ups." When a mob chief was ambushed or murdered out on a suburban back road, there would be "garish displays of flowers at funerals attended by judges and aldermen."[28]

The Irish became skilled at sharing the rewards of power and soon came to dominate Chicago politics after working their way up from jobs as canal diggers and policemen. They honed the art under Mayors Edward J. Kelly and Patrick Nash from 1933 to 1947, first by sharing with other white ethnic groups and then with the city's growing black population. By 1940, Democratic ward committeeman William Dawson was the top black political boss in the white-dominated Cook County Democratic party. He was among those who urged the party to drop Mayor Martin J. Kennelly in 1955 and replace him with new party chairman Richard J. Daley. Dawson delivered five wards in the primary to put Daley over the top. Daley's majority of 125,000 votes over Democrat-turned-Republican Robert Merriam came largely from margins provided in Dawson's wards and four other black wards.[29]

Daley became legendary during more than two decades as both Cook County Democratic Central Committee chairman (1953–76) and mayor (1955–76). He skillfully gathered immense political power over patronage, nominations for office and policymaking in local, state, and even the federal government. Anyone who wanted one of the thirty thousand patronage jobs or hundreds of elective offices that he controlled had to go through the local Democratic ward committeeman and the mayor's office. In return, loyalty to the mayor and the Democratic party was obligatory.

RACIAL POLITICS IN CHICAGO

Chicago's power base encountered a crisis, however, when blacks, and, more recently Hispanics, increased in population. By the late 1960s, resentment was rising among blacks over Daley's use of power. Even though the black population was growing rapidly, from 13.3 percent of the voting age population in 1950 to 27.1 percent by 1970,[30] the mayor's housing and school policies were clearly designed to keep blacks locked in their own neighborhoods and away from the best-paid jobs. Daley's strong ties to contractors and building trades unions were central to his power base and represented tens of thousands of politically connected jobs, but the work crews on city-connected projects were virtually all white, as were the unions for plumbers, electricians, carpenters, steelworkers, and even laborers. Little changed after Daley's death in 1976 until a savvy black congressman and former state legislator, Harold Washington, decided to take on the machine.

Vowing to open up the city's bureaucracy, Washington became the black candidate in the Democratic mayoral primary of 1983. He was pitted against Mayor Jane Byrne and state's attorney Richard M. Daley, son of the late mayor. Washington was opposed by nine of the fifteen black aldermen and eighteen of the twenty-three black state legislators, who were still tied to the Cook County Democratic organization. Nevertheless, Washington garnered 73 percent of a huge black voter turnout. With Byrne and Daley dividing most of the white vote and all three candidates winning shares of the Hispanic vote, Washington earned a narrow primary victory, with 36 percent of the votes cast, and went on to win a close election against a Republican who benefited from the votes of many whites who normally voted Democratic.

Washington filled his cabinet with reform-minded black, white, and Hispanic leaders, and though quite a few were chewed up and spit out by the bureaucracies they were trying to fix, the new administration won a reputation for relatively fair and equal administration of city services. Early on, Washington faced a full-blown revolt from his city council, still dominated by old-line forces, but by 1987, when he won reelection, the "council wars" had been ended and Washington was enjoying the prospect of four more years to build on his achievements. He died unexpectedly in November of that year, and the old line in the city council maneuvered quickly to elect Eugene Sawyer, a black with machine ties, as interim mayor. In the 1989 mayoral elections, Cook County state's attorney Richard M. Daley defeated Sawyer in the primary and then topped black alderman Timothy Evans, running as an independent, in the general election.

Even though whites recaptured the mayor's office in 1989, the Washington years forever changed Chicago's political landscape, according to Michael Preston, a leading student of black politics. From the late nineteenth century to 1983, black political leadership in Chicago meant allegiance to a white patron first and the black community second. Black politicians were not allowed to develop independent black power bases and thus generally had to practice defensive, often conservative politics, based on what was possible rather than what was needed.[31]

By 1990, the U.S. Census Bureau showed Chicago's population in a four-way split: 38 percent black, 38 percent white, 20 percent Hispanic, and 4 percent Asian and other. The population parity between blacks and whites suggests that Hispanics could become the balance of political power. Hispanic political and community leaders, however, are hampered by geographic dispersion, population undercounts, low voter eligibility, low average age of population, and fragmentation by nationality.

The Hispanic vote can be important, nevertheless. According to one estimate, Hispanics gave Harold Washington 75 percent of their votes in his 1983 primary. This would translate into a forty-five-thousand-vote margin for Washington, who won the primary by forty-eight thousand votes.[32] Hispanics strongly supported Richard M. Daley in his successful 1989 primary and general election contests, both of which included black opponents.

Like immigrants who arrived before them, Hispanics are learning how to play political hardball. In 1989 Illinois senator Miguel del Valle collaborated with black legislators in refusing to vote for a temporary tax increase sponsored by their Democratic leaders. Del Valle and the blacks had enough votes among their forces to hold the tax legislation hostage until the Democratic leadership in both houses agreed to a bill to elect Cook County circuit judges by districts, which would increase the potential for minorities to be elected to the bench.

After Harold Washington was elected mayor in 1983, he declared the old Chicago political machine "a mortally wounded animal." His reelection in 1987 tended to confirm this taunt; yet as of 1993, a Daley was once again ensconced in the mayor's office. And in 1994, John Stroger, a black who ran with the backing of Mayor Richard M. Daley, was elected president of the Cook County Board. Will Richard M. build another disciplined coalition of political lieutenants to reforge a machine equal to his father's? Almost certainly not, though he may have the resources and skills to become a strong player in Illinois politics and to stay in office for several terms.

Part of the reason is that the city is a smaller part of the state population than it was under Daley's father, down to less than one in four Illinois residents. Richard J. Daley's political power came primarily from his chairmanship of the Cook County Democratic Central Committee, which controlled about thirty thousand jobs and access to nomination to elected office and judgeships.[33] Party organizations in the 1990s are weaker than in the past, the courts are more separate than they used to be, and Richard M. Daley has emphatically eschewed a party leadership role. It is improbable that a lasting political or community coalition will develop that approaches the strength of the Daley machine at its zenith. More likely, a multiracial coalition will slowly develop as Chicago fights for its fair share of state and federal resources.

THE EROSION OF DOWNSTATE

The first region of the state to rise to power historically is the weakest player on the field today. The river transportation that led to the founding of towns like Kaskaskia, Alton, and Shawneetown is now nearly meaningless from a commercial standpoint. Although most of the land is as fertile as before, the farm economy is no match for the mixed industrial-service economies of the collar counties and Chicago. Much of downstate is troubled and poor in the 1990s, struggling to regain economic and political health.

Boasting only three cities of more than one hundred thousand people, downstate's checkerboard landscape (which despite the name includes all rural areas north and west of metropolitan Chicago) is dotted with eight hundred mostly small towns, like South Beloit (population 4,072) on the Wisconsin line and Cairo (population 4,846), south of Paducah, Kentucky. In between is the desperately poor, isolated black community of East St. Louis, and cutting diagonally across rich farmland from the St. Louis area toward Chicago, along old Route 66, is a string of nearly all-white market towns— Litchfield, Lincoln, and Pontiac among them. Indeed, there is little sense of a single downstate, other than as a geographic identifier.

Significant change occurred downstate during the 1980s. Industrial cities such as Rock Island, Peoria, and Decatur experienced job loss and population decline, while the nearby Champaign-Urbana and Bloomington-Normal—with economies based on education, services, and technology— prospered and grew. Net farm income was only 5 percent of total income in Illinois's rural counties in 1990.[34] Although this net income figure understates overall agribusiness activity, the farm sector is now a smaller component of downstate economic activity than the eye would perceive on a drive through the endless corn and soybean fields of eastern and central Illinois.

Even areas with economic bright spots face a demanding period of modernization. Job recruiters for Diamond Star Motors in Bloomington, touted as the most advanced auto assembly operation in the world, have gone to high schools in the area to warn that a high school diploma will not be enough to qualify for a place in their computer- and robotics-driven workplace. Gone are the days when a young man in Peoria or Rock Island could drop out of high school and still land a secure, lifetime, middle-class job "on the line" at Caterpillar or International Harvester. Better education is a key; yet like the school systems in Chicago and poorer collar county suburbs, many downstate communities must make do with chronic underfunding and worn-out facilities.

Downstate Illinois is politically balanced, not the Republican stronghold of dated conventional wisdom. Three of downstate's six congressmen are Democrats. The 1990 Democratic gubernatorial candidate, Neil Hartigan of Chicago, carried forty-one of the ninety-six downstate counties, and in 1992 President Bill Clinton carried downstate handily.

The most prominent downstate leader as of 1995 was Republican governor Jim Edgar. Born, reared, and educated through college in Charleston (population 20,000) in eastern Illinois, Edgar has deep affection for the people and politics of downstate Illinois. The governor emphasizes this loyalty by noting that he and his wife, Brenda, took their honeymoon in Springfield, where they appreciated the many shrines to Abraham Lincoln.

Even so, political influence downstate is fragmented and weak. Rather than leading any downstate coalition, Edgar often finds himself mediating disputes between Chicago's Mayor Daley and a suburban spokesman, Senate President James "Pate" Philip. Among major statewide organizations, only the Illinois Farm Bureau is dominated by downstate members. Downstate companies such as Caterpillar and John Deere may loom large within such major business organizations as the Illinois Manufacturers Association, the Illinois Business Roundtable, and the Taxpayers' Federation of Illinois, yet the organizations are controlled by their metropolitan Chicago members.

The increasing concentrations of population, wealth, and media in Chicago and the collar counties have drained downstate of the influence and prominence it enjoyed in an earlier era. Even Springfield is less visible. Politicians must go to Chicago if they want major television coverage because the Chicago stations do not staff the Capitol pressroom. Meetings of statewide public advisory councils are more likely to meet in the futuristic State of Illinois Center in Chicago's Loop (which could have served as Darth

Vader's headquarters in *Star Wars*) than in Springfield, simply because members, including downstaters, generally find it more convenient to meet in or near Chicago. Former governor James R. Thompson even eschewed the executive mansion in Springfield in favor of a house on Chicago's north side; he was the first governor to live outside Springfield during his tenure.

Simply put, downstate has been shrinking relative to the collar county region—in population, political strength, economic wealth, and media visibility. Big chunks of Illinois farmland are being transformed into new subdivisions around metro Chicago and St. Louis. The growth envelops small towns where the main-street coffeeshop regulars never dreamed they would one day become part of the suburban ring and, by extension, of the suburban power bloc. Yet the erosive process continues, suggesting, however paradoxically, that the two declining powers, the city and downstate, might yet find common ground to face their new competitor, the suburbs.

REGIONAL DIFFERENCE STILL HAZY

The separation of Illinois into three apparently distinct blocs might suggest that geopolitical groupings would shape Illinois politics in the years ahead. Thoughtful observers suggest that it may not be that simple.

Political scientist Peter F. Nardulli decided in 1986 to test the conventional wisdom that Illinois is a state sharply divided by regions. He and his colleagues conducted lengthy interviews with a scientifically drawn sample of nearly three thousand adults throughout Illinois. They asked respondents how they perceived regions of the state, how they viewed people in other parts of the state, and about their own positions and values on policy issues.[35]

Most respondents considered Chicago and northern and southern Illinois regions of the state; however, few thought of the suburbs as a region, even though social scientists do.[36] More than half of both the Chicago and downstate respondents perceived that they were different from one another in how they were reared, how they live, and what they consider important. According to Nardulli and Michael Krassa:

> Many people (especially Chicagoans and downstaters) did not feel that others thought highly of them, and even more felt that others were not concerned about their welfare. Moreover, the vast majority in a region did not feel that others would support a program that would primarily benefit their region. . . . [Legislators] were viewed as obstructionists who were not concerned with the

welfare of the entire state. Downstaters were most likely to feel that others and their legislators were unconcerned and/or ignored their interests.[37]

These perceptions appear unjustified, however, based on the respondents' own attitudes. For example, only 17 percent of downstaters favored giving Chicago its own statehood, even though 51 percent thought such an action would either help downstate or have no effect on it. On support for spending increases for various programs, more Chicagoans (68 percent) than downstaters (57 percent) favored increased spending to aid farmers. It might be assumed that if there were strong strains of different political cultures across regions, there would have been less support for education in southern Illinois than in northern Illinois, but there was not.

There were statistically significant differences between southern Illinois and Chicago respondents on several social issues. For example, 40 percent of those from southern Illinois supported discrimination against homosexuals compared to 23 percent of those from Chicago. Only 31 percent from the southern part of the state felt a woman should have a right to choose an abortion whereas 49 percent from Chicago favored the woman's right. On the death penalty, family values, and several other social issues, feeling was generally consistent across all regions.

These shared values as well as differences across regions have generally been confirmed by the annual Illinois Survey conducted by Northern Illinois University. In the 1993 survey, about three-quarters of respondents from each region favored increased spending for public schools, and fewer than 10 percent wanted to decrease spending. Although a significantly smaller percentage of downstaters (33 percent) favored making abortion legal in all cases than did either Chicagoans (46 percent) or collar county residents (44 percent), there was similarity across regions in the percentages opposed to abortion under any circumstance (downstate, 16 percent; Chicago, 15 percent; and collar, 11 percent).[38]

Nardulli and his associates concluded: "It would be difficult to support the view that regionally-based subcultures exist in Illinois which lead local residents to markedly different political orientations. . . . It is clear . . . that residents of various regions analyzed are not as distinct as Illinois folklore would suggest."[39] This does not mean all Illinoisans think alike; views vary widely throughout the state on virtually any matter of significance, and "each region is far more diverse than is acknowledged in casual political discourse. It makes no more sense to talk about the suburbs as homogeneous than the city of Chicago."[40]

The same is apparently true about leaders in each political party. Sociologist Mildred A. Schwartz ranked the twenty-seven Illinois Republican state senators in 1979 on a conservatism-liberalism scale, based on rankings by seven interest groups.[41] The GOP senators were split about evenly between the collar counties and downstate. Schwartz found significant differences in the ideologies of the senators, from strong conservatism to moderation; yet the range and distribution of differences were about the same within each of the two regions. That is, the ideological mix of suburban GOP senators was about the same as that of those from downstate.

Why do regional differences appear less marked than might have been expected? Several factors may play a part: the continuing cross migrations of residents; the dispersion of ethnic and racial groups across regions; statewide policies that provide somewhat common educational services and requirements; and a single television market (Chicago) that provides news for more than two-thirds of all Illinois residents.

"WHERE'S MINE?" LIVES ON

For all the variety within each region and the policy values shared by the regions, there are important distinctions in the 1990s that provide powerful political justification for perceiving and acting upon regional differences. The differences are mostly economic, and the response by all parties is traditional: to fight for resources among the groups even when a unified statewide approach might make more sense.

Chicago remains the eight-hundred-pound gorilla simply because it has more than twenty times the population of the next largest city in the state. The metro-east area of Illinois, the second largest urban area, has only a fraction as many residents (about 600,000) and is not a city at all but a collection of small municipalities and suburbs linked to St. Louis, Missouri, just across the Mississippi. There are no other big cities. In 1992, only five cities besides Chicago had more than 100,000 residents: Rockford (142,000), Peoria (114,000), Springfield (106,000), and two suburban communities, Aurora and Naperville (104,000 each).

The city is thus distinctly urban and dominated by minorities. There are greater concentrations of poverty, poor children, crime, and social disarray in Chicago than elsewhere in the state. At the same time, the city continues to lure wealth to its financial markets and corporate offices, creativity to the performing arts venues, and, like moths to the flame, political figures to Chicago's media outlets.

The collar counties are unified to an extent because they are well outside Chicago and relatively well off. They face the challenges of building and paying for infrastructure fast enough to keep up with growth and to maintain roads and sewers, and they must find ways to cope with growing poverty and crime.

Downstate is unified mostly by its suffering during the deep recession of 1981 to 1983, which diminished the region's vitality and shattered the self-confidence of many community leaders. Downstate is markedly poorer, older, and less well-educated overall than the collar counties.

The contrasts in wealth among the regions generate periodic calls from each region for its fair share of the state's largesse. This has become a serious issue that divides the regions. In 1987, a research unit of the state legislature looked at where state taxes came from and how state spending for selected major programs was distributed by region.[42] The collar counties paid 46 percent of the taxes but received only 27 percent of state spending. Downstate was the big net beneficiary, paying 33 percent of taxes while receiving 47 percent of spending. Chicago paid 21 percent of the taxes and received 25 percent of the spending.

The approach used to resolve most regional conflict has been to divide up the pot as needed to gain a majority vote. For example, when Chicago leaders pushed in the 1960s for a new campus for the University of Illinois in Chicago, their efforts were met by demands from downstate leaders that Southern Illinois University be awarded funding for a new campus in Edwardsville. Both campuses were constructed.

The formula for allocating state aid to local schools provides another illustration. Collar county legislators argue that their voters are already paying much more than other regions in state taxes (true) and getting much less back (also true). Downstate and Chicago legislators retort that their schoolchildren are getting less financial support per pupil from all sources than are the suburban children (also true, generally speaking). At the heart of the problem is a school funding structure based on local property taxes rather than a major state contribution, which could even out differences between rich and poor communities. The inability of the regions to forge a solution prompted former state school superintendent Ted Sanders to lament, "Education reform has been 'slip-slidin' away into the quicksand of politics and provincialism."[43]

Regional conflict is also generated when proposed legislation would have varying regional impact. Property tax relief offers an illustration. During the 1980s, property assessments rose rapidly in many parts of Chicago and the collar counties but declined sharply in many downstate areas. There was strong public pressure for property tax limitations from the city and collar counties, while many downstate legislators and local governments opposed limits, primarily out of fear of reduced local funding in the future, when assessed property values might rebound.

Thus voting in 1989 on a property tax limitation bill in the Illinois House was primarily on geographic rather than partisan lines. Thirty-two Democrats, mostly from the Chicago area, favored; seventeen Democrats, primarily from downstate, opposed. Twenty-four Republicans, nearly all from the suburbs, favored; twenty-one Republicans, nearly all downstaters, opposed.[44] The bill failed to win the votes required for passage. The regional conflict was resolved to some extent the following year, when property tax "caps" were approved, but solely for the five suburban counties that surround Cook. This legislation was groundbreaking in part because it provided a legal and political acknowledgment of the five collar counties as a formal entity.

In summary, regional political differences result largely from self-interest, differences in wealth, and strong perceptions that the other regions are out for themselves, not primarily from sharp cultural or attitudinal differences among the regions. Political struggle and conflict across the regions of Illinois will continue. There may be more—and more complicated—regional conflict now that the old Chicago-downstate regional division has been supplanted by a Chicago–collar counties-downstate triad. As historian Robert M. Sutton put it: "The public interest in Illinois today is a kind of common denominator hammered out by the interplay of these powerful regional forces."[45]

CHAPTER THREE

Power and Influence,
Illinois Style

Let us hypothetically consider two legislators of the same party with the same number of years in office. Each has the same formal vote, yet one is an ally of the governor and has supported the representative who was elected Speaker of the house. She is respected as an expert on complicated revenue issues and comes from a politically safe district.

The other lawmaker has none of these traits in his favor but is independently wealthy, a magnetic and telegenic speaker, and the recipient of frequent praise by the state's leading newspaper, the *Chicago Tribune*. Who is more powerful? The answer depends on the level of skill each legislator can muster in applying his or her respective strengths.

Politics is a serious game in which the players apply their respective bundles of power and influence as skillfully as they know how to achieve their objectives. Power is the application of coercion, threats, control, even force to cause someone to do something he or she would not have done otherwise, to stimulate, as Bertrand Russell has said, "the production of intended effects."[1] Influence is a subtler form of power centered around persuasion. The person who is influenced acts freely, unlike the victim of a power play. Power is wielded when a legislative leader coerces another legislator to cast a vote that the lawmaker was not planning to cast. Influence is displayed when a lobbyist provides persuasive information to convince a governor to veto a bill that the governor had been planning to sign.[2]

Power comes in many forms. Formal powers of elected officials include the vote of a legislator, the appointment powers of legislative leaders and the governor, the veto powers of a governor, jobs and contracts, and the perquisites of the office such as invitations to the executive mansion and use of state airplanes. Informal powers can be wielded not only by elected officials but also by others on the political stage. These are money, organizations, charisma, specialized knowledge, media coverage, coalition-building skills, and creativity.

Skillful use of power and influence has been a hallmark of Illinois politics. But as the state's political landscape changes, the methods of using power continue to evolve and different players become more or less prominent. The governor's office will always be a focal point, of course, and the legislature the biggest and most diverse arena. Yet the game is played in many other venues and at all levels of government, and increasingly important roles are played by interest groups, lobbyists, grass-roots organizations, and the media. Illinois is not unique, of course, in the way power and influence are used, but without question the state has produced some masters of the art. This chapter begins with portraits of some of those experts, then profiles the major sectors that have an impact in the ongoing struggle for power and influence in Illinois.

ARRINGTON'S SENATE "MAJORITY"

The late W. Russell Arrington was Evanston's representative to the General Assembly from 1944 to 1972 and president of the Illinois Senate from 1965 to 1970. A Republican lawyer-businessman, Arrington was smart, wealthy, and strong of personality, even intimidating.[3]

When first elected senate president, Arrington and his fellow Republicans held a thirty-three-to-twenty-five majority, but their ranks were soon cut to thirty-one by the deaths of two members. The Illinois Constitution requires a minimum of thirty votes to pass legislation in the senate, which created a challenge for Arrington, who knew that several Republican senators were known to stray from the fold on matters important to certain special interests or to the Democratic mayor of Chicago.

Because there was a Democratic governor and a Democratic majority in the house, Arrington convinced his fellow GOP senators that in light of their tenuous majority, the only way to have any real power in the state was to operate as a tightly disciplined bloc. He persuaded the Republicans to agree that on important issues, a majority vote of the Republican caucus, taken behind closed doors, would bind all Republicans to support the caucus position on the senate floor. Thus a sixteen-to-fifteen vote among Republicans in caucus would be—and indeed was—transformed into a thirty-one-to-twenty-five vote on the floor. For the six months of the 1965 session of the legislature, the closed-door Republican caucus was, for all important purposes, the Illinois Senate. Inside the caucus room, to be sure, emotional debates took place; grown men were known to cry at the thought of casting votes that would be anathema in their districts. But on the floor of the senate, the Republicans were a model of unity. The senators voted as they did because they knew the caucus system increased the power of each of them in passing their own pieces of legislation. They were also fortified by the solidarity displayed by their elite, disciplined band. When a senator showed signs of defecting from the caucus—for they were bound by no law, only personal commitment—Arrington cajoled, offered financial help with campaign finances, made commitments on legislation important to the wavering soul, or simply intimidated the lawmaker into staying in line.

To make the binding caucus acceptable to the Republican senators, Arrington created one of the first legislative campaign committees. He solicited business leaders to help raise funds, which in turn were spent on behalf of members of the caucus who faced tough election challengers. Arrington also developed legislative staff support for his members so that they could devise alternatives to the Democratic governor's budget and legislative program.

Even so, individual interests sometimes threatened to break up the bloc, as happened in 1965, when the reapportionment process was getting under way. Reapportionment of districts was an issue of overriding importance on which Arrington thought he had convinced his members to vote together. But because nothing is more partisan to a lawmaker than the shape of his or her district, one Sunday late in the session, Arrington's staff learned that three GOP senators had agreed to a Democratic reapportionment map whose district boundaries would help them be reelected.

Arrington immediately called an unprecedented Sunday evening meeting and revealed to all the caucus members the conspiratorial plans of the wayward senators. Using the anger of the other caucus members along with his own withering personality, Arrington forced the three to abandon their plans and to come back into the fold.

From time to time, Arrington had to bend. He wanted to increase taxes on race tracks, for instance, but strong opposition by veteran GOP senators convinced him to relent. Nevertheless, by making disciplined use of an informal device called the party caucus, Arrington was able to transform a tenuous majority in one legislative chamber into a powerful bloc that gave Republicans parity on most issues not only with the Democrats who controlled the governorship and the other chamber but with the master of bloc voting himself, Mayor Richard J. Daley of Chicago.

DALEY'S GOLDEN TOUCH

Daley, mayor from 1955 to 1976, was the most powerful player in the legislature in 1969,[4] even though his days as a state senator were long past. Daley was chairman of the Cook County Central Committee of the Democratic party, a post he had won in 1953. As chairman of the party in the county with half the state's population, he had come to dominate the awarding of thousands of city and county patronage jobs. In addition, he chaired the slating process by which the Democratic party endorsed candidates for city, county, state, legislative, congressional, and judicial offices.

Inside Cook County in the late 1960s, a candidate simply could not—or so most were convinced—win the party nomination unless endorsed by Daley's slating committee. Anyone could run for the party nomination, but without the money, precinct workers, and formal endorsement, he could not win. For nearly all offices in Chicago and Cook County, nomination at the Democratic primary election was tantamount to election at the November general election. So if you wanted to hold office, you had to win the endorsement of the slating committee of the Cook County Democratic Central Committee, chaired by the man newspaper columnist Mike Royko called the Boss.

Most of the sixty-two house and senate members elected from Chicago in 1969 were career politicians. Many simultaneously held patronage jobs with Chicago or Cook County; each wanted to keep his or her job(s) and possibly be elevated to the Chicago City Council, the Congress, or the judicial bench. All knew they were beneficiaries of the political organization that had been solidified and strengthened by Daley. Their future in politics depended on reciprocal loyalty to the organization and to Daley.

On a busy day during the 1969 legislative session, leaders of the Chicago Democrats in the house would distribute to their members cards that listed the positions favored by the Chicago leadership, which the members followed faithfully. Republicans derisively referred to these as "idiot cards," but GOP leaders were impressed and often envious of the discipline across the aisle, which their party lacked.

The critical issue in 1969 was Governor Richard B. Ogilvie's proposal for a new income tax of 2½ percent on individual income and 4 percent on corporate income, a concept that had been resisted for decades. Daley needed additional income for his city government and for Chicago's public schools, but he did not want to take responsibility for increasing local taxes. Knowing that he needed Daley's support, Ogilvie proposed that one-twelfth of all state income tax revenue be returned to local governments on a population basis. That was good enough for Daley, who agreed to assure passage of the controversial tax.

On the day of the final house vote, the Republican speaker of the house "called the question" at the close of debate. He then opened the electronic voting switches. Everyone could see the tally of green (yes) and red (no) lights on giant scoreboards as members cast their votes. Eighty-nine votes were required for passage of the tax bill. The final tally could be delayed while members explained their votes. Republicans pushed their green or red buttons early. As expected, Republican support alone was far from adequate at sixty-nine votes.

While votes were being explained, Democratic minority leader John P. Touhy, a Chicagoan, orchestrated the addition of Democratic votes onto the tally board, five at a time. With his eyes on the board, Touhy would wave an arm and, in prearranged order, another five votes would go on the board. The first votes from Chicago Democrats were generally from the least important, often black, members of the organization. To professional politicians, votes in favor of a major new tax are of potentially great cost later at the polls and are thus not to be squandered.

After about ten minutes of gesticulations by Touhy, the magic total of eighty-nine votes flashed on the screen.[5] The Republican Speaker of the house quickly took the tally and declared the bill passed. Twenty-two Democrats, sixteen of them members of the Cook County Democratic organization, voted for the bill. Daley could have put ten to fifteen more votes on the board if necessary, but he was able to spare many important members of the Chicago delegation from that duty. One observer in the gallery commended Touhy's performance as comparable to that of Sir George Solti, conductor at that time of the Chicago Symphony Orchestra.

MADIGAN'S GENIUS FOR COMMITTEES

In 1969 Michael J. Madigan was sitting in the old state Capitol as a member of the Illinois Constitutional Convention. In 1970 he was elected to the Illinois House, where he has served continuously since. During this period, Madigan has also been the Democratic committeeman of the thirteenth Ward in Chicago. On the side he has also developed a reportedly lucrative Chicago law practice.

Madigan was elected Speaker of the house in 1983 and held that office until 1994, when Republicans won a majority of house seats. During that decade Madigan methodically enhanced the powers of the Speaker. He did this by centralizing power in the house within the Speaker's office; developing fund-raising committees whose war chests outstrip those of other legislative leaders; using his campaign funds to help elect and reelect Democrats in contested races; and convincing powerful interest groups that the Speaker controls or is the key to passage or defeat of their legislation.

As house minority leader in 1981, he combined luck and skill to craft a redistricting map that was extremely favorable to Democratic candidates. The complicated redistricting process was directed by a bipartisan committee whose swing vote was determined by a pick from the hat; the Democrats were lucky enough to win the draw in 1981 and, making use of new computer software, "drew districts that were more Democratic than even legislators living in them thought possible."[6] As a result, throughout the 1980s and early 1990s, Democrats enjoyed comfortable majorities in the house, with a margin of sixty-seven to fifty-one in 1994.

Another of Madigan's tactics was to shift control of staff appointments from committee chairs to a committee on committees, which he controls. He further increased his influence in committee by changing rules to allow him to substitute committee members sympathetic to him for those less so.

His two campaign committees (one in his name, the other in that of the Democratic house) raised $2.2 million in the two years from July 1987 to June 1989. Madigan spent much of it on behalf of fellow house Democrats from the suburbs and downstate who needed—and were grateful for—his help. One downstate house member received almost $40,000 in 1988 to fend off a challenger who attacked the Democratic lawmaker's support of a tax increase. Another downstate Democrat, a novice vying for a seat vacated by a Republican incumbent, received $20,000 from Madigan and was elected.

Once elected, new members continued to receive help. Madigan arranged for staff assistance with legislation that would make them look good at home, and, when Madigan had a comfortable majority, new members were generally excused from voting with the former Speaker on controversial legislation. "He is more than willing to feed those guys and burp them," said one lobbyist. "The majority are willing to let him do that. He's made the water nice and warm."[7]

Many Springfield lobbyists and Democratic legislators have become willing participants in a Madigan-engineered system that some compare to one-stop shopping.[8] Well aware that Madigan controls the fate of house legislation, lobbyists often contribute directly to one of the Speaker's funds or seek his advice as to which Democratic incumbents need help the most.

Using a classic "you scratch my back and I'll scratch yours" argument, Chicago personal injury lawyer Philip H. Corboy in 1986 wrote a "give until it hurts" letter to members of the Illinois Trial Lawyers Association. "Mr. Madigan uses the money obtained at his reception for assisting all Democratic legislators throughout the state," Corboy wrote. "Obviously, allegiances to him are then acquired from those that he himself has helped. . . . We must be in a position to help him so that he can retain his majority vote in the House and so that he in turn has a rapport with his legislative constituency."

Madigan's power was illustrated dramatically one day in May 1989. For three years Governor James R. Thompson had unsuccessfully sought an increase in the state income tax. Various proposals had been debated extensively, but Madigan had always blocked a vote, undoubtedly to the relief of many of his members, who were unenthusiastic about voting for an increase even though they were under significant pressure from education groups to do so.

Then on May 17, 1989, to the astonishment of everyone, Madigan introduced, debated, and passed from the house a temporary two-year increase in the state income tax—all in one day. Half the revenues would go to education and half to local governments. The Illinois Municipal League had not even been asking for an increase, but it was clear that new Chicago mayor Richard M. Daley needed the financial help. The Madigan proposal was subsequently adopted in the senate and signed by the governor.

Each of these masters of the art put together and applied power in different ways. Each, too, faced limits; even Speaker Madigan has been rebuffed by the veto of a Republican governor and by counterattacks from the other legislative chamber. None of these people work in a vacuum. They are affected in various ways by outside influences that use their own methods to affect decisions and outcomes. The key players discussed in this chapter are the party organizations, interest groups and their lobbyists, grass-roots organizations, and the media.

DECLINE OF PARTY ORGANIZATIONS

Political party organizations in Illinois were generally weak in 1996. The typical state or county party organization had little power to induce one of its elected public officials to do something he or she would not do otherwise. It was not always thus. The Democratic party of Illinois held its first nominating convention in 1835[9] and came to dominate the opposing Whig party for the next two decades. By 1856, Abraham Lincoln and many fellow Whigs had defected to join other anti-Democrats in forming a new Republican party. They became the state's leading party, with few lapses, until 1932, but the tables turned again during the Depression, when Democrats in Chicago solidified into a generally unified organization that made their party dominant in Chicago and competitive statewide, as it is today.

Party organizations were originally developed to help like-minded political activists elect their partisans to government office in hopes of influencing, even controlling, government processes. Originally party organizations were informal, unregulated entities. Slowly statutes were adopted, primarily by the states, to regulate these organizations. The most important activity became the nominating of candidates to contest general elections.

The formal party organization chart in Illinois has the shape of a pyramid. At the base of each organization is a precinct committeeman for each of the state's nearly twelve thousand precincts, each representing about five hundred voters. For all counties except Cook, precinct committeemen are elected every two years by those who vote in the party's primary nominating election. In Cook County, party voters elect thirty township committeemen outside Chicago and fifty ward committeemen in the city. Each committeeman theoretically appoints a captain to keep in touch with voters in each and every precinct, but where parties have little public support, these slots often go unfilled.

After each primary election, precinct committeemen elect a chairman from their ranks. They "vote their strength," each casting for chairman the total number of votes cast in their respective precincts in the primary. In Cook County, the township and ward committeemen elect the county chairman.

Above the county chairs on the organization chart are the state central committeemen, one for each of the state's twenty congressional districts. In 1989, the Republican party was successful in passing legislation that gives each party the option of either continuing to elect state central committeemen at the party's primary election or to elect them by a vote of the precinct committeemen (township and ward committeemen in Cook). In theory, election by the precinct committeemen would link the base of the party pyramid with the crown and conceivably infuse the top with whatever influence exists at the county level. Republicans have used this option since 1990, while Democrats continue with election by primary voters.

Though the statewide organization implies that power peaks at the top of the hierarchy, in practice party power has traditionally been strongest at the county level. State chairmen have generally wielded little influence. Political party power varies greatly from locale to locale and can change over time. It depends on the local political culture, individual leadership, the resources available to a party organization, and the party's effectiveness in influencing nominations. The Cook County Democratic Central Committee was once the model of the strong party machine. It had access to huge resources in the form of party workers, money, and campaign savvy and used them skillfully to dominate the nominations process.

According to Illinois parties specialist Kent Redfield, the best places to look for signs of strength or weakness in parties are in the traditional functions of recruiting and influencing nominations, running election campaigns, raising money, getting voters to the polls, and providing voters with cues on how to vote.[10] Although the two major parties are highly competitive statewide, one party or the other has tended to dominate in local areas. As a result, a party organization's power lies in its ability to control or heavily influence party nominations. That is, if a party organization dominates access to nomination and then election, officeholders tend to do what the party organization leaders want.

The influence of party organizations over elections has been eroding since about the turn of the century. In 1889, Illinois adopted the Australian secret ballot. In place of ballots distributed by the respective parties, the Australian ballot put all parties and candidates onto a single ballot, which was cast secretly. It allowed voters, for the first time, to split their general election votes among candidates of more than one party.

The primary election, adopted in the early 1900s in Illinois, replaced the convention as the parties' nominating mechanism. Primary elections allowed party voters to challenge party-endorsed candidates for nomination. By the 1960s, the influence of party organizations in primary elections began to wane. Patronage jobs for party loyalists had been declining in number as a result of expanded civil service protections and court decrees that prohibited political firings and, by 1990, political hirings. Thus party leaders had fewer resources with which to reward active precinct workers.

Another factor was the growing influence of television, which allowed candidates to appeal directly to voters and diminished the need to depend on party organizations to carry candidates' messages to the voters. Television also caused sharp increases in the costs of campaigns, which exceeded the resources of most party organizations. As a result, candidates began to raise most of their own campaign funds, further reducing their link to party organizations. Finally, consultants emerged who specialized in campaign management, media, and fund-raising. Candidates could now "rent" their own campaign organizations without the need to rely on the skills of party organizations.

As a result, the formal political party organizations provided for in statute, such as the Illinois Republican State Central Committee or the Democratic Central Committee of McLean County, have often become little more than enthusiastic boosters of the party label. For the most part, candidates achieve success on their own and thus have little obligation to the formal party organizations whose banners they carry.

The lack of party organization influence was clear in 1990 in the nineteenth Congressional District in eastern Illinois. That year every one of the eighteen GOP county chairmen in the congressional district endorsed the same candidate for the party nomination to the U.S. House, yet their candidate lost at the party primary election.[11]

Fighting to retain influence, the Illinois Democratic State Central Committee has become more effective at raising money. During the two-year 1983–84 presidential election cycle, the state Democratic party raised only $700,000. By 1987–88, the party raised and spent $4.4 million.[12] Even so, in 1994 the organization was a paper tiger. In the era of Richard J. Daley, statewide aspirants went hat in hand to party leaders to seek endorsement— and dutifully dropped out if they didn't receive it. In 1994, for the first time in memory, the Democratic state party avoided making any endorsements. "Why fool each other?" said Democratic party chairman Gary LaPaille. "We know these people are going to run regardless of what happened in this room. . . . In the old days if you weren't endorsed that sent a pretty strong signal that you wouldn't have the money or the political support to wage a primary campaign. Today, it makes no difference."[13]

The Republican State Central Committee continues to operate in the shadow of its Republican governor. Both former governor Jim Thompson (1977–90) and Jim Edgar (1991–) have dominated their party's formal organization. It has not been unusual for the same person, selected by the governor, to serve as executive director of both the Republican State Central Committee and the governor's campaign committee. The Republican state party reported raising more than $4 million in the 1987–88 cycle, but most of the money was "pass-through" revenue raised by the national party and legislative candidate committees for purchase of direct mail services and special-rate mailing privileges.

Both state parties play limited financial roles in political campaigns. Of $46.7 million spent by candidates in the 1989–90 election cycle, the Democratic state party made $2.65 million in direct expenditures and the Republicans, $2.19 million.[14] Observes Redfield: "Participation in party activities is declining at all levels. The public is dissatisfied with party politics. The state parties have almost no role in the recruitment of candidates for statewide office and little impact on those statewide campaigns. The electoral power of Illinois legislative leaders is growing. Both office seekers and officeholders generally act independently of their party organizations at all levels."[15] The only hope for increased power among state party units, it seems, is to continue to expand their financial bases and spend that money on behalf of candidates. As of 1994, however, most state and local party organizations in Illinois would have to be classified as rather weak.

THE RISE OF INTEREST GROUPS

As political parties have declined in influence, interest groups have aggressively sought to fill the vacuum. They have done this by helping candidates, especially incumbents, meet the escalating costs of campaigns and by providing campaign managers and other election tools to candidates for state office and the legislature, supplanting roles once the preserve of party organizations.

In 1994, more than twelve hundred organizations employed 3,450 lobbyists in Illinois.[16] This was nearly ten times the number registered fifteen years earlier, when registration requirements were less comprehensive. Registered groups range from the Illinois State Acupuncture Association to Zion Township in Lake County. Business interests dominated the field, but labor, education, professional associations, and social service organizations are also heavily represented.

The power of a group can be measured by membership numbers, intensity of membership feeling, and the group's prestige. The Illinois AFL-CIO union affiliates claim nine hundred thousand member families; the Illinois Farm Bureau, one hundred thousand farm families, though many hold membership only to purchase insurance and other services. The Illinois State Medical Society (ISMS) claims a decidedly smaller membership of seventeen thousand, few of whom are active politically. But the physicians contribute generously to the society's political action committee. Because physicians represent a prestigious elite, the society organizes its members to serve as individual contacts with lawmakers; often these contacts are the lawmakers' own personal physicians—no doubt an effective and highly personal approach to influencing government.

Interest groups draw on many of the informal elements of power. They

Table 1: Legislators' Perceptions of Lobbying Group Influence

Ranking of Lobbying Group Influence	Ranking of Top Contributors to Legislators 1983–84	1991–92
1. Illinois State Medical Society	1	1
2. Illinois Education Association	3	2
3. Illinois Manufacturers Association	2	4
4. AFL–CIO	*	20
5. Illinois Chamber of Commerce	–	–
6. Illinois Association of Realtors	6	5
7. Illinois Bankers Association	4	6
8. Illinois Trial Lawyers	–	3
9. Illinois Retail Merchants Association	–	–
10. Illinois Farm Bureau	–	–

Source: Interest Group Politics in the Midwestern States, ed. Ronald J. Hrebenar and Clive S. Thomas (Ames: Iowa State University Press, 1993), 20–49.

* Contributions are also made by individual unions affiliated with the AFL–CIO.

provide not only valuable information to policymakers but also a sense of the intensity of feeling that groups—and supposedly their members—have toward an issue. Interest groups routinely report back to their members on the favorable and unfavorable votes cast by legislators. The "Legislative Ratings" from the Illinois State Chamber of Commerce Political Action Committee (PAC) are typical. Such rating systems are relatively common among interest groups, and because they display the percentage of favorable votes cast by a legislator on issues of interest, they help determine endorsements and campaign contributions to be made by the group's PAC.

When legislators are asked to name the most influential interest groups in the Illinois General Assembly, they tend to list those that are also the largest contributors to legislative campaigns. Table 1 shows that the top three groups in influence have consistently been among the biggest contributors, and seven of the ten groups are major contributors. The other three groups all have large and/or prestigious memberships as well as respected, multimember lobbying and research staffs.

Clearly, money is the "mother's milk of politics." Governor Jim Thompson's campaign committee raised $7.11 million for his final campaign in 1986. Almost half came from interest groups and their PACs.[17] Another 30 percent came from individual contributions above $150, most more than $1,000. Though the connection between interest-group donations and political influence is not always easily discerned, some links are obvious: Thompson's 1986 reelection campaign received $100,000 from an agribusiness company that had earlier received a $6 million state grant to build a special coal furnace at its plant.[18]

Committees organized to support Democratic candidates in the 1992 elections expended $31.4 million, and those supporting Republicans spent $30.1 million.[19] In the same election cycle, $20.8 million was spent by candidates for the legislature, with an additional $6.7 million provided "in kind," that is, the receipt of goods or services in lieu of money.[20] This total works out to an average of $155,000 in spending for each of the 177 senate and house districts.

The ten biggest-spending interest groups alone provided almost $8 million to candidates in 1992.[21] The Illinois State Medical Society topped the list at $1.7 million, followed by the Illinois Education Association (IEA) at $1.4 million. The medical society made contributions in 83 of 118 Illinois House races and 42 of 59 senate districts. It contributed $5,000 or more to 21 candidates, and $88,000 to a single candidate (a physician), who lost. ISMS also contributed heavily to Republican legislative leaders, giving $107,000 to house GOP and $41,000 to senate GOP leaders.

Interest group support has been escalating. In 1986, the top six contributor associations gave a total of $1.5 million directly to legislative candidates, about three times the amount given by the same groups a decade earlier. By 1992, the top six groups had upped the ante to $3.7 million.[22]

In an illuminating study of investing in the Illinois General Assembly, Kent Redfield illustrates the possible direct impact as well as the limits of campaign contributions.[23] In 1993, it appeared that legislation requiring parental notification of abortion would become law. The bill had passed the house and the senate and had been returned to the house for concurrence in a senate amendment. The ISMS, which had not taken a position on the bill earlier, became concerned with penalty provisions that could be applied to a physician. When the bill's sponsors said they were not interested in entering negotiations on the bill at that point, the medical society opposed final passage. When the bill came up for concurrence, thirteen house members who had previously voted for the bill changed their votes to "present" or "no." As a result, the bill received eleven fewer votes and fell seven short of passage. Votes on the abortion issue are considered difficult under any circumstances because of intense feelings on all sides of the issue. Changing a vote and running the risk of "flip-flopping" is even more difficult.

Of the thirteen lawmakers who switched votes, twelve had received campaign contributions from the medical society. Eight had received from $1,250 to $3,000 during the two-year election cycle and four had received from $10,000 to $36,000. If, however, campaign contributions were the only consideration, then seven other house members who had received $5,000 or more in ISMS contributions would have switched their votes but did not. Although Redfield acknowledges that no one can know why the thirteen lawmakers changed their votes, "What is clear is that the medical society's campaign contributions give them instant access to legislators and with it the opportunity and ability to influence votes."[24]

The influence of campaign contributions is limited, certainly. Evidence that campaign contributions alone cannot influence the outcome of some issues came in 1993, when a major increase in the cigarette tax was passed. Taking full advantage of direct corporate contributions, which are allowed in Illinois, the tobacco industry contributed $240,000 to legislators during the 1992 election cycle. "Once the cigarette tax increase had the backing of the governor and the four legislative leaders," according to Redfield, "no amount of intense lobbying by the tobacco interests was able to defeat the increase. The unified position of the governor and four legislative leaders provided political cover for the members and left the tobacco interests with a rare and major defeat."[25]

INFORMATION IS POWER

In addition to money, powerful interest groups have been contributing experienced campaign managers from their staffs to candidates. For years the Illinois Education Association has provided its endorsed candidates in hotly contested state legislative races with professional managers, get-out-the-vote workers, and polling services. In 1990, ISMS loaned two of its top executives to work full-time in Jim Edgar's gubernatorial campaign.

Although money and campaign services might grease the wheel, information is often the overriding ingredient in gaining or losing a vote. Lobbyists are the primary conduits of this information, sharing it with legislators and staff, the governor's office, other interest groups, and anyone else who can have some impact on policymaking. Lobbyists are strategists, tacticians, builders of coalitions among groups, experts, and communicators. They testify in committees, buttonhole lawmakers one-on-one, organize meetings between their members and legislators, stage rallies and demonstrations, and try to put a favorable "spin" on media coverage of their issues.

Senior lobbyists develop political action strategies that dovetail with the needs and resources of their association or client, helping decide, for instance, if contributions should be oriented to leadership or candidates, be partisan or bipartisan, and favor incumbents or challengers. They also shape the way information is conveyed and, when possible, do a little horse-trading with other lobbyists to develop compatible strategies on related issues.

One organization of lobbyists is the Business and Industry Federation of Economic Concern (BIFEC), which meets weekly in Springfield when the legislature is in session. The thirty-plus members brief each other on the status of bills. Requests are sometimes made that a group or corporation join a coalition in support of or opposition to legislation. BIFEC holds a workshop before each primary election to evaluate legislative races, which provides intelligence that is useful in allocating political action committee campaign contributions.

Many lobbyists are regular employees of corporations, unions, and trade associations. Others have their own lobby firms or work for law firms and contract their services to corporations and groups. Some lobbyists are known to have strong relationships with the Democratic house leadership or with Republican senators. Thus on issues important to well-financed interests, several contract lobbyists will be hired to supplement the work of lobbyists employed by the organization.

Lobbyists come in all styles. Some are congenial fellows and women who are appreciated for putting on dinner parties following the day's session. Others eschew the nightlife and are skilled at getting critical information, in the right format, to the right people, at just the right time.

Information and expertise are the keys to influence for Saul Morse—lobbyist, attorney, member of the state human rights commission, and paraplegic. Morse worked earlier for the Illinois Commerce Commission and as a senate Republican staffer. He has represented several major clients in Illinois, including the Illinois State Medical Society. Morse belies the stereotype of influence-peddling lobbyist and emphasizes the "education" aspects of the role. In 1989, the General Assembly passed a major revision of the Illinois Medical Practice Act. The 123-page bill was drafted entirely in Morse's office.[26]

DAY IN THE LIFE OF A LOBBYIST

Most lobbyists devote most of their efforts to narrow issues of particular interest to their employers or clients but of almost no interest to the public. To illustrate the arcane nature of much day-to-day lobbying, coauthor Nowlan recalls the work that he and colleague Joan Parker did one day late in the 1992 spring legislative session, when they were president and vice president, respectively, of the Taxpayers' Federation of Illinois.

Joan calls Garland Allen of the Hopkins & Sutter law firm to get his reaction to new language for voluntary disclosure of tax liability. Gar says there must be legislative intent to make it crystal clear that the Department of Revenue (DOR) has certain latitude to provide waivers from tax liability. Joan prepares language and takes it to Rep. Jack Kubik and his Revenue Committee staff aide Mona Martin. They agree to arrange a colloquy on the house floor if Joan will talk with Rep. Barbara Flynn Currie (*D*-Chicago), revenue chair, about participating.

Joan talks with Doug Whitley, director of the Department of Revenue, and Kevin Conner, DOR lobbyist, about a flap that may block senate concurrence on the house amendment to the Uniform Penalty and Interest legislation that Joan and others have been working on for two years. Whitley will talk with Jim Sweet, senate Democrat Revenue staffer, and Joan calls Marc Weinstein of Sears to have him call Sweet and explain the legislative history of the bill. Joan briefs Sen. Judy Baar Topinka, who had agreed to put the uniform penalty changes into one of her bills.

Sen. Walter Dudycz (*R*-Chicago) catches Joan out near "the rail" (the brass rail that encircles the rotunda on the Capitol's third floor; when not otherwise engaged, lobbyists and lawmakers "polish" the rail to exchange intelligence). He thanks Joan for her analysis of a report on property taxation and asks us to write a one-page explanation of the property tax in Cook County, for use with his constituents. We agree to what is no mean task—one page!

We catch—on the run—Marcia Thompson, the director of the senate Democratic staff, to see that she understands our opposition to the governor's proposed changes in net operating loss (NOL) rules, and we apprise her of the minor stir regarding uniform penalties. I compare notes on NOL with Caterpillar lobbyist Don DeFoe and call Brian Whalen and Bob Osing at Navistar to report to them on the issue and coordinate our mutual efforts on it.

Rep. David Leitch (*R*-Peoria) tells me via my pager to meet him outside the house chambers. David is upset that the Taxpayers' Federation has apparently blocked a bill of his in the senate, which he amended on the house floor to help some folks in his district who want to assess themselves to make neighborhood improvements. I'm not aware of the situation, so I check with Joan. She had been alerted by Julie Ward of the Illinois Association of Realtors that the amendment would extend authority to impose special assessments without referendum, which the Realtors and TFI have always opposed. Joan and I put Leitch and Ward together. Ward offers to draft language to provide a "front-door" referendum for those to be affected.

Back on the uniform penalty front, Joan keeps in continual contact with the dozen or so players involved. Looks like the problem with senate Democrats will be resolved, following a meeting in the office of Sen. Richard Luft (*D*-Pekin), senate revenue chair, who has been helpful throughout. Later in the house gallery, Joan watches as Kubik and Currie pose the questions and answers that become part of the legislative intent for the voluntary disclosure provision. She also exchanges information with Rich Clemmons, chief lobbyist for the Illinois Farm Bureau, on a school finance bill. The hour has reached six and the two houses are adjourning. Joan heads off for dinner with Sue Sikes, lobbyist for Cook County assessor Tom Hynes, to compare notes. I end up slicing onions for a cookout at Nancy Couter's, senate GOP revenue staffer, where I discuss the Ohio local income tax option with Sen. "Babe" Woodyard, who would like to see the option made available in Illinois. (The evening before, Joan and I had hosted twenty-five lawmakers and staff for a buffet supper at my place.)

These recollections describe a fairly typical day in the life of a lobbyist. More important than what actually transpired that day, however, is all that preceded it during the six years that Joan has been lobbying for the federation. Beleaguered lawmakers don't just agree to conduct colloquies on the house floor or to allow amendments to be tacked onto their bills, nor do staffers and fellow lobbyists willingly share valuable information—not unless they trust you, and not unless they expect that you will work to reciprocate whenever you can.

GAUGING INTEREST GROUP STRENGTH

In 1981, political scientist Sarah McCally Morehouse classified Illinois as having "moderately strong" interest groups.[27] Evaluating the importance of interest groups in 1988, David H. Everson and Samuel K. Gove confirmed this assessment.[28] The influential interest groups are provided seats at the table at which public policy issues are bargained. Governors regularly convene task forces on major issues, and appointments to these panels appear to be meticulously balanced among the most influential interest groups.

Interest groups are more effective at protecting a benefit won earlier than at achieving a major change. It has always been easier to beat a bill in the legislature than to pass one. The Illinois Education Association has been able to protect teacher tenure laws but has been less successful in getting the legislature to pass tax increases for education. And the time-honored practice of asking competing interest groups to work out an "agreed bill" tends to result in modest change from the status quo, not in dramatic victory for one side or in total defeat for the other.

Because of the perception in the 1980s of increased power among the legislative leaders and the governor, many interest groups have been concentrating their campaign contributions on the legislative leaders and gubernatorial candidates and away from individual legislators. This increases the likelihood that the groups will be consulted closely by several if not all of the five leaders during their negotiations on issues of importance to the groups. As Redfield observes: "Being a significant player in the financing of legislative elections insures that you have a seat at the table when issues are raised, defined, and decided. It will be impossible to craft a state response to whatever new federal health care program is enacted that does not take into account the interests of public and private labor unions, large corporations and interest groups representing organized health care professionals and facilities. These groups may not be able to dictate the exact terms of the response, but they will be able to exercise a veto."[29]

GROWING GRASS-ROOTS INFLUENCE

As Democratic ward organizations have withered and well-funded interest groups have become more important, another group of players has loudly claimed a place on the game board: community action and neighborhood groups. Alliances of the poor and the disfranchised have been cobbled together on shoestring budgets for more than one hundred years in Chicago, where the social worker Jane Addams was one of the earliest and most skilled practitioners. Her settlement house in Chicago's turn-of-the-century slums provided social support for new immigrants and raised their expectations about the government's responsibilities to provide proper schooling, restrict child labor, and occasionally collect the garbage.[30] Saul Alinsky added his voice half a century later, organizing residents of the Back of the Yards neighborhood and later, at the dawn of the civil rights era, helping found the Woodlawn Organization in one of Chicago's south-side ghettoes.[31] Alinsky taught Hell Raising 101, training thousands of neighborhood residents in Chicago and elsewhere that a raucous protest and a good crowd at the barricades was the first step to getting attention from city hall.

Mayor Richard J. Daley unwittingly fueled the growth of Chicago's neighborhood organizations by refusing to acknowledge their demands or ideas for community improvements. The groups redoubled their efforts, found friends in the leading Chicago-based charitable organizations, such as the John D. and Catherine T. MacArthur Foundation, the Joyce Foundation, and the Chicago Community Trust, and began developing expertise in housing rehabilitation, community redevelopment, and public policy advocacy.

The election of Chicago mayor Harold Washington gave a big boost to the relative power of community organizations. Of necessity, the antimachine mayor had to work around the elements of the Democratic political organization that he defeated; that meant working closely with community groups. He parceled out small stipends to community organizations to act as "delegate agencies" in the neighborhoods and industrial districts and redistributed city housing funds to fledgling nonprofit development corporations. Such organizations were growing in cities around the country, but thanks in part to Washington's support, Chicago built one of the strongest networks of community-based organizations and neighborhood development corporations in the nation. "We realized that city government didn't have all the answers," said Jim Capraro, whose nonprofit corporation has helped attract $40 million in investment to his racially changing southwest-side neighborhood. "You would suggest something to them and they would respond with a blank look; they had never thought of it from the local perspective before."[32]

Politicians took notice as the neighborhood groups' political importance became evident. Washington would not have been elected without the backing of community groups, among them the Midwest Community Council on the city's black west side. The late Nancy Jefferson was a visible, strong-willed leader of that group, and as the *Chicago Tribune* reported, "Washington rarely made a move on the West Side without first consulting Nancy."[33] In 1990 Republican gubernatorial candidate Jim Edgar openly courted and received Jefferson's support, which helped him solidify a stronger black vote than Republican candidates typically garner.

Another example of a neighborhood power broker is the United Neighborhood Organization of Chicago (UNO). Founded in the Alinsky mold in 1980, UNO has affiliates in four lower-income, largely Mexican American neighborhoods served by about twenty Catholic parishes. UNO has about a thousand members and several thousand supporters.[34] According to Wilfredo Cruz, UNO takes credit for winning the construction of several public schools, renovation of a public health clinic, and other public works in Hispanic neighborhoods.[35] UNO has also recruited and supported Hispanic candidates who have won city and state legislative offices. One of UNO's leaders, Danny Solis, has become a key ally of Mayor Richard M. Daley.

Rising to power in Illinois traditionally is followed by opportunities to be cut in on the action; that has been the case for scores of nonprofit community organizations now paid by the city, state, or federal government to provide child care services, housing development, industrial retention, job placement, and social services. This can be a tender trap; while working out a contract with a government agency, it is rarely good form to criticize one of the agency's officials in the daily newspapers. For that reason, some organizations have remained relatively independent of government and corporate sponsorship, believing that independence on a shoestring may be more effective than playing the insider role.

One organization that maintained its outsider status was the Public Welfare Coalition, a statewide advocacy group that has used the media to amplify issues of poverty and welfare reform. The group's former executive director Doug Dobmeyer found that his lobbying trips to Springfield and entreaties to the public aid bureaucracy were not effective, even though one in ten Illinois residents in 1990 was dependent on a meager welfare payment of only one-half the state's poverty level. He turned to the media instead, developing a full arsenal of tools including numerous press conferences in Springfield and Chicago, regular letters to the editor, heavy airtime on radio and TV talk shows, and a blizzard of faxed press releases during budget negotiations and legislative sessions.[36] Making four hundred or more press contacts each year, the organization coaxed the media into telling the true stories of mothers running out of food or being unable to afford warm coats and hats for their children during Chicago's brutal winters.

The media heat helped pave the way for a 7.5 percent increase in aid in 1990 but more often was used to beat back proposals to reduce or eliminate programs. For three years running, Dobmeyer scrambled up a media plan when conservative senators sought legislation that would bar an increase in payments (from $268 to $367 per month) if a woman had a baby while on welfare. Each time the bill came up in committee or was scheduled for a floor vote, a press release or letter to the editor was sent off and Dobmeyer worked the phone with reporters. In 1993, the bill's chances were scuttled after the *Chicago Defender,* the city's daily black newspaper, quoted Governor Edgar as saying he would not support such a move. The following spring, senate president James "Pate" Philip gave the order to his Republican majority and passed a similar bill, which died later only when another power player, house Speaker Michael Madigan, gauged strong opposition among his core constituencies and gave it the thumbs down. In 1995, however, with Republicans in firm control of the legislature, even Dobmeyer's skills were not enough to prevent enactment of the welfare limitation bill.

POWER OF THE PRESS

Exposure in the media is a time-honored way to raise an issue, pro or con. In the nineteenth century, many community newspapers were started primarily to promote the platforms of political parties. Present-day reminders include the *Quincy Herald-Whig,* the *Belleville News-Democrat,* and the *Belvidere Daily Republican.* The impetus for the Republican party of Illinois came from newspaper editors when Paul Selby, editor of the *Morgan Journal* in Jacksonville, issued a formal call in 1856 for a conference of newspaper editors.[37] Twelve influential editors plus Abraham Lincoln, the only noneditor admitted to the gathering, met in Decatur and put together a platform that advocated full restoration of the 1820 Missouri Compromise, which limited the extension of slavery. This stimulated the call for a convention to organize an Illinois Republican party.

Today the media influence public policy in at least three direct ways: public and behind-the-scenes lobbying; editorial positions and endorsements of candidates; and investigative and in-depth public policy reporting. The Illinois Press Association lobbies openly to protect state requirements that legal advertising must appear in local papers and, more important, to keep generous the dollar amounts set by various statutes for the advertising lineage. The Illinois Broadcasters' Association has worked for statutes that require public bodies to hold open meetings. During the 1960s George Tagge, the political editor of the *Chicago Tribune,* used his press box privileges (the boxes are adjacent to the house and senate floors) to lobby vigorously for a new exhibition center in Chicago to be named after the *Tribune*'s late publisher Colonel Robert McCormick. Called McCormick Place today, in the 1960s it was referred to by state lawmakers as "Tagge's Temple." In part because of this strong-armed advocacy, a ranking of top interest groups in Illinois, done in the 1980s, included the *Tribune.*[38]

Newspaper endorsements in Illinois have never been restricted to the editorial pages, often showing up in a subtler form in news stories. Heavy and generally positive coverage of the 1970 Constitutional Convention, for instance, helped soften up the voters for the constitution's eventual passage. Advertising can also play a role. In October 1978, columnist Mike Royko, then with the *Chicago Sun-Times,* wrote three columns that were highly critical of the Democratic challenger to U.S. senator Charles H. Percy. With Royko's blessing, the Percy campaign spent $200,000 to enlarge and reprint two of the columns as separate full-page advertisements in every daily newspaper in Illinois. The columns and reprints generated great public comment and were considered highly significant by Percy's campaign managers in their candidate's come-from-behind victory.[39]

The supportive editorial nonetheless remains the essential bit of padding in most political campaigns and on many public issues. Shoestring advocacy groups and pinstriped corporate executives alike ask for and generally receive time with the editorial boards of the state's major newspapers, and if they state their case clearly and persuasively enough, an editorial may appear a few days later.

Politicians are less comfortable with the media's other political device, the investigative report. Though expensive, investigative reporting has been practiced with some vigor by many Chicago and downstate newspapers and some television stations, usually to uncover corruption or expose a dysfunctional bureaucracy. Television commentators Len O'Connor and Walter Jacobson spent years digging up and broadcasting embarrassing material about Chicago political shenanigans, and the *Chicago Sun-Times* went so far as to open a tavern, the Mirage, to expose the kickbacks and bribery of the city's various inspectors.

Perhaps because blatant corruption and freeloading on the job are not so common as in years past, more recent investigative reporting has taken on a more educational, almost academic, character. The *Chicago Tribune* in particular periodically assigns large teams of reporters, editors, and photographers to analyze in minute detail the social or economic ills of the city. A 1985 series titled "The American Millstone" described the sad and broken world of Chicago's so-called underclass,[40] and set off a firestorm of protest from black residents who felt the series was blaming the victims for their plight. Later work by *Tribune* teams chronicled the physical decay of Chicago's public schools, the troubled public housing system, and the wholesale killing of children on Chicago's streets. To a lesser extent, the *Sun-Times,* the *Daily Southtown,* and the *Peoria Journal-Star* have done similar work, though they lack the financial resources to duplicate the exhaustive coverage of the *Tribune*.

Investigative reporting provides political mileage in a circular way. To show the value of their own work, media outlets are typically generous with airtime and news space when a lawmaker announces a legislative proposal that responds to the investigation. The media benefit as well because national news associations that make awards for investigative work consider changes in public policy as one of the criteria of a successful report.

Elected officials are clearly sensitive to the media, and most are fully aware that media space, time, and comment—positive and negative—are powerful elements in Illinois politics. But by far one aspect of media influence overshadows all others in its influence on political strategies: television. Until about 1960, candidates for statewide office charted their campaigns according to a map of the 102 counties of Illinois. Although the counties varied dramatically in population, candidates felt an obligation to proclaim that they had campaigned in all of them. Candidates would often travel in small caravans and be met at county lines by caravans from the receiving county.

In those days, there was no substitute for personal campaigning, either by the candidate or by party workers. Today there is. What television lacks in personal touch, it makes up in its ability to present the candidate to literally everybody in the state and to do so with controlled, polished messages.[41]

Ten television markets serve Illinois, as shown in map 3. Virtually all households have one or more television sets, and the average one is on for nine hours per day. As a result, television can and does bring candidates to almost every voter in the state, via paid advertisements and news broadcasts.

Because of this reach, candidates now consider campaigning in every county counterproductive. Instead, schedules are arranged around the cities that have network-affiliate television stations. Schedulers try to find or create events that will be attractive to station assignment editors. The criteria are to make it convenient so that little crew time is needed; make it visual because the television medium craves an interesting, lively background; and make it short and simple because most television news stories are one hundred words or less and the crews need to move on to cover other stories.

Though there has been little direct evidence to prove its power, a study of a 1982 statewide campaign confirmed that television can have a strong impact.[42] In the Republican primary for state treasurer, candidate John Dailey spent more than $150,000 for television ads in the five media markets in northern Illinois and nothing in the five markets that serve southern Illinois. His opponent, Robert Blair, a former Speaker of the Illinois House, had much less to spend in his campaign and spent nothing on television. Endorsements by county Republican party organizations were split about evenly between the two candidates.

Dailey won the primary. He carried nearly all the counties in which he ran television ads, and he lost most of those in which he did not use television.

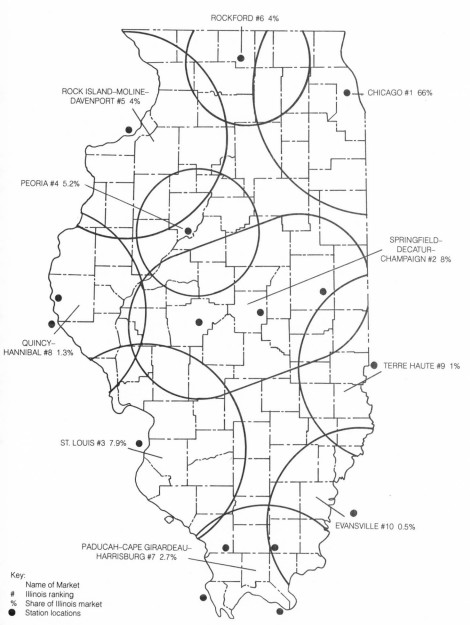

ROCKFORD #6 4%

CHICAGO #1 66%

ROCK ISLAND–MOLINE–
DAVENPORT #5 4%

PEORIA #4 5.2%

SPRINGFIELD–
DECATUR–
CHAMPAIGN #2 8%

QUINCY–
HANNIBAL #8 1.3%

TERRE HAUTE #9 1%

ST. LOUIS #3 7.9%

EVANSVILLE #10 0.5%

PADUCAH–CAPE GIRARDEAU–
HARRISBURG #7 2.7%

Key:
    Name of Market
\#   Illinois ranking
%   Share of Illinois market
●   Station locations

This information on Illinois major television media markets is taken from the *Broadcasting and Cable Yearbook 1994*. The percentage figure for each market represents that portion of Illinois households considered to be in each market area of dominant influence. These percentage calculations are assigned on a county basis with no provision for overlapping market signals. The rounded market boundaries are for illustrative purposes only. They provide a rough approximation of market signal reach.

Map 3. Major Media Markets in Illinois

Dailey consistently fared better in counties where his advertising aired than where it did not. Television helped him fare well even in those counties whose Republican organizations had endorsed his opponent. He did poorly, despite county party backing, in those areas where he did not advertise on TV.

The problem for candidates—and perhaps for voters—is that television is expensive and tends to benefit those who have money to spend, while hurting those without big campaign treasuries. In 1990 the Illinois candidates for governor and U.S. Senate raised from $6 million to $10 million each. More than half of this money was targeted for television ads. Because political party organizations lack the capacity to raise that much money for the many candidates running under party banners, candidates must raise their own funds. This situation has enhanced the power of the individuals and interest groups able to make large contributions. Fueled by this money, television has largely replaced the party organizations as the primary conduit of messages from candidates to the voters.

That money is central to power and influence in Illinois should come as no surprise. It drives campaign strategies, nurtures legislative leadership, provides support to the governor of whichever party is in power, and even influences Chicago's robust grass-roots organizations. All of this is consistent with the individualistic political culture of Illinois, where government and politics are a marketplace in which participants exchange credits and debits as they pursue their goals.

CHAPTER FOUR

Loosening the Constitutional Straitjacket

State constitutions provide the dimensions of the fields on which the game of politics is played. They provide the structure of government, offices to be elected, and, more important, certain limits on government and the powers of its legislative, executive, and judicial branches. In Illinois for many years, those limits were a defining factor in state and local politics—a straitjacket from which the people struggled to free themselves.

Unlike the federal government, which has had only one Constitution since the Articles of Confederation, Illinois has had four constitutions since its admission to the Union in 1818. The number may be misleading, though, because the first "frontier" constitution was written hurriedly. Drafted, debated, and passed in three weeks, it was a rough document in a state with little knowledge of its future. Twice in the next fifty-two years, as the state evolved and Chicago emerged, the constitution was rewritten, but the versions of 1848 and 1870, like the first constitution, often created new problems while trying to resolve earlier ones.

For one hundred years between the 1870 vote and the 1970 approval of the current constitution, the state moved forward in spite of the constitution's restraints; leaders tried again and again to rewrite or amend the state framework but failed each time. They were victims not only of the restrictions written into the constitution they hoped to improve but of poor preparation, a leaning toward partisanship, and opposition from special interests. Then, in a triumph of nonpartisan effort, 116 delegates gathered in 1969 in the Old State Capitol building in Springfield. This was no ordinary bunch—many of the state's future leaders were delegates—and they took on the task with vigor. Over a nine-month period under the skilled and energetic leadership of longtime constitutional advocate Samuel W. Witwer, they overhauled the law of the land and engineered a political alliance to gain voter support. It was a major achievement in Illinois history and one of the best examples of the state's occasional ability to overcome its individualism to address a common problem.

THE NATURE OF CONSTITUTIONS

Constitutions are designed to serve as the bedrock on which a government's structure is built. This is a risky engineering feat in almost any case, and it certainly was in early Illinois, where the constitutional framers were unsure of what kind of building was to be erected on their foundation. Still, they made use of a central concept that shows up in all state constitutions except that of Delaware: the constitution must be harder to change than a simple state statute; rather than being amendable by the legislature alone, the constitution cannot be changed without approval of the voters.

As evidenced by the United States Constitution, this primary set of rules need not be long, and many argue that it should not be. Rather than filling a constitution with detailed provisions of just how government should be structured and what offices should be filled at what salary, a short-form constitution is little more than a framework of rights and responsibilities. Idealists say that a constitution should contain "fundamentals" (though there is disagreement on what is "fundamental") and that "nonfundamentals" should be in legislation or statutes. For instance, idealists would say the basic organization of state government into three branches is fundamental but that creation of a specific state agency by the constitution (e.g., the state board of elections created by the 1970 Constitution in Illinois) is not fundamental. Another point of contention among constitution writers is how restrictive a state constitution should be. A "negative" constitution is one that contains many restrictions on state and local governments. Illinois's second constitution had a number of such negatives, many intended to rein in the power of the legislature. One of them limited legislators' pay to a penurious two dollars per day; this backfired by spurring creation of a system of "fees" paid by private interests for introduction of legislative bills.[1]

When the Illinois Constitution is compared to that of California, for example, the Illinois document looks very good. The current Illinois document does not include many "negatives" and "nonfundamentals," whereas the California Constitution is very lengthy and full of details. The other major difference is that the California document provides for the "general initiative" by which voters can propose constitutional amendments by petition (rather than through the legislature). The initiative is widely used in California, and it is common for the voter to face twenty constitutional and other initiatives and referenda at a primary or general election. Although this system provides far more avenues for debate over constitutional issues, it also turns constitution writing into a highly politicized undertaking in which advertising and financial backing play major roles. A general initiative for Illinois was discussed by the 1970 Constitutional Convention but was not given serious consideration because of the negative reaction to the California experience.[2]

Although important in establishing basic general rules for a state's government, state constitutions and constitution making do not often attract the public's attention. The exception is when a controversial amendment is proposed or, as happened in the 1960s in Illinois, a complete rewrite is contemplated. This is the case even though by law in Illinois, high school students and some college students have to pass a test on the contents of the state's constitution.

CONSTITUTIONAL COMPROMISE IN 1818

The first Illinois Constitution was adopted in 1818. It was a requirement for statehood and its creation was rushed because Illinois hoped to become a state before its neighbor, Missouri. The thirty-three elected delegates appointed a committee of fifteen to draft the document, a process that was kept short by borrowing heavily from the new constitutions of other states. When the whole group convened to discuss the document, the central provisions stood up relatively well. A bicameral legislature would be elected, with each house reapportioned according to the census every five years. The executive branch, which in the eastern states had been seen as too powerful, would be relatively restrained. The governor would be allowed only one consecutive four-year term, no exclusive veto power, and limited powers of appointment.

One issue that received much attention—and had national implications—was the question of slavery. The original draft language, borrowed from Ohio, prohibited both slavery and involuntary servitude, and although indentured servants were to be allowed, the indenture had to be voluntary and for no longer than one year. Proslavery delegates argued that use of slaves would bring economic benefits to Illinois and would keep the salt springs in Gallatin County producing revenue. They were smart enough to avoid advocating full slavery, knowing that such a provision could doom the constitution's review by the U.S. Congress and president. But they inserted language that protected existing property rights, including indentured servants, and a second clause that allowed continued "renting" of slaves from Tennessee and Kentucky to perform the backbreaking work in the salt mines.

The final constitution also omitted a provision, which had been included in the Ohio and Indiana constitutions, expressly prohibiting amendment to allow the introduction of slavery. The phrase's absence sparked debate when the U.S. Congress reviewed the document, but opposition from northern states was insufficient to prevent passage. On December 3, 1818, Illinois became a state.

That this omission was intentional was later confirmed when proslavery forces pushed for a constitutional convention in 1824. They succeeded in both houses of the legislature but were defeated at the polls after a vigorous antislavery campaign by many of the state's leaders.[3]

AFTER WEAKNESSES EMERGE, A SECOND CONVENTION

The first constitution gave the legislature so much power and the governor so little power that the system was ripe for abuse. Because delegates at the first convention wanted to assure the appointment of Elijah C. Berry as the first auditor of public accounts, they provided that the General Assembly would appoint that position and "such other officers for the state as may be necessary." Janet Cornelius recounts that this tiny opening soon became a large enough loophole that the legislature "appointed canal commissioners and agents, fund commissioners, commissioners of the board of public works, bank directors, state's attorneys and others,"[4] setting the precedent for the next 150 years of patronage in Illinois. The legislature was often clumsy in using this power and had even greater difficulty with the constitution's highly restrictive banking provisions, which led to a series of financial debacles as the state's economy grew. By 1841, when Jacksonian Democrats urged a shift of power back toward the executive branch, Illinois was ready to write its second constitution.

Despite a strong campaign to convene the convention in 1842, a provision of the first constitution prevented it from happening. Calling a convention required approval not only of both houses of the General Assembly by a two-thirds majority but also by a majority of "all the citizens of the state voting for representatives." Because many of those who voted for representatives in 1842 did not cast a vote on the convention issue, the initiative failed despite a majority of 37,476 votes for a convention versus 23,282 against. A more aggressive campaign four years later gained approval for a convention in 1848, but the need for a majority of those voting remained a serious barrier to convention calls and constitutional amendments until 1950, when the so-called gateway amendment relaxed the restriction. Passage of an amendment was then allowed with approval by two-thirds of those voting on the amendment itself.

The second convention provided more lessons in the difficulty of writing a good constitution. Delegates seeking to correct mistakes in the first document inserted restrictive language in the second, effectively tying the hands of future Illinoisans. To avoid recurrence of irresponsible borrowing by the state, for instance, one section restricted the state from contracting debts of more than $50,000, a figure that would soon hobble state development efforts. Legislative "misdeeds" in the creation of corporations under the first constitution were restricted by a prohibition against such establishment (though an unintended loophole allowed for hundreds of incorporations under "special" circumstances). Another section attempted to loosen the restrictions on amendment of the constitution by allowing approval by only one house of the legislature but then created a whole new web of conditions around that provision. "On the one hand," wrote Cornelius, "the delegates inserted policy-making legislation into the constitution in the excessively detailed sections dealing with salaries and judicial reorganization. Yet, when faced with the possibility that their work might be amended or changed, they regarded their document as a broad, unchanging statement of fundamental principles, assuming that 'wisdom would die with them and that nobody else should by permitted to disturb their labors, and interfere with what they had done.'"[5]

The 1848 Constitution nonetheless contained some improvements and was approved by the voters. It reduced the legislature's ability to control the judiciary through appointments, provided legislative authority to create corporations or associations with banking powers, and eliminated the option of using a "viva voce" system of voting (in which the voter calls out his vote and thus must publicly show his preference) in favor of the written ballot.

The convention also pioneered the use of "side issues," controversial concepts that, if included in the constitution proper, might have led to its failure. These issues were presented to voters separately from the constitution and included only if they passed. One foreshadowed Illinois's future troubles with black-white relations: it prohibited immigration of free blacks into Illinois and was strongly approved. The other, permitting the levy of a property tax to pay the state debt, passed by a relatively close margin.

FRESH LAW TURNS STALE

Concern for further constitutional change came almost immediately after the approval of the 1848 Constitution. Illinois was in transition from a state with an exclusively rural economy to one having the features of a modern industrial state. Railroads were a central part of the state's economic life by 1850. Antibank and anticorporation sentiments were by-products of this transitional period, and they were the focus of the new drive for constitutional change.

In 1856, only eight years after the previous convention, a referendum to call another convention was submitted and decisively defeated, in part because of limited voter awareness of the issues. A successful call, however, was held four years later in 1860. The convention met in 1862, with the southern part of the state dominating the leadership. The Democrats wrote a partisan constitution with antibank, anticorporation, and profarmer provisions. But they meanwhile became embroiled in various extraneous issues, including a quarrel with the state, then under a Republican governor, over whether the convention could hire its own printer instead of using one chosen by the state. The clearly partisan final document was signed by only fifty-four of the seventy-five original delegates and only three Republicans. Most Republican newspapers, including the *Chicago Tribune*, editorialized against it, and the constitution was defeated at the polls.

Constitutional change became an issue again after the Civil War. The call for a convention was urged by Governor Richard J. Oglesby, approved by the 1867 legislature, and approved by the voters in 1868 by a close vote. The delegates were elected in November 1869 and seated the next month. The convention organized on a bipartisan basis, with a mood of conciliation and compromise prevailing, a mood difficult to establish in the immediate post–Civil War period.

The product of the 1870 convention was longer and more detailed than earlier documents, signifying the growth in complexity of the state's needs and problems. The convention delegates, according to historian Robert Howard, "cured most of the faults of the 1848 constitution. They drafted a new basic law that was voluminous in detail and in time would be criticized as being a straitjacket on progress. Nevertheless, the new constitution endured for a century as Illinois kept abreast of its sister states while advancing from a predominantly rural civilization into the atomic age."[6]

One of the most controversial side issues put to the voters provided a new method of electing members to the House of Representatives. The cumulative voting method was devised to reduce regional tensions by a controversial system of "minority representation." The system allowed each voter to cast three votes for representatives, splitting them or giving them all to one candidate. Because many voters took advantage of the three-in-one "bullet" vote, a Republican could often be elected in a predominantly Democratic district and vice versa. This provided a rough if somewhat artificial balance of power between the parties until the cumulative vote was eliminated in 1980.

The 1870 Constitution falls into what Daniel Elazar calls the "commercial republic pattern." It was built on "a series of compromises required by the conflict of ethnic and commercial interests and ideals created by the flow of various streams of migrants into their territories, and the early development of commercial cities."[7]

The 1870 Constitution was the basic document of Illinois for a hundred years. It proved to be very difficult to amend "because the leaders of the state's important interests were afraid to upset the balance of forces established by the compromises," according to Elazar.[8] It presented many problems for state officials, especially in regard to financial matters. For example, because of the strict limitations on local government debt, a large number of special districts were established that would later be blamed for Illinois's and especially metropolitan Chicago's parochialism and lack of coordinated planning. Because delegates did not learn the lesson of 1848, when dollar amounts were written into the constitution without regard for rising costs, the 1870 document provided that the General Assembly was not to appropriate "a sum exceeding, in the aggregate, three and a half million dollars" on the new statehouse in Springfield. As might have been expected, the money ran out and the statehouse was never completed according to the original plans.

In addition to the limitations and detail, narrow court interpretations of the constitution made it difficult for elective officials to govern. For example, a 1932 state supreme court decision ruled that the constitution did not permit the state to levy an income tax, which would remain a badly needed revenue source for several decades to come.

The constitution received relatively little attention until the election of reform-minded Governor Frank O. Lowden in 1916. The governor's inaugural message contained a strong plea for a constitutional convention. The legislature approved the call in 1917, as did the voters the following year. Like the ill-fated convention of 1862, however, partisan lines were drawn and the Republicans this time came out on top. They were poorly organized, and the convention became known for lengthy recesses and absenteeism among delegates. The process dragged on for three years. Despite improvements such as a clause that "laws shall be applicable alike to all citizens without regard to race or color," the document was overwhelmingly defeated in December 1922. The lopsided vote provided a sign of times to come: because the proposed constitution failed to provide Chicago with full powers of home rule, the Democratic Central Committee of Cook County opposed it and Mayor Anton Cermak urged voters to "snow it under."[9] The vote tally in Cook County was twenty to one against approval.

WITWER'S LONG ROAD TO REFORM

The 1922 failure did nothing to improve the 1870 document, and Chicago's need for home-rule powers, among other issues, hung heavy in the following decades. After World War II, a coalition that included the League of Women Voters and the Chicago Bar Association decided to push once more for a convention. They appointed a Committee on Constitutional Revision and asked a respected Chicago attorney, Samuel W. Witwer, to be chair. "As Witwer recalls it, 'in a weak moment,' he agreed to do so, being assured by them that the committee would have its work done in a matter of only a few years."[10] In fact, it would take the next twenty-five years of his life.

Witwer recruited a blue-ribbon committee to help him plan the campaign but found to his dismay that there was almost no written documentation about the weaknesses of the 1870 Constitution. So he set out to become an expert on the subject and was well prepared in 1947 when he appeared before a senate committee to lay out the need for change. The senators, it turned out, "had no real desire to hear from the Witwer committee,"[11] and some hardly listened to the presentation. Witwer was infuriated and became more determined than ever.

Constitutional reform gained momentum when Adlai E. Stevenson became governor in 1949. Stevenson presented a constitutional convention package to the legislature that year. Handling the matter for Stevenson in the legislature was Richard J. Daley, later Chicago's mayor but then Stevenson's director of revenue. The proposition lost on a close vote in the House of Representatives.

The Republicans in the legislature offered an alternative to Stevenson's "con-con" package—the gateway amendment. It eased the vote needed on constitutional amendments by providing that an amendment could be adopted by a favorable vote of two-thirds of those voting on the amendment itself, loosening the prior requirement of a majority of those voting in the election. It also provided that three amendments instead of one could be submitted in each general election. The legislature, with Stevenson's support, approved the gateway amendment and submitted the question to the voters on a separate blue ballot that bore the notice: "The failure to vote this ballot is the equivalent of a negative vote."[12] The blue ballot has been identified with constitutional revision questions to this day. Thanks to the special ballot and a strong campaign, the gateway amendment received an overwhelmingly favorable vote.

It was felt by many at the time that constitutional revision by amendment was more desirable than a constitutional convention. The gateway provisions were used by the General Assembly in 1950 and in subsequent years. But enthusiasm for this approach diminished because the track record of constitutional revision was not impressive. From 1950 to 1966, fifteen amendments were submitted to the voters and six were approved. Only two of the adopted amendments were far-reaching—a 1954 reapportionment amendment and a 1962 judicial reform amendment. Discouraging to reformers were three defeats for amendments to revise the revenue article, which was badly out of date in its restrictions on government taxation powers.

The major development that gave renewed attention to constitutional revision was the 1964 at-large election for the House of Representatives, a result of the failure of the legislature and governor to redraw house district lines. Many new faces were elected. They were "blue ribbon," and when the legislature convened in 1965, they were ready for change. Among their reform enactments was the creation of a legislative Constitution Study Commission. The commission, composed of legislators appointed by the legislative leaders and public members appointed by the governor, was given an open ended charge to "study any and all provisions" of the constitution; to determine whether "any part or all" should be revised; and to determine whether any revision should be by a constitutional convention or by piecemeal enactment. After two years of study, the commission concluded that "a Constitutional Convention is the best and most timely way to achieve a revised Constitution."[13]

As recommended by the commission and approved by the legislature, the call for a convention was on the November 1968 ballot. After a strong campaign by a citizens' organization, the Illinois Committee for Constitutional Revision, the call was approved by 71.4 percent of those voting in the election.

CONVENTION SUCCESS AT LAST

The delegates were elected in the fall of 1969 on a non-partisan basis, and the Sixth Illinois Constitutional Convention convened December 8, 1969—one hundred years to the day after the start of the 1869 convention. Witwer, who had been quietly building trust and alliances over the last two decades, was elected convention president. He knew many of the 115 other delegates and many knew each other as well because the room was filled with rising stars in the state's political hierarchies. Richard M. Daley, son of the Chicago mayor, was there. So was Michael Madigan, future Speaker of the house; black civil rights leader Al Raby; future senator and gubernatorial hopeful Dawn Clark Netsch; Chicago Democrat and future judge Paul Elward; young reformer Peter Tomei; and a broad spectrum of representatives from labor, women's groups, and other walks of life. Witwer negotiated hard to create twelve balanced committees that would not break down on partisan lines or be overwhelmed by a single controversial issue. For the most part he succeeded. The committees set to work in a collegial atmosphere with a strong staff behind them. Executive director Joseph Pisciotte oversaw a small army of clerks, lawyers, writers, researchers, committee aides, a parliamentarian, messengers, and doorkeepers. This staff and structure were based on those of other states' conventions and help explain the volume and quality of work that was turned out by the delegates.

The Sixth Illinois Constitutional Convention had a long and sometimes controversial history before adjourning on September 3, 1970, but could have been worse had not an important decision been made before the convention: the approval of the flat-rate income tax in 1969. The tax was upheld by the state supreme court in August 1969;[14] if this decision had been reversed, the tone of the convention might have been quite different because the give-and-take on the revenue article might have overshadowed debate on other controversial issues.

Many of the changes made in the 1970 Constitution were important; others were relatively minor. The convention delegates were concerned with "cleaning up" the ancient document; they revised, deleted, and reorganized the old material, cut four thousand obsolete words, and excised many outdated provisions such as references to the 1893 Columbian World's Fair and the Illinois Central Railroad.

Of more importance was the constitution's clarification of the separation of powers, especially between the legislative and executive branches. Thus the lieutenant governor was removed as the presiding officer of the senate, and the legislature was given the power to call itself into special sessions. The office of auditor general, created in the new constitution, was clearly spelled out as that of a legislative officer. The provision with the biggest impact in this area was the new veto power given to the governor. Before 1970 the governor had the regular veto and line-item vetoes and used them with some frequency. Added in 1970 were the reduction veto on appropriation bills and the amendatory veto. The governor's strengthened hand changed the gubernatorial-legislative relationship because the governor no longer has to be a major actor during the legislative process; after the fact, he could modify legislation through his veto powers. (See Chapter 6 for a discussion of gubernatorial use of these expansive veto powers.)

Another significant change was the grant of home rule to cities and counties. Before 1970, Illinois had been a Dillon's rule state—local governments had only those powers granted to them by the legislature. Home rule reversed this relationship by providing that, with certain limitations, local governments had all the powers not denied them by the legislature. The home-rule provision proved instrumental in the later political alliance that helped pass the final document; it was one of four items on Mayor Richard J. Daley's "must" list. The others were classification of property taxes in Cook County, an elective judiciary, and continuation of cumulative voting. Home rule and property tax classification were put in the main package; the other two were advanced as side issues. With all four of the key issues under control, Daley endorsed the main body of the proposed constitution (though not until two weeks before the public vote) and swung his machine behind it. The endorsement made support clearly bipartisan and resulted in a noticeable jump in favorable ratings in public opinion polls, paving the way for victory.

Less noticed by the voters were numerous smaller changes that most observers felt strengthened the state's foundation. To oversee sometimes unwieldy state and local bureaucracies, the constitution created a new state board of education and state board of elections. A Judicial Inquiry Board was created to provide a method of investigating courtroom misconduct, and new rights were added to the Bill of Rights, the most important being anti-discrimination provisions based on sex and provisions protecting the rights of handicapped persons. The new anti-sex-discrimination section (Equal Rights Amendment) was surprising because of the role the Illinois legislature played in 1980 in defeating a similar amendment to the U.S. Constitution.

The 1970 convention, like most of its predecessors, submitted a "package" and four side issues. These provided for lowering the voting age to eighteen, abolishing the death penalty, choosing between appointive and elective selection of judges, and continuing cumulative voting for state representatives.

Upon finishing their business in an atmosphere of tired jubilation, the convention delegates decided to submit the proposed constitution to the voters at a special election on December 15, 1970. A new citizens' campaign, Illinois Citizens for the New Constitution, was established at the urging of Governor Richard B. Ogilvie. Many interest groups supported the new constitution; others opposed it. Special campaign groups were organized to support or oppose certain issues, such as an appointive judiciary.

The new constitution passed statewide with bipartisan support by a favorable 56 percent margin but a low voter turnout. On the side issues, the death penalty was retained; cumulative voting was chosen over single-member, single-vote districts; the elected judiciary was retained; and the option of reducing the voting age to eighteen was rejected.

The vote was more favorable in Cook County than in downstate Illinois. Only 30 of the state's 102 counties supported the document, but they represented three-fourths of Illinois's population. Sixty-five percent of Cook County's voters supported the main document, as opposed to 45 percent of the downstate vote. Voting followed historic geographical patterns set by constitutional amendments (1950–66) and the call for the 1969–70 Constitutional Convention: northern counties generally voted favorably on constitutional questions and southern areas consistently voted negatively.

Thus Illinois had a new constitution. It was a remarkable achievement in a large and divided industrial and partisan state and in turbulent times. Also, it was remarkable because Illinois is not considered a "reform" state. Daniel Elazar said the new constitution was "one of the most advanced in the country."[15] It was a compromise between the political and managerial approaches to governance.[16]

STANDING UP OVER TIME

The test of time has shown that the package approved in 1970 seems to be working for the people and the special interests of Illinois; no major efforts have been initiated to discard it. Unlike the constitution that preceded it, the 1970 document allows two ways to create improvements without undue hardship: through amendments, which have been used fairly frequently, and by reconvening a convention, which is required to be put to a public vote every twenty years.

There have been some attempts in the legislature to reverse the decisions of the constitutional convention, but few have gotten on the ballot. Since 1970, only fourteen amendments have been placed on the ballot, and of these, seven have been approved. One amendment with a major statewide impact was the so-called cutback amendment in 1980, which reduced the size of the House of Representatives and eliminated the controversial minority representation system (cumulative voting). The cutback amendment was approved by the voters in 1980 by a two-to-one margin. Another important amendment was approved in 1988, when the voting age was reduced from twenty-one to eighteen years to conform with the U.S. Constitution.

One amendment, passed in 1992, falls in the "motherhood and apple pie" category. It amends the Bill of Rights to add a crime victims' rights section. Crime victims shall have "the right to be treated with fairness and respect for their dignity and privacy throughout the criminal justice process" and nine other rather innocuous "rights."[17] It was adopted during a "tough on crime" period, and some academics say it illustrates the inclusion of "nonfundamentals" mentioned at the beginning of this chapter. Two more changes were added in 1994. Voters ratified a proposal to encourage earlier passage of bills by the General Assembly; the new deadline of May 30 means that bills passed after that date are not effective until June 1 of the following year unless passed by a three-fifths majority. Voters also approved changing the right of an accused criminal "to meet the witnesses face to face" during trial proceedings. Children who have been sexually abused may now testify from a separate room, via closed-circuit television, to prevent intimidation and additional psychological harm from the alleged abuser.

The strongest measure of the value of the staying power of the 1970 convention is that voters rejected an opportunity to call for a new convention. The 1970 Constitution provided for a vote every twenty years on whether to call a convention; the attorney general ruled that the first call would be on the ballot in November 1988. In preparation for the debate on the question, the legislature created a Committee of 50 to provide material to help the voters. The Committee of 50, which included political and civic leaders, held hearings and reconvened the living delegates from the 1969–70 convention. There was no strong sentiment for another convention by the committee or the 1969–70 delegates.

In the media and the public, there was considerable opposition. Interest groups such as the State Chamber of Commerce, the AFL-CIO, and the League of Women Voters opposed the call for different reasons. Some felt that the 1970 Constitution had served the state well; others questioned the cost of another convention (the 1970 affair cost about $14 million). Still others felt that new controversial issues, such as abortion rights, would be brought up in a convention.

There were some vocal supporters for another convention. Some wanted merit selection of judges, others wanted the initiative and referenda as in California. Supporters mentioned other changes, such as a revised tax system with more progressive taxes. But in November 1988 the voters agreed with the opponents and overwhelmingly defeated the call by a vote of three to one.

By most measures, then, the 1970 Constitution was a distinct improvement over the 1870 version. It was a political document and thus not perfect from the reformers' perspective, continuing, for example, the election of officials to a number of state offices that are filled by appointment in other states. Neither did it do away with election of judges, which has been blamed for corruption and favoritism in the courts. One national observer, Neil Peirce, wrote in his book *The Megastates* that the 1970 Constitution was "not a terribly distinguished piece of work."[18]

From a national perspective this may be so, but from the vantage point of Illinois, whose history of constitution making has been less than brilliant, the document was a major step forward. At least as important as the content of the constitution was the process it created. Illinois leaders from both sides of the aisle and all walks of life, respectful of each other and mindful of the state's needs, convened and hammered out solutions to long-standing problems. In the individualistic culture of Illinois, such a process is rare enough that the 1970 Constitutional Convention can fairly be called a triumph for the common people.

CHAPTER FIVE

Inside the Legislative Machine

In the 1950s and 1960s, many journalists raked state legislatures over the coals with articles such as "The Octopus in the Statehouse," "The Two Ring Circus under the Capitol Dome," and "The Illinois Legislature: A Study in Corruption." In self-deprecating defense, legislators framed the quotation from an 1866 New York court decision which declared, "No man's life, liberty, or property are safe while the legislature is in session."

Until the mid-1960s, the Illinois legislator had no office, no staff, no telephone, and insignificant pay. The constitution authorized each lawmaker only fifty dollars per biennium for postage, and lawmakers traditionally met only in the spring of odd-numbered years.[1] But if being a part-time and poorly paid politician wasn't much of a prize on the surface, many legislators found it to be lucrative in other ways. Some were landowners or businessmen whose interests were well served by their legislative position and their friendships with government officials. Others found that money could be made on the side, as Representative Charles A. White admitted in a letter to the *Chicago Tribune* in 1909. The legislature at that time elected U.S. senators; White and other representatives had accepted a thousand dollars each to cast their votes for a wheeler-dealer named William Lorimer, who would later be expelled from the U.S. Senate. White also told of a general slush fund, known as a jackpot, that helped sway legislative decisions. White had earned nine hundred dollars for various votes, a tidy sum at the time.[2]

Illinois legislators rebelled in the 1960s against both their poor image and their self-imposed structural inadequacies. Under the leadership of the late senate president W. Russell Arrington, the Illinois General Assembly initiated rapid modernization. A subsequent study rated Illinois as having the third most effective legislature in the nation.[3] It credited the Illinois legislature with having one of the strongest staffing patterns, relatively good compensation, and private offices for each lawmaker. Burdett A. Loomis reported in 1990 that the Illinois legislature ranked in the top ten among the fifty states on indicators of professionalism (staffing, compensation, information capacity), percentage of full-time legislators, and low membership turnover.[4]

The high ratings notwithstanding, the Illinois legislature remains similar in many essential ways to its counterparts in other states. It is a fiercely partisan body where horse-trading and sophisticated political stratagems are often more important to the lawmakers than the particular issues to be decided. It is tied closely to business and special interests by high-pressure lobbying and generous contributions to election campaigns. Whereas the early legislatures were marked by short hours and low pay, today's legislature is a full-time endeavor for many, and good pay and better pension benefits have enticed many to make a career of the legislative game.

Experience in the legislature can be valuable because it is a complex business in which byzantine procedures and layers of committees and staff are only the first barriers to turning a bill into a law. Control has always been shared with the governor, whose veto can destroy years of work, and has always been well guarded by the majority and minority leaders of the house and senate, known most recently as the Four Tops. Along with the governor they control legislation in Illinois, and to have an influence on them, a legislator must be savvy, well connected, willing to bend, and tough in the trenches.

LEGISLATORS OF EVERY STRIPE

Illinois legislators are among the best paid in the nation. In 1995 their annual salaries ranged from $45,668 to $65,000. The higher amounts are based on committee and party leadership roles; there are so many such positions that four-fifths of all lawmakers received a leadership stipend of at least $11,500. Legislators also received $79 per day when the legislature was in session, health insurance, a generous pension plan, and $47,000 per year for district offices ($57,000 for senators).

Legislators tend to reflect the habits and mores of the districts they represent. In the Capitol rotunda, you might see kelly green sports jackets and white shoes standing toe-to-toe with black wing tips and somber pinstripes. Southern Illinois lawmakers are likely to be deeply concerned about jobs and capital improvements for their relatively poor region. Chicago legislators pay special attention to funding for the city and protection of its home-rule authority. Suburban lawmakers are most concerned about improving the transportation network to unclog crowded roadways while somehow keeping property taxes from rising.

Most Illinois lawmakers are white males, though blacks and women have increased their representation significantly.[5] In 1963, only 2 percent of the state lawmakers were women; by 1993, it was 23 percent. Blacks increased their representation from 3 to 11 percent in the same period, approaching their 14.8 percent of the Illinois population. By 1995 there were 6 Hispanics among the 177 lawmakers, not yet proportional to their 7 percent share of state population.

Members elected to the 1993–94 General Assembly had extensive experience. Seven in ten had college degrees and one-third had earned graduate or professional degrees. More than half the senators had been elected to three or more terms (a senator has one two-year term and two four-year terms between decennial redistrictings), and just under half of the representatives had been elected to at least five terms of two years each. New blood is infused periodically after decennial redistricting, as incumbents confront new territory and sometimes increased competition. After remapping in 1993, 40 percent of the 177 lawmakers were newcomers.

Increasingly, the legislature has become a full-time occupation. In 1963 only 7 of the 236 legislators described their commitment as full-time; by 1993 almost half (84 of 177) so described it, and many others were heavily dependent on their legislative compensation.[6] More women (82 percent) than men (40 percent) considered themselves full-time legislators.[7] Of those with other major pursuits, 34 listed their occupation as attorney, 10 each were farmers and businessmen, and 7 each listed education and insurance.

These legislators are real people with needs, ambitions, doubts, and anxieties. It takes great motivation to raise up to $500,000 in campaign funds and devote endless evenings to run for a position that may undercut one's nonpolitical career. People are spurred to candidacy for varied and personal reasons: a sense of civic responsibility; a need to prove oneself; the challenge of the game of winning; professional advancement, especially for Chicago Democrats for whom politics is often a lifelong career; the salary and attractive pension benefits; and opportunities to get involved with well-known figures and on important issues. Many legislators, especially those from downstate, see the General Assembly as the culmination of their public service. Others see it as a stepping-stone to higher office.

Legislators want to feel good about what they are doing. They want to feel their work is important and to take pride in having contributed to a better hometown and state. For all these reasons, legislators enter the General Assembly with high hopes. Often these hopes go unfulfilled. Each lawmaker is but one in an unwieldy group of 177. A legislator's direct participation in most issues might be limited to a final passage vote on policies shaped without his or her involvement. The legislative leaders and the governor and their unelected staffs often seem to be in charge.

LIFE IN THE POLITICAL TRENCHES

This is not to suggest that there is little for legislators to do. Usually there is more to do than time permits. Legislators must shepherd bills of their sponsorship along the winding legislative path; help process legislation in committees and on the floor; respond to scores or hundreds of letters weekly; and host visiting constituents. They also must read until their eyes cross: bills, staff analyses, interest group position papers, letters, newspapers, and research reports. They must return endless phone calls from lobbyists, constituents, and reporters.

Back home they serve as advocates for their constituents, for example, with the secretary of state on drivers' license matters; the department of transportation on road improvements; revenue on tax matters; professional regulation on occupational licenses; conservation on park improvements; public aid on social services; and public health on nursing home care. This is the bread-and-butter work of a career politician. Taking care of a problem or guiding a citizen through the bureaucracy generates appreciation that is often rewarded on election day and, perhaps, at fund-raising events.

To build visibility with voters, lawmakers maintain from one to three offices in their districts. Some do regular "circuit-riding" to meet constituents at courthouses throughout the district. Several host cable television shows or write columns for local newspapers. If there is any time and energy remaining, lawmakers look after what might remain of their law practices or businesses.

As a result, lawmakers must establish priorities. First and foremost for nearly all legislators is reelection. All other activity may be regarded as a means to this end. Many legislators specialize. For the sake of simplicity, the lawmakers might be placed in four categories: the issues advocate, the district advocate, the committee specialist, and the broker. The issues-oriented lawmaker might be either a committed conservative, populist, antitax, or gay rights advocate who sponsors legislation that supports his or her ideological commitment. The district advocate focuses more on issues of specific benefit to his or her constituents such as highway and park projects, the location and staffing of a new prison, or funding for university campuses. All legislators sit on committees, but some sit on the same one for many years and become known as experts in the area covered by that committee. Finally, there is the broker, a legislator who enjoys the bruising work of stitching together bipartisan, regional, and other majority coalitions for controversial bills.

Despite cultural and regional differences among lawmakers, the legislature is a fraternity in which a degree of camaraderie develops. Liberals and conservatives may disagree on issues just as country boys and Chicago corporate lawyers enjoy different cuisine, but they also have a great deal in common. All have run for office, raised campaign funds, and endured abuse from voters. All were elected, and all those who want to stay will have to go through the process again. All must respond to constituent inquiries, meet visiting school groups, listen to lobbyists, and spend up to eighty nights a year in Springfield, eating and drinking in the same few places.

For this reason, patterns of mutually useful behavior have developed. Legislators generally treat their colleagues with respect, avoid becoming personal in the heat of debate, keep their word and commitments, reciprocate favors done, and help one another whenever possible. These patterns help explain some otherwise irrational behavior. For example, legislators will often help a colleague, even one from the other party, get his or her bill out of committee. If the committee vote looks close, a committee member might change his vote "so that my respected colleague can get his bill reported to the floor for the full debate it deserves, even though I may have to vote against it at that time." This helps the colleague get a little favorable publicity in the home district; it also clogs the legislative process with bills that must be considered even if they are unlikely to be enacted.

The cost of admission to this exclusive club is often high, especially for candidates in competitive districts who have contests in both the primary and general elections. In the general elections of 1992, there were ten house districts in which combined candidate spending exceeded $250,000; in five senate districts, the spending surpassed half a million dollars.[8] But money does not guarantee success. Nancy Masterson spent $118,000, or $27.91 per vote received, in a losing house bid in a suburban Republican district. Chicago Democratic representative Al Ronan spent $133,000, or $19.79 per vote, in a 1992 primary contest in which he was unseated. That same year in a Republican primary contest, Rosemary Mulligan spent $167,000 to defeat Representative Penny Pullen, who spent $149,000. They each spent about

$25 per vote. Costs continue to escalate. In the general elections of 1994, Republican and Democratic candidates for the state senate spent an average of just under $150,000. In the most expensive senate race, winner Kathleen Parker (*R*-Northbrook) spent $789,000 to defeat incumbent Grace Mary Stern (*D*-Highland Park), who expended $556,000.[9]

CONFLICT AND RESOLUTION

Once they have indebted themselves to become elected or re-elected, legislators typically find themselves in a pressure tank where conflict, accommodation, and interdependence characterize the relationship among themselves, the governor, and interest groups. Conflict between lawmakers and governors is natural, for there is an inherent clash of perspectives. Lawmakers focus on their districts, the governor on the whole state. Legislators go about their business in a piecemeal fashion, each developing bills based on individual interests and special knowledge, whereas the governor has to be comprehensive in his or her annual state of the state and budget messages. The legislator's job has a short-term focus because seven of ten Illinois lawmakers are up for election every two years. A governor is elected every four years and is expected to take a long-term view, to present a vision for the future.

As a result, each branch frustrates and exasperates the other. They contend on fairly even terms. The governor has greater formal powers, information resources, stature, and visibility; as a single actor, the chief executive can be decisive. But the legislature has its own strengths: sophisticated committee staffs, nearly full-time commitments by many legislators, strong leadership that can block gubernatorial initiatives, and the will to live up to its billing as a coequal branch. Adding further pressure on both the executive and legislative players are the interest groups, which make their presence felt through one-on-one conversations with legislators, generous financial support of legislative leaders, and memberships on state advisory committees and policy task forces.

The give-and-take process winds through a full cycle every two years in Illinois, each known as a biennial session; the 1995–96 biennium is formally referred to as the Eighty-ninth General Assembly. The legislature convenes each year on the second Wednesday in January and continues to meet, with periodic recesses, for the two-year period. The cycle is separated into three phases each year, beginning with the main event, the regular spring session.

The spring session generally begins slowly and has traditionally ended with a roar in late June or early July. Laws can be enacted by bills only, and bills may originate in either house with the sponsorship of one or more members. Typically, about five to six thousand bills are introduced in the course of the biennium, most during the spring of the first year and hundreds of these during the very first week. Bills are assigned to standing committees by the Committee on the Assignment of Bills (or Rules Committee), which is controlled by the Speaker in the house and by the president in the senate, who are the leaders of the majority party in each body.

In contrast to the U.S. Congress, where committees control bills, sponsors steer their bills through the Illinois legislative process. Tradition dictates that the committee hearing date for a bill is scheduled at the pleasure of the sponsor, if at all possible. Timing is important because a sponsor must gather support and "count heads" in committee as well as at passage stage. Each bill receives three formal readings on the floor of each house on three separate days. The first reading occurs at introduction; the second after committee action, when amendments are considered by the entire house; and the third, final reading, when the bill is approved or rejected. In contrast to the U.S. Congress, where voice votes are allowed, all votes at the bill passage stage in Illinois are recorded electronically.[10]

Even with the imposition of successive deadlines, a logjam of unfinished bills typically develops as the spring session approaches its scheduled June 30 (or May 31 in 1995 and thereafter) conclusion. This is understandable because the pressure of a deadline is a critical component that induces brokering and compromise among lawmakers. The parties are often evenly balanced, and no region—Chicago, the collar counties, or downstate—has a majority. Coalition building thus is often imperative. As in the U.S. Congress, bills must receive a majority of the votes of all those elected—sixty in the house and thirty in the senate—rather than just a majority of those voting.

During June the daily calendars of pending legislation expand to many pages, and hundreds of bills may be voted on in a single day. Drafters of the Illinois constitutions of both 1870 and 1970, seeking to encourage negotiation and final legislative action by June 30 (or May 31 in 1995 and thereafter) of each year, required that bills passed after that date cannot take effect until the following July unless passed by three-fifths of those elected. Attaining an extraordinary majority generally requires cooperation from the minority party in each house, so it was assumed that the presiding officers in the General Assembly would do their best to get the job done before or very close to the deadline. Leaders have even been known to stop the clock in their chambers at five minutes to midnight on June 30 to pass bills on time.

In recent years, however, when control of the governorship and at least one house of the legislature was divided between the two parties, the three-fifths proviso actually discouraged on-time adjournment. After the deadline votes from both parties would be required to adopt the annual budget and controversial legislation. Thus the governor and legislative leaders tended to delay serious negotiations until the political necessity for compromise and shared responsibility was formally imposed by the three-fifths proviso. Thus, for example, budget cuts and increased cigarette taxes could be enacted only with bipartisan support. In 1991 with a new governor, agreement was not reached until July 18, and in 1993 the final bills were not passed until July 13.

At the 1994 elections, the constitution was amended to move from June 30 to May 30 the date after which the three-fifths majority is required. The amendment was enacted by the legislature without a dissenting vote; the electorate then ratified the action. This earlier deadline reflected the reality of the political dynamic of divided control.

After the legislators depart for the summer, during the so-called interim period, the governor's staff, his Bureau of the Budget, and agency managers face the task of reviewing the eight hundred or so bills that are passed in a typical year (see figure 2). The constitution requires that the governor receive a bill within thirty days of passage. The governor then has sixty days to sign the bill or impose one of several types of vetoes.

Legislative staff members are busy during this period compiling summaries of the spring session and analyzing gubernatorial actions on bills. The budget staff monitors implementation of the budget to assure that legislative intent is being fulfilled. Other staff members prepare for and attend public hearings of subcommittees, special committees, or task forces that have been directed to deliberate on unresolved issues.

The lawmakers reconvene in the fall for a veto session that allows further debate and action on bills vetoed or amended by the governor. In odd-numbered years, the veto session generally opens in October; in even years, lawmakers reconvene following the November elections. The fall session typically lasts only seven to twelve days.

When a vetoed bill is returned to the house where it originated, the members have fifteen calendar days to act. If a veto is overridden there, the bill is sent to the second house where the same fifteen-day deadline applies.[11] Ve-

Figure 2. Bills Introduced and Passed, 1979–92

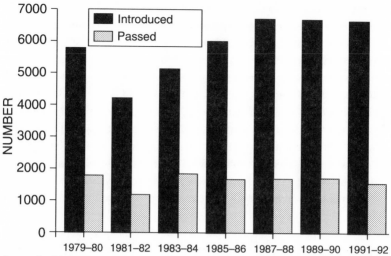

Source: Legislative Research Unit, Illinois General Assembly, Springfield, IL.

toes are not the only matters considered. Tax increases, pay raises, and other difficult political issues may receive more favorable consideration than they would in the spring. Because of retirements and defeats at even-year elections, there are numerous lame-duck lawmakers who may feel less need to respond to party leaders and constituency pressures. Some will even reverse themselves and become proponents of certain parts of the governor's program because the governor can provide a job with good pension benefits in addition to salary. In other words, all bets are off during even-year fall sessions.

CHANGING ROLE FOR COMMITTEES

Three decades ago respected observers of the Illinois legislature declared, "As an independent determinant of the fate of legislative proposals, the standing committee is of scant importance."[12] This is no longer true. On the surface, committees appear to be ineffective at screening and shaping legislation, but a closer look shows that in the 1980s committees were used significantly by the majority party, especially in the house, to block some bills and amend others.

Even so, much of the work of committees is routine and has little effect on the policies embedded in a bill because even if a bill dies, the main idea may be resurrected later. "Committees are almost meaningless," said one exasperated lobbyist. "Bad bills can get out so easily." Few bills are openly killed in committee, and fewer than one in ten receive a "do not pass" rating.[13] Said Bill Edley, a freshman house member in 1989: "The biggest negative I can say about the legislature is that we pass too damn much legislation. We don't have the opportunity to review the bills and to craft them as well as one would like."[14]

Nevertheless, smaller percentages of bills are being reported favorably from committee. In 1993, senate committees passed 40.3 percent of their bills onto the floor, while house committees forwarded 42.7 percent of their bills, down from 80 percent in the 1960s.[15] Bills typically die in committee in one of two ways: a sponsor does not request a hearing, allowing the bill to die at the deadline for reporting bills, or the bill is put on the "interim study calendar," where it very often is not studied.

The committee system in the house is becoming more like that in the U.S. Congress, according to Michael E. Pollak, parliamentarian for former Democratic Speaker of the house Michael Madigan. "Committees are beginning to take bills away from sponsors to develop committee-sponsored bills, and ideas from several bills are being bundled into a single bill. And if a Republican has a good idea, the Democratic majority in committee may even allow the Republican to become a cosponsor of the Democratic bill that adopts the idea."[16] and vice versa when Republicans are in charge.

Party leadership is felt strongly in committees. Democratic leaders frequently circulate bill lists with arrows that point up or down to indicate the position of the leadership. Because of fairly strong party discipline in recent years among the Democratic majorities on house committees, lobbyists often considered a bill dead if it had "down arrows" from former Speaker Michael Madigan's office. Thus they lobbied hard with the Speaker, his staff, and assistant leaders to get the arrows reversed or at least removed (a neutral position). The legislative leaders also have authority to replace committee members from their party's legislative caucus. On an important bill, a party member unfavorably disposed to the legislation can be replaced for that day with a member who will support the leadership.

STAFF PROFESSIONALS WORK THE SYSTEM

Thirty years ago there would have been very little to write about legislative staff because there were so few, but today staff members far outnumber legislators and thus affect the dynamics of the legislative process.

There are four staffing categories: those who work for leadership, committees, or individual legislators and those who work for the legislature's various support agencies, including the bill-drafting reference bureau, research unit, committee on administrative rules, and information service. Those in the first three groups are appointed on a strictly partisan basis, while those who work for the support agencies do so for the most part on a bipartisan, or neutral, basis.

In 1965 there were 24 professional staff working for the legislature. In 1990 more than 348 professional staff served the leadership and committees, and legislative service agencies employed about 125 more, and there was a well-regarded legislative staff. The total staff numbers about 750.[17] By tradition the majority and minority party in each house divide staff funding equally, with leaders of each party hiring chiefs of staff, parliamentarians, legal counsel, press aides, and budget and research directors.

Legislative staff are typically in their twenties and hold, or are working on, master's or law degrees. Like the legislators for whom they work, staff members have ambitions, priorities, and frustrations. Some see staff work as a stepping-stone. Illinois governor Jim Edgar, lieutenant governor Robert Kustra, and U.S. representative Richard Durbin are among scores of former staffers who have subsequently served as elected officials, agency heads, gubernatorial aides, and lobbyists.

In the shorter term, however, what most staff members want is to see their ideas, bill drafts, amendments, and budget recommendations implemented as public policy. This objective should be appreciated by those who work and negotiate with staff because to have one's idea adopted by a respected legislative staffer is an important step in the public policy game. They also want recognition for the work they have done, despite the frustrating institutional requirement that all credit goes to the boss. Staff members appreciate people who thank them for their contributions to the process. Finally, staff members can often be expected to be open to bipartisan cooperation, even within the context of partisan assignments. Committee staff from both parties often share information while their bosses engage in partisan public debate.

Each committee has at least two staff analysts—one for each party. Before each committee hearing, staff members prepare analyses of each bill, typically including a synopsis; descriptions of possible problems; discussion of the positions of the party, affected agencies, interest groups, and the governor's office; and suggestions for questions at the hearing. In most cases, the analysts will have contacted the pertinent state agencies and other interested parties to generate information. This detailed groundwork provides the foundation on which the state's lawmakers build legislation.

A SOMETIMES TORTURED PATH

Some bills will work their way, step by proper step, toward passage without major incident, but a likely path for major appropriations bills and controversial pieces of legislation is convoluted and winding; a bill might seem irretrievably lost before its essence suddenly reappears in another bill, making a frantic dash for the finish line.

Persuasion of fellow legislators is stock-in-trade in the legislative arena, but subtler techniques such as timing and personal knowledge of other legislators are often just as effective. A legislator shepherding his or her bill through a committee hearing tries to match the timing to the moods of the committee. For example, the lawmaker may have arranged for testimony on a bill by interest group representatives and other experts. Some of these people may have come hundreds of miles for the hearing and will want to have their full say on the matter. But if other bills have consumed a great deal of time, and if tired committee members are fidgeting in their chairs, the lawmaker may well size up the chances of a favorable vote and, if the count looks promising, curtail or eliminate his team's testimony to request a timely vote.

Most committee work is more hard-headed, especially when money is involved. The governor must make his budget recommendations to the legislature by the first Wednesday in March. The Bureau of the Budget (BOB) prepares individual appropriations bills for about sixty agencies; together these bills represent the governor's budget, which in fiscal 1995 totaled about $33 billion. Although the executive branch develops its budget over an eight-month period, the legislature must react, evaluate, and authorize the budget in the four months between March and the traditional early July adjournment. Each house conducts this work through one or more appropriations committees.

Since the 1980s, the appropriations committees have actively altered the governor's proposed budgets, sometimes reducing agency budgets across the board by two or three percentage points. This has been largely the result of a partisan split between the governor's office, controlled by Republicans from 1977 through 1994, and the legislature, where Democrats controlled one or both houses. Strong, experienced, and knowledgeable committee chairs and staff directors have also reallocated spending authority away from a governor's objectives to those that reflect the preferences of the committee leaders.

The appropriations bills provide a good example of how the professionalized legislature, with its full-time and bipartisan staff, exerts a role as a full counterweight to the executive branch. The appropriations bill for each agency proposes dollar amounts by line items such as personal services (personnel), contractual services, equipment, travel, and telecommunications. Appropriations committee staffers require agency responses to detailed questions to justify what each line item would buy. Because staff analysts specialize in different areas, their questions cannot be derailed easily. Analysts from one or both parties will meet with the agency's fiscal officer and sometimes the agency head to discuss the proposed budget, laying groundwork for future legislative debate or actually brokering a deal in advance of the committee hearing. (Not surprisingly, staffers representing the same party as the governor are generally, though not always, more cooperative with executive branch agencies than staffers from the opposing party.) Legislators are brought back into the loop before each budget hearing, when appropriations committee staff directors meet with their respective chair or minority spokesperson, along with other committee members, to discuss each agency bill. This is the point at which legislative positions on an agency's bill are determined. Any remaining differences among agency, legislative staff, and the two parties are thrashed out during the public committee hearing.

Conference committees, "shell bills," and "agreed bills" represent important and sometimes stealthlike vehicles for crafting compromises on controversial issues. A conference committee reconciles differences between the house and senate versions of a bill. Five members are appointed from each house, three by the presiding officer and two by the minority leader. Generally, the bill sponsor and committee members who are specialists on the bill's subject matter are appointed to the conference committee.

These short-lived committees were traditionally not required to meet publicly or to meet at all. One freshman senator noted in the 1970s that "in the two years I've been here, I've been appointed to nine and I've yet to attend a meeting."[18] Often a legislator or staffer would simply circulate a conference committee report based on agreement between two or more key conferees, seeking the six signatures needed to file the revised bill with the two chambers. On more important bills, legislative leaders, the governor's office, and key lobbyists would often hold a quick meeting in a corridor off the senate or house floors or in the privacy of a leader's office.

Such a system allows bills to be changed significantly, even completely rewritten, by conference committees. During the sometimes chaotic windup of the spring session, a score of conference committees may be in existence simultaneously. Keeping track of the action can be hard work; a bill defeated in the morning may be resurrected in the evening as an amendment to another conference committee's report.

Because this process was often manipulated by skilled legislators and staff, senate Republicans in 1989, under the leadership of then-minority leader James "Pate" Philip, forced a change in Senate rules to require that a conference committee report lie on senators' desks for one day before a vote can be taken; sponsors of bills be appointed to conference committees that will deal with their bill; and all amendments adopted in conference committees be germane (i.e., pertinent, to the subject matter of the original bill). After a decade of being outmaneuvered by the Democratic majority, Philip and his senate Republicans in 1993 took advantage of their new majority and adopted rules requiring a hearing on conference committee reports before a senate Rules Committee. If retained, these rules ought to reduce the ability of a few people to make changes in legislation without the knowledge of other members, let alone the public.

The "shell" bill is another vehicle for resurrecting dashed hopes. It allows legislative leaders to introduce, late in a session, new proposals as well as compromises hammered out among leaders and the governor. Because new bills cannot be introduced after a certain date set by rule each session, the party leaders and various executive branch departments introduce early a number of innocuous shell bills, empty of substantive content, which can be used later as rootstock on which to graft new legislation or amendments. Not any bill can be used because amendments must deal with the same chapter of the state statutes as the bill they would amend. Thus dozens of shell bills are moving along at any given time, available at strategic moments to carry forward late-developing compromises or to resurrect ideas killed off earlier.

The "agreed bill" process is attempted when legislators feel caught uncomfortably in the middle of intense conflicts between major interest groups on subjects about which the lawmakers are less expert than the interests. For example, proposed changes in workers' compensation for injuries divide labor unions and management. Legislative committees sometimes direct the interest groups to try to iron out their differences outside the legislative chambers and then come back with an agreed bill, which the legislators would likely ratify. The agreed bill process sometimes works, especially if the interest groups think the legislative solution might be worse than their agreement.

FOUR TOPS GUIDE THE ACTION

The complexity of any legislative structure ensures that a leadership core will develop to guide the membership. The structure and political makeup of the General Assembly has led to the institution of a four-leader system. In the 1980s and early 1990s, these leaders controlled the legislature to a degree not seen since the 1960s.

These Four Tops in the late 1980s were the Democratic Speaker of the house Michael Madigan; senate president Philip Rock, an experienced Democratic power broker who retired in 1993; and the minority leaders of each house, Republican Lee Daniels in the house, and James "Pate" Philip in the senate, both of whom would later become the majority leaders.

In close consort with Republican governor James Thompson, these four leaders managed to consolidate their legislative hold for five principal reasons: increased centralization of powers within the leadership; dramatic increases in fund-raising and campaign support for rank-and-file members provided by the leaders; increased need of legislators to be reelected because of increased reliance on legislative compensation and benefits; the deep experience of recent leaders; and the long period (1977–94) of a Republican governor and Democratic control in at least one house of the legislature.

In the 1994 elections, Republicans captured a sixty-four-to-fifty-four majority in the house, giving one party control of the governorship and both chambers of the legislature for the first time since 1972. Because bills passed after May 31 cannot take effect until July 1 of the following year unless passed by a three-fifths majority, however, participation of the minority party may continue to be required in most years to adopt the annual budget. If the Republican majorities are unable to analyze and act upon the $33 billion budget and some four thousand bills in the two months between the governor's March budget address and May 30, Democratic support will be needed to put together enough votes for the required extraordinary majorities.

As presiding officers, the Speaker of the house and the president of the senate dominate the appointments of chairs of all committees and the assignment of bills to committees. This can provide the leaders with extraordinary leverage, as former Speaker Madigan often displayed by refusing to call Republican-sponsored bills for a vote. Because they also control the important rules committees, the Speaker and senate president can determine which bills are assigned to committees for further consideration, thus breathing new life into or snuffing out a lawmaker's pet bill.

This leadership power was strengthened in the early 1980s when leaders centralized selection and management of the partisan staffing for committees. Staffers are now loyal to the leadership and not to the committee leaders who once had a say in the selection. Many of these staff assistants have also become skilled at campaign management and take leaves of absence during campaigns to help direct reelection efforts of members with difficult races, further tying them into the political apparatus of the legislative leaders.

Because of their powers, the leaders have become aggressive and successful at raising campaign funds which, along with campaign management services, they allocate to their members. Each of the four leaders directs campaign funds that spent from $1 million to $8 million during the 1994 election cycle.[19] Most big interest group contributions flow not to individual members but to the leadership funds. In 1992 the average leadership contribution to Democratic candidates in twenty-one "targeted" (highly competitive) districts was $81,000, compared to an average of $45,000 for the Republican candidates.[20] This was often more than the candidates raised through their own campaign committees.

With nearly half of Illinois lawmakers calling the legislature their full-time vocation in 1992, these members have a greater need than ever to be reelected. This need increases the value of the financial help and campaign skill provided by their leaders, which in turn increases the loyalty of members to their leaders.

The leadership of each party targets a small number of legislative districts for special effort based on the potential for gaining a seat or protecting a seat targeted by the opposition. The leadership helps its targeted members by sponsoring popular bills and assisting in getting the bills through the legislature. Members targeted for tough re-election contests sometimes vote the way the opposition might vote, with the tacit approval of their leadership, to avoid becoming vulnerable to attack by the opposition's candidate.

Leadership protection of candidates in marginal districts can become quite dramatic.[21] In 1993, house Speaker Madigan had agreed to provide votes for passage of a fourteen-cents-a-pack increase in the cigarette tax as part of a budget package negotiated by the four leaders and the governor. As votes on the issue were being explained during voting, Madigan was alerted that a vulnerable freshman lawmaker was thinking about voting for the tax increase. The newcomer's hand hovered nervously over her voting switch.

Madigan rushed to the legislator's desk, locked his eyes onto those of the freshman, and said forcefully, "We do not need your vote! We do *not* need your vote!" Indeed, most of the Democrats targeted for defeat by Republicans voted against the tax increase, which passed with the bare majority needed.

Leadership powers are limited, nevertheless. Each party's membership is diverse, with varying ideologies, personalities, ambitions, and rivalries. Perfect discipline is impossible. A lawmaker's loyalty to district interests may often be stronger than that to a leader. Leaders also need support of their members to win and retain their leadership positions. As a result, leaders cannot run roughshod over members. Instead, they generally try to apply their powers in positive ways, in expectation of generating credits that can be drawn on as needed.

THE BALANCE OF POWER

The power of legislative leaders is matched by that of the governor, especially since 1970, when the rewritten Illinois Constitution provided the governor with two additional powers of veto, the reduction veto that allows appropriation amounts to be lowered and the amendatory veto that permits substantive changes to a bill. The same constitution made it easier for the legislature to override a governor's veto, reducing the required majority to three-fifths from the previously insurmountable two-thirds.[22] Both sides soon tested these new powers and were ultimately forced into a showdown.

The stage was set by Governor Thompson's heavy use of the amendatory veto in the 1980s. After the legislature in 1982 sent the governor a measure prohibiting use of a particular method of taxation for multinational corporations, Thompson recast the bill with his amendatory veto so that it *required* the method in certain cases.[23] Both houses of the legislature at this point had firm Democratic majorities, and they fired back by overriding Thompson's vetoes twenty-five to fifty times per biennium. Thompson kept the veto pen busy until, in 1987, Madigan refused to call up a number of bills that Thompson had sent back with amendments. These were bills that Thompson wanted, and Madigan's action had the effect of killing them. The following year, Thompson could not even get his proposals to increase taxes introduced into the legislature. According to Alan Rosenthal, Thompson "got the speaker's message and began to temper his use of the amendatory veto."[24]

The four leaders and the governor found over time that accommodation could prove helpful to both sides, and because of the continuity that Thompson and the leaders brought to their positions, they developed effective working relationships. Major issues were often resolved by a "summit process" in which the five would meet to hammer out agreement. If consensus could be achieved, the four leaders and the governor then generated the votes to ratify their agreements.

In many cases it was money that made agreement happen. In 1985, Thompson put together a $2 billion public works program he called "Build Illinois." Although it was initially couched as a strategic economic development program for the state, Thompson and legislative leaders ultimately turned it into a vehicle for gaining support when they needed it. Thompson adopted many projects selected by legislators and divided part of the funding equally among the two party caucuses in each house, where the leaders dominated the allocations.[25] Build Illinois became known as a pork barrel program, but, in the process, it illustrated well the strengths and weaknesses of accommodation.

Also playing a role in decision making are the interest groups which, as in Washington, D.C., are almost a third arm of the legislature. Indeed, an informal association of lobbyists is called the "Third House." Whereas the legislature is bisected into Republican and Democratic camps, interest groups are fragmented by economic philosophy and specialization. One of the few positions they all agree on is that campaign contributions are a worthwhile approach to gaining influence.

From July 1988 through June 1989, for example, 210 Illinois political action committees spent more than $13 million on elections, of which nearly $5 million went directly to candidates for the legislature.[26] Not all that money went to the 177 sitting members, but most did, to the tune of about $25,000 per lawmaker.

Taking note of the power structure in the legislature, interest groups have recently directed more of their contributions to the campaign committees of the four leaders and several assistant leaders. This represents mutually advantageous accommodation as well as interdependence. In the eighteen months preceding March 1990, nearly two-thirds of the $6.2 million received by campaign committees of the leaders came from interest groups, businesses, law firms, and lobbyists.[27] These contributions increase the power of the leaders as they dole the money out to their appreciative rank and file. Life is also made easier for interest groups because their lobbyists can focus more time and effort on four leaders and less on the full complement of 177 legislators.

HOW DECISIONS GET MADE

A legislator makes thousands of decisions each year—from the insignificant to the momentous—in committee, on second reading, at passage stage, and in response to lobbyists, constituents, and reporters. The lawmaker must apply a split-second calculus to many of these decisions. Should he help a colleague get his dubious bill out of committee (an easy affirmative decision for most)? How should he or she vote on possibly career-threatening tax increases or abortion legislation? A legislator cannot blithely or out of indecision abstain from voting, allowing those who know more about an issue to make the decision. The Illinois Constitution requires that bills receive a majority of all those elected so failure to vote or a formal "present" vote operates as a "no." There is no easy way out.

A lawmaker's political party affiliation and the position of his or her leadership provide the most important guides to decision making. On routine and noncontroversial matters, the party line is a good guide to how a legislator will vote, but on difficult votes, leaders impose on their members only to the extent necessary to achieve their objectives. Leaders appreciate that attitudes in a legislator's district may be at odds with a party position. In those cases, the leaders try to put together majority roll calls without asking for support from those who would have to vote against their constituents.

Constituents' attitudes reflected in mail and personal contact also provide important cues for lawmakers, especially for those in competitive districts. Most voters have little or no idea how their legislators are voting, let alone who they are. Legislators understand this, so one might conclude that lawmakers could act without concern for constituents' attitudes. This is generally not the case, for careerist lawmakers view their political world in terms of actions that might increase or decrease their electoral base. Endorsement by large membership organizations of realtors, farmers, and labor unions can add scores or hundreds of votes to one's base of support, as can support from advocates of gun ownership or the so-called pro-life and pro-choice abortion causes. This is why small but intense groups often wield more influence than their numbers would seem to represent.

The legislative institution has developed approaches to reducing conflict in decision making, especially for the many issues that are deliberated without strong partisan, constituent, or regional considerations. One of these is "going along," that is, voting for legislation unless there is visible opposition. In committee, as members try to wrap up a long hearing, one often hears a legislator ask, "Is there any opposition to this bill? If not, I move the last unanimous favorable roll call." As one legislator put it, "Bills are judged innocent 'til proven guilty."

Reciprocity is another consideration. It makes more sense to help a colleague than to stand in his way, for his assistance may be useful another day.

Reciprocity often takes place in committees; it is one reason bad bills get out of committee to clog floor action later. Passing a problem along seems to simplify decision making: "Let the senate clean up the problems," or "Let's send it to the governor, and let him resolve the conflict."

Making commitments early reduces conflict as well. Keeping one's commitment has been a hallowed norm though one breached more frequently in recent years. Thus an early commitment to a colleague or lobbyist on a controversial bill that is going to plague the legislature all session effectively takes the committed lawmaker out of the lobbyists' cross fire.

Not all conflict, of course, can be resolved, pushed along, or reduced. For the scores of decisions that involve conflict, the lawmaker complements his or her own values and knowledge with cues provided by the leadership, staff, colleagues, lobbyists, the governor's office, the press, and constituents.

Information is an important factor. Legislators have more information available than they can digest, and the amount they do absorb is impressive. Nevertheless, on any one decision, the information absorbed and available is likely to be incomplete. Thus the credibility of the information and the person who delivers it becomes critical. The best cues tend to come from expert colleagues, veteran lobbyists, senior legislative staff, and longtime state agency experts. A former legislator recalls one use he made of informational cues on the house floor: "I respected my seatmates to my left, right and in front of me. One was on the judiciary committee, another on local government and agriculture, the third on revenue. I was on appropriations and education. We had most of the committees covered among us. So on third reading as each bill came up, we would ask who had it in committee, what he remembered, and how he was going to vote. While we didn't always agree, it was an invaluable set of cues."[28]

REASONS FOR PUSHING ON

Even with good pay, skilled staffs, and strong information support, the legislator's job is more demanding and imposes greater stress than in decades past. Campaigns are longer and more costly; the job is nearly full-time. Legislative leaders try to assist those members with outside jobs by scheduling as many Tuesday through Thursday sessions as possible, leaving Mondays and Fridays for work. But even this is impossible near the end of a session, when five days or more are required each week. Family life may suffer as well. When the legislator is home, the family faces competition for his or her time from business matters, constituent inquiries, obligatory civic club speechmaking, and political meetings.

To get elected or reelected, the legislator must further squeeze business and family time to raise funds and solicit votes. In his first race for the house in 1988, Democrat Bill Edley, a small business owner-operator, spent every afternoon from 2 P.M. until dark from June until November going door-to-door in a district that reached from near Peoria in central Illinois to the Mississippi at its far western bulge. He knocked on thirteen thousand doors.[29]

Why do they run? According to Alan Rosenthal, they do it for personal needs of power and display, predisposition toward politics, sense of self, pay, pensions, ambitions, and career advancement.[30] Although most do not go on, the legislature is a good path to higher office. In 1994, both U.S. senators and ten of the twenty congressmen from Illinois had served in the Illinois legislature, as had the governor, lieutenant governor, secretary of state, comptroller, mayor of Chicago, and numerous judges and Chicago aldermen. For those who want to make a career in the legislature, once elected, chances of being reelected are extremely good. More than 90 percent of those legislators seeking reelection were successful in most elections during the 1980s and early 1990s.

Another reason is strictly financial. Election to the legislature brings with it a solid pension plan that has been sweetened by legislation coming from the very people who benefit from it. Before 1994, all former legislators could increase the value of their pensions simply by taking another government job with higher pay; many worked their connections to land such jobs and, in the process, guaranteed themselves pensions that often exceeded their earnings as legislators. Former senator Ted Lechowicz, for example, boosted his pension from $42,921 to more than $61,000 per year by taking a six-week job with the secretary of state that paid $6,000 per month. That salary plugged into the state pension formula yielded an annual bonanza of $18,279 in extra benefits.[31] Public pressure ultimately forced the legislature to scale back the benefit, but only for new members of the legislature; existing and former members could still take advantage of the program.

PARTISAN BATTLES HEAT UP

Although pensions and other perks may keep some legislators coming back for more, lawmakers who have made a career of it are undoubtedly also in it for the action and adrenalin-pumping legislative battles. The level of conflict has gone up and down over the years, but in the 1980s and early 1990s it was clearly at a high level. For a good nose-to-nose political match, the Illinois legislature was a sure thing.

The new polarities were decades in the making, and the growth of suburban power was a major factor. The 1980 elimination of cumulative voting and the reduction of the house from 177 to 118 members played an important early role. Cumulative voting, which allowed a voter to cast up to three votes for a single candidate, tended to give the minority party, that is, Republicans in Chicago and Democrats downstate, one seat in each three-member house district. This diminished regional conflict because both Republicans and Democrats had colleagues in each geopolitical region of the state. It also tended to blur partisanship, for a suburban Democrat might now and then vote against a Democrat from Chicago on a matter dividing city and suburbs, such as mass transit, election laws, or education funding.

Because 118 house members are elected from single-member districts, conflict and partisanship intensified throughout the 1980s, when Democrats controlled both houses, and came out in the open by 1993–94, when Republicans, after redistricting, took control of the senate. In both houses, bills sponsored by minority party members were frequently killed simply because of their sponsorship, and major issues of statewide importance, including budgeting and education, became bogged down in vitriolic region-against-region stalemates.

Ideological differences between Republicans and Democrats are quite distinct in Illinois, according to sociologist Mildred Schwartz. She ranked state legislators on a single dimension of liberalism-conservatism, drawing on a roll-call analysis of bills in 1979 that were important to seven interest groups. The rankings showed all Republican senators on the conservative side of the scaling and all Democrat senators on the liberal side. In the house, only four of eighty-eight Republicans were found alongside the liberal Democrats, and none of the Democrats shared the Republican view.[32]

Another study by Julie Hamos compared Democratic and Republican votes on controversial bills in the 1980s. These bills included guaranteed unpaid family leave for care of newborn children, ninety days advance notice on plant closings, and an affordable housing trust fund. In most cases, 90 percent of Democrats supported the legislation while 90 percent of the Republicans were opposed.[33]

Of great importance in the balance between these two parties is the drawing of new election districts every ten years. Reapportionment represents the essential trench warfare of politics, for after a mighty struggle among the political combatants, new battle lines are set for a full decade.[34] The process begins following the decennial census and is purportedly to be a bipartisan effort of the legislature. But since elections are won or lost depending on where the lines are drawn, the last two redistricting processes became deadlocked in the legislature. The task was sent, according to the constitution, to a commission of legislators and nonlegislators, four Democrats and four Republicans, selected by the legislative leaders. Because these politically balanced commissions could not reach agreement by August of the redistricting year, the constitution provides for a ninth tie-breaking commission member who is added by drawing one name from a hat that contains two names, one Democrat and one Republican. In 1981–82, the Democrats won the draw; the following decade the Republicans did. Not coincidentally, the Democrats controlled the senate in the 1980s, but after remapping in the 1990s, the Republicans took over.

Districts are to be equal in population, compact, contiguous, and nondiscriminatory. Within those rules, the players draw boundaries that include as many favorable voters as possible. Computers are at the heart of the procedure, processing census information on a precinct-level basis so that legislators can tell instantaneously how moving a district line by one city block will change the population, political, racial, economic, age, and other dimensions of the proposed district.

Conflict is inherent. While party leaders want to increase their respective total membership numbers, individual lawmakers are more interested in "safer" districts from which they can easily win reelection. Leaders of black, Hispanic, downstate, collar county, and Chicago interests want both safer districts for themselves and more of them.

The basic techniques for achieving partisan advantage are to pack your opponents and their voting strength into as few districts as possible or dilute your opponents' strength. Districts that are equal in population and acceptably compact and contiguous can be drawn to benefit either party.

In 1981, under the leadership of Speaker Madigan, the commission's Democratic majority adopted a map that extended Democratic district lines from Chicago, fingerlike, into the adjacent suburbs to capture enough Republican votes to make districts of proper population without ceding Democratic control. By diluting Republican strength, Chicago Democrats controlled 19 senate districts, even though the city's population by itself would have supported only 15.5 districts.

In 1991, Republicans redrew the district lines to make maximum use of their growing suburban power base. In 1992 they gained control of the senate by a thirty-two-to-twenty-seven majority and reduced the Democratic majority in the house from seventy-one to forty-seven to sixty-seven to fifty-one, losing seven other seats by fewer than a thousand votes each. In 1994, Republicans captured those seven seats and picked up five more, to take majority control of the house, sixty-four to fifty-four.

SUBURBS GRAB FOR FAIR SHARE

The remap in 1991 created, for the first time ever, a legislature that reflected the emerging political dominance of the collar county suburbs. In 1992, the senate elected its former minority leader, DuPage County veteran James "Pate" Philip, as senate president. Two-thirds of Philip's Republican majority came from the collar county districts, and enough downstate Republican votes could be depended on to block Democratic initiatives. As a result, Philip joined a downstate governor and Chicago Speaker of the house as an equal at end-of-session bargaining over the budget and other controversial issues.

Philip brought more than experience with him to the job; he was known and admired by some, detested by others, for his role as an unrelenting city-basher. He called Chicago schools "rat holes," suggested that increased welfare benefits would only be spent on more lottery tickets, and in 1994 raised a furor when he blamed a recent case of child abuse on lax work ethics by "minority" workers and supervisors in the state's Department of Children and Family Services. If his statements infuriate Chicagoans, they often play well to the mostly white and middle-class voters in his suburban district. "I look at suburbanites as a (special) class of people," said Philip to senate colleagues in 1991. "We're hard-working. We pay our bills. We're not on welfare. We don't take public aid. We're the powerhouse of this state."[35]

Direct and brusque, Philip took delight in the 1993–94 legislative session in thwarting his opponents, especially Chicago Democrats and the Chicago public schools. Chicago mayor Richard M. Daley blamed Philip and his GOP senate colleagues for blocking development of a third major airport in the city and for delaying authorization of riverboat casino gambling in Chicago. (Gambling boats had been generating revenues for local governments in the suburbs and downstate for several years.) In another case, Daley and Madigan were forced to bargain with Philip, reducing seniority protections for some Chicago teachers in return for Republican support of a budget plan for Chicago schools. Even Governor Edgar of Philip's own party had to contend with the suburban leader, who blocked passage of a ban on assault weapons sought by the governor.

In 1995, the house elected Lee Daniels, also of suburban DuPage County, to be Speaker of the house. The Republicans had control of both houses of the legislature and the governor's mansion for the first time in two decades. The GOP quickly enacted a series of pro-business and school reform bills, proposals that had been blocked repeatedly when Democrats controlled one chamber of the legislature.

Democrats have responded to the collar counties' increased influence in the senate by intensifying efforts to win seats in the suburbs, while downstate legislators of both parties, concerned that they could be reduced to marginal roles, have organized downstate caucuses to build unity around issues of regional priority.

The three-way regional split raises the question of whether the Illinois legislature, with its professional staff and nearly full-time lawmakers, is any better equipped to solve state problems than the part-time body it replaced. The answer is both yes and no.

Because of increased capacity, professionalism, and self-confidence, the legislature can play a larger role than in the past in initiating and crafting major policy change. For example, the process of developing complicated education reform in 1985 was dominated by legislators who specialized in education. Arthur Berman, chair of the Senate Education Committee in 1985, and Gene Hoffman, veteran education specialist in the house, organized statewide hearings, negotiated with the education interests, and shepherded the legislation through to enactment. The subsequent major reform of the Chicago school system, which transferred some power from the central bureaucracy to parents, teachers, and community members at local schools, could not have been accomplished without the legislature's work.

On the negative side, the primary difficulty facing schools statewide is uneven funding so that poor communities generally are unable to provide as much as their richer counterparts. This problem, too, requires legislative action because solving the problem will cost $1 billion or more and will pit suburbs against Chicago and downstate. On this point the legislature has been ineffective and probably will continue to be until regional differences are put aside in favor of statewide interests. The statewide perspective has been further compromised by the increased careerism of the legislators, whose focus on re-election tends to create a parochial, district orientation. Even with increased information resources and time commitments from lawmakers, the legislature still has little interest in comprehensive review and evaluation of public policy.

The regional, careerist, and partisan orientations of lawmakers appear also to have induced a politics of caution that often frustrates constructive change. For example, Speaker Madigan in 1993 kept many controversial bills bottled up in committees even though he dominated his chamber with a comfortable sixty-seven-to-fifty-one majority. Seven of his Democratic members, several from the suburbs, had been elected with razor-thin margins, and Madigan felt that keeping his majority was more important than risking the wrath of voters.

In the same period, Governor Edgar's unwavering commitment to his pledge of no new taxes dampened enthusiasm among fellow Republican lawmakers to confront their standard-bearer with proposals on school finance, state pension underfunding, and fiscal reform. They feared embarrassing him with legislation he would veto for reasons of politics rather than merit. As a result, the legislature accomplished little of substance in 1993 despite a backlog of festering problems. Funding differences between rich and poor schools widened, the state budget deficit deepened, and children's services continued in disarray. Management of the state Department of Children and Family Services was largely taken over by a federal court monitor.

A veteran observer of the Capitol characterized change in the legislature this way: "In the old days, legislators might take money from time to time, but their word was as good as gold. Today's lawmakers won't pocket money, but their word's no good." That is, although lawmakers' public ethics have improved, their personal relationships and institutional ethics have deteriorated. Careerist legislators are more concerned about individual objectives than about the institution of the legislature and the state as a whole. For the near term, partisanship and regional politics, fueled by an individualistic approach, show every sign of continuing to dominate the legislative arena.

CHAPTER SIX

Management from the Governor's Chair

James R. Thompson was elected governor four times and served from 1977 to 1990, twice as long as any Illinois governor before him. He decided not to run for a fifth term that many observers thought he could win. Most remarkable about his string of victories was that Illinois went through a tough economic transformation on Thompson's watch. Hundreds of thousands of well-paid manufacturing jobs were wrung out of the state's economy and replaced by comparable increases in jobs in a rapidly developing service sector that ranged from fast-food restaurants to financial services and information technologies. Illinois suffered a deep recession in the early 1980s and uneven economic growth thereafter, with strength in the collar counties but weaknesses in rural areas and Chicago. Yet Thompson kept on winning.

Thompson responded to the economic woes as did governors in other struggling states. He expanded the state's economic development agency, infused it with money for job retraining, and created incentives for industry. He established more state offices overseas than any other state (eleven by 1990) and became the state's chief salesman abroad.

Thompson declared that governors ought not to devote much time to direct management once they have learned the job. Indeed, many agency directors did not see him personally on state business in a year's time. Yet Thompson will probably be given his highest marks for having administered the state effectively. Overall, he hired and retained high-quality staff and agency directors, and he gave them the latitude to do their jobs. Remarkable for Illinois, with its well-known history of political corruption, no scandals were reported during his fourteen years in office. Thompson came into office without a clear picture of where he wanted to lead the state. He addressed problems as they arose, with intelligence and an attitude that government could make some, if not fundamental, difference. Though he tried and had good people to help him, he became resigned to the limits of government in solving fundamental social problems. He did not, however, see it as his role to exhort the larger society to transform itself. Maybe he, like other policymakers, did not know what to prescribe for society's shortcomings.

Thompson thought of himself as a builder.[1] He constructed the State of Illinois Center in Chicago, which resembles a huge, glimmering, ungainly spaceship, plopped awkwardly in the heart of the city's Loop. He embarked on what appeared to be a major infrastructure renovation program, called Build Illinois, which evolved instead into a potpourri of projects awarded in large measure to the districts of favored lawmakers or those whose support was needed.

Thompson was elected as a crime-busting U.S. attorney who promised reform. At his first inaugural in 1977, Thompson declared: "No job will be bought, no favors will be sold. No citizen seeking help will be asked his or her party allegiance or political loyalty."[2] But by his final year, most state job vacancies were filled on the basis of party allegiance or sponsorship by lawmakers, and in 1990 the U.S. Supreme Court struck down elements of his extensive patronage system.[3] In 1986, he raised an unprecedented $7.11 million for his final campaign,[4] much of it in contributions of $10,000 to $100,000 from businesses, interest groups, law firms, and individuals who did business with the state or who were interested in legislation that would come to his desk.

There was nothing illegal in these patronage and fund-raising practices, but there was no reform. Illinois politics appeared to change the onetime reformer more than he changed the state, repeating a pattern that has marked political life throughout the state's history. Big Jim Thompson probably reflected the values, aspirations, and individualistic political culture of Illinoisans better than most governors before him.

APPROACHES TO MANAGING ILLINOIS

Illinois has shaped thirty-eight governors—and been shaped by them—since Shadrach Bond first took on the job in 1818. Twenty have been Republicans, eighteen Democrats. Like Thompson, each brought his own approach to the job of governing. As the late Robert P. Howard explained in *Mostly Good and Competent Men*, several of the chief executives left lasting imprints as managers, builders, or social reformers.[5]

Thomas Ford (1842–46) was one of the managers. He inherited a huge debt from an overly ambitious internal improvements scheme to build rail-roads, canals and plank roads throughout Illinois. Ford determined that, painful as it would be, the state must pay the principal and interest so as to restore the state's integrity as a place to invest. He sold government land and passed a permanent tax to pay off the debt, and he arranged new mortgage terms for completion of a canal between Lake Michigan and the Illinois River, which would link the Great Lakes to the Gulf of Mexico. In so doing, Ford "made possible the future solvency and prosperity of Illinois."[6]

Another manager was Republican Frank O. Lowden (1917–21), who re-organized 125 boards and commissions, many of which operated as political fiefdoms, into nine executive departments. He also centralized the state's budgeting and accounting systems and became a leading candidate for presi-dent at the 1920 GOP convention. But after nine ballots in which Lowden was deadlocked with General Leonard Wood and Senator Hiram Johnson of Cali-fornia, the convention turned to Warren G. Harding.

The most recent manager was Richard B. Ogilvie (1969–73), who cre-ated the executive Bureau of the Budget and staffed it with bright young pro-fessionals. Ogilvie established a strong Environmental Protection Agency before the federal government took similar action. He also imposed the state's first income tax and shared part of the revenues with local governments.

A different breed of governor, Thompson among them, were the builders who measured the success of their tenure by the amount of concrete poured and steel erected. Helped by a bond issue and planning initiated by his prede-cessor, Governor Len Small (1921–29) took Illinois out of the mud and onto seven thousand miles of concrete pavement. Year after year he set new na-tional records as a road builder. He rejected road bids of $40,000 per mile, threatened to have the state rather than contractors do the work, and ulti-mately reduced the costs to $27,000 a mile. Small also put state aid to schools on an equalization basis designed to help fiscally weaker districts.

William G. Stratton (1953–61) widened U.S. Route 66 to four lanes and by the end of his eight years in office took credit for 7,057 miles of new road-ways and 638 bridges. Stratton imposed tolls to finance a network of super-highways for the burgeoning metro-Chicago region. He sponsored major bond issues that won referendum approval and financed creation of new uni-versity campuses and a network of mental health centers. In addition, Strat-ton reformed the state court system and revised the state's malapportioned legislative districts for the first time in half a century.

Thompson's claim as a builder is based on the $2.3 billion parceled out as part of his Build Illinois program. Although some of the resources were dissipated among a hodgepodge of small projects dictated by legislative bargaining, the program also created significant science and engineering additions at the University of Illinois and constructed the people-oriented State of Illinois Center in Chicago, subsequently named in his honor. Another legacy of Thompson's program was the ten new prisons built to house a rapidly expanding prison population, created in part by longer sentencing policies championed by Thompson.

The social reformers were perhaps the least easy to fit in the mold of individualistic Illinois politics. Edward Coles (1822–26) was an idealistic aristocrat from Virginia who freed the slaves he inherited. Robert Howard credited Coles with preventing Illinois from becoming a slave state: "Coles reacted quickly when the legislature's pro-slavery majority ordered an 1824 referendum on the calling of a constitutional convention that would have legalized the de facto human bondage that existed in early Illinois. Lacking power to veto the resolution, he assumed leadership in defining the issue, raised money for publicizing his views, and mobilized public sentiment against supporting the pro-slavery movement. In what seemed to be a hopeless campaign, the cause of freedom triumphed—6,640 to 4,972."[7]

John Peter Altgeld (1893–97) became one the heroes of American liberalism. Altgeld spent surpluses built up by his predecessor to open teachers' colleges at DeKalb and Charleston and insane asylums at East Moline and Bartonville; he increased appropriations for the University of Illinois and encouraged its expansion in graduate programs and medicine. Altgeld made his mark, however, in social reform. He appointed Florence Kelley, a protégé of Jane Addams, to enforce a new factory inspection law; the law also limited employment of women to eight hours a day and strengthened an earlier child labor statute.

According to Howard, the turning point in Altgeld's career was his eighteen-thousand-word justification for pardoning three anarchists who had been convicted on flimsy evidence of a bombing at the famous Haymarket Square labor rally in 1886 in Chicago. "This courageous but belligerent action made him the most hated man in Illinois and wiped out any prospect of his being elected to another office. Thereafter he devoted his multiple talents to the protection of the poor and downtrodden and to the enactment of progressive legislation."[8]

It is easier to leave a lasting imprint when financial resources are available to build lasting infrastructure, as was true of several of the governors whose careers are sketched above. Henry Horner (1933–40), the state's first Jewish governor, presided during the depths of the Great Depression. He financed unemployment relief by shifting the state's major tax burden from property to sales and worked effectively with fellow Democrats from the New Deal administration of President Franklin D. Roosevelt. "By background and performance, he was ideally suited to serve as Depression governor," according to Howard, who considered Horner among the state's best governors.[9]

EDGAR THE LOW-KEY MANAGER

Thompson's protégé and successor was Jim Edgar, a study in contrasts to Thompson and many of his predecessors. Edgar was the first governor in sixty-two years to succeed a governor of the same party, a reflection of the state's competitive partisan balance. Thompson is a native Chicagoan who operated state government primarily from that city, where he resided during his governorship. Edgar, who grew up and went through college in Charleston (population 20,000), was the first downstate governor in thirty years. Edgar was also the first nonlawyer governor in three decades. Thompson had had no previous state government experience; Edgar has spent his entire career in state government and state politics.

Thompson is open and gregarious; Edgar is reserved and private. Thompson relishes the black-tie social life and spends expansively on fine art and antiques. Edgar is a family and church-oriented person; alcohol is not allowed in the executive mansion.[10] Edgar was even known to mow his own lawn at a cabin-style home north of Springfield, where he and his wife spend as much time as possible. His image is so squeaky-clean that reporters filed stories when they observed a state trooper assigned to him atop the riding mower at his retreat home.

Because of his restrained personality and lifestyle, Edgar appeared to have more limited objectives and less power than his predecessor. There were no major initiatives during his first term, in part because of a campaign pledge that there would be no tax increases, a promise he fulfilled. When the *Chicago Tribune* in 1994 endorsed Edgar for a second term over challenger Dawn Clark Netsch, it had to acknowledge that "if Edgar thinks he can glide along for another four years, then the state is headed for trouble."[11] The editorial noted that Edgar had backed down on several legislative initiatives during his first term—for a ban on assault weapons, for riverboat casinos in Chicago, and for experimental "charter" schools—and pointed out that the opposition had come not only from Democratic nemesis Michael Madigan in the house but from Republican senate president James "Pate" Philip. In contrast, Big Jim and Pate Philip got along famously, and Philip would often sponsor Thompson initiatives that he opposed personally.

Edgar and Thompson are alike in one respect—neither is a reformer. Like Thompson, Edgar courted big campaign donors and rewarded his political friends with contracts and patronage whenever possible. Edgar, by contrast, trimmed the state bureaucracy and scaled back Thompson's propensity to award big incentives to lure jobs to the state or help existing companies expand. If he had to be assigned to a category, Edgar would be a manager.

A SPRAWLING EXECUTIVE BRANCH

Like the suburbs around Chicago, the executive branch of government in Illinois is a huge and sprawling operation, with 82,900 employees and 40,400 more at the state universities in March 1994.

In the early 1990s the state employed more Illinois residents than all but the biggest corporations. If estimated state revenues of about $26 billion in fiscal year 1995 were equated with corporate income, Illinois would rank twelfth on the Fortune 500 list of leading American corporations, ahead of Amoco Oil of Chicago and Procter & Gamble.

The executive branch is complex and highly diversified. It delivers health and social services each year to 2 million of Illinois's 11.7 million residents, two-thirds of them poor or troubled children. There are eighty-three state programs for children, delivered by fifteen agencies. A different function is provided by the small Department of Professional Regulation, which examines, licenses, investigates, and sometimes disciplines about eight hundred thousand persons across forty-one occupations, from physicians and real estate agents to boxers and wrestlers. The Department of Natural Resources helps start recycling programs around the state, and the Department of Corrections houses thirty-five thousand residents crowded into forty-five correctional facilities.

The organization of Illinois state government is about as complex as the state is diverse. By the second decade of this century, the bureaucracy had grown into a sprawling, unmanageable collection of 125 agencies, boards, and commissions, which Governor Frank O. Lowden cut down into nine executive departments in 1917. Since then, the number of departments has expanded to twenty-six, and thirty-three major boards and commissions have been created, each linked to the governor on the organization chart and through members that he appoints. The executive branch has become so layered, in fact, that the first "cabinet meeting" of Governor Thompson in 1977 had to be held in the ballroom of the executive mansion.

The first problem a chief executive faces in Illinois is that the executive branch is not his or hers alone. The executive powers are divided by the Illinois Constitution among five independently elected officials: the governor, secretary of state, attorney general, treasurer, and comptroller[12] (see table 2). This system contrasts with the executive branch of the U.S. government, in which the president appoints all other constitutional officers.

Independently elected officers can try to make life difficult for their fellow executives. In 1994, the governor and lieutenant governor (elected as a team) and the secretary of state were Republicans; the attorney general, treasurer, and comptroller were Democrats. The attorney general, who is responsible for representing the legal interests of the state, has often differed with the governor's Environmental Protection Agency over how and when to prosecute alleged violations of environmental laws. The comptroller, Dawn Clark Netsch, frequently criticized Governor Edgar's management of his budget and even ran against him in the 1994 election.

The attorney general is the chief legal officer for the state. Among other responsibilities, the AG and his staff provide advisory opinions for state and local officials and represent in court more than three hundred boards, departments, and commissions of state government (though the governor retains legal counsel for his office and that of most of his agencies). The AG also collects monies owed the state and works with county state's attorneys to prosecute certain criminal cases.[13]

The secretary of state is best known for administering motor vehicle registration and drivers' licensing; in addition, the office oversees the state library and archives and administers laws relating to incorporation in Illinois. The secretary of state has far more employees (more than four thousand) than any other state elected official except the governor.

The comptroller keeps the state's "checkbook" and pays all the state's bills. Comptrollers have used the information at their disposal to evaluate and comment on the financial condition of the state. The treasurer is responsible for receiving, investing, safeguarding, and disbursing (upon the order of the comptroller) all monies paid to the state.

Although these thumbnail sketches fail to describe all that the governor's fellow elected executives do, their offices remain, when compared with the office of the governor, narrow and generally ministerial. For this reason, these officials have worked over the years to broaden the scope and visibility of their offices through enactment of statutes that assign them responsibil-

Table 2: The Executive Branch of Illinois State Government, January 1994, with Major Agencies that Report to the Governor (number of employees in parentheses)

Secretary of State (4,125)	Treasurer (142)	Governor (186)	Lieutenant Governor (29)	Comptroller (397)	Attorney General (762)

Bureau of the Budget

Civil Administrative Code Departments
Aging (105)
Agriculture (618)
Alcoholism and Substance Abuse (129)
Central Management Services (1,277)
Children and Family Services (3,618)
Commerce and Community Affairs (409)
Natural Resources (1,985)
Corrections (12,780)
Employment Security (2,831)
Financial Institutions (161)
Historic Preservation (193)
Human Rights (127)
Military and Naval Affairs (323)
Insurance (337)
Labor (86)
Mental Health and Developmental
  Disabilities (12,056)
Mines and Minerals (120)
Nuclear Safety (218)
Public Aid (9,205)
Public Health (1,286)
Professional Regulation (396)
Rehabilitation Services (2,099)
Revenue (2,570)
State Police (3,190)
Transportation (8,292)
Veterans Affairs (996)

Other Agencies, Boards and Authorities

Environmental Agencies
Environmental Protection Agency
  (1,167)
Pollution Control Board

Public Safety Agencies
Criminal Justice Information
  Authority

Emergency Services and Disaster
  Agency
Local Government Law Enforcement
  Officers
Training Board
Prisoner Review Board
State Fire Marshall

Regulatory Boards
Banks and Trusts Companies
  Commissioner
Commerce Commission
Industrial Commission
Liquor Control Commission
Racing Board
Savings and Loan Association
  Commissioner

Financing Authorities
Development Finance Authority
Education Facilities Authority
Export Development Authority
Farm Development Authority
Health Facilities Authority
Housing Development Authority
Independent Higher Education Loan
  Authority
Medical Center Commission
Toll Authority

Miscellaneous Agencies
Arts Council
Capital Development Board
Civil Service Commission
Court of Claims
Education Labor Relations Board
Guardians and Advocacy Council
Human Rights Commission
Property Tax Appeal Board
State Historical Library
State Labor Relations Board

Source: Office of the Comptroller, Springfield.

ities beyond those few set forth in the constitution and added by personal initiative.

For example, the lieutenant governor has no constitutional duties other than to fill the office of governor when it is vacated. Yet the report on that office in the *Illinois Blue Book* (1991–92) has sections on the lieutenant governor's activities in voluntarism, economic development, rural affairs, substance-abuse prevention, senior citizen services, and abandoned mined lands reclamation.[14] Recent attorneys general have been active in environmental protection and in concerns for senior citizens and consumer affairs. When he was secretary of state, Governor Edgar expanded his motor vehicle responsibilities to crack down on drunk driving and used his role as state librarian to champion adult literacy programs.

These activities make political sense because these offices are often used as launching pads to higher office. In 1990, the Republican secretary of state, Jim Edgar, faced Democratic attorney general Neil Hartigan in the race for governor. Seeking to move up the ladder, the other three executive officers that year ran for the posts being vacated by the gubernatorial candidates.

POWERS OF THE GOVERNOR

The governor has strong formal and informal powers, thanks in part to the enhanced veto and management powers provided by the 1970 Constitution. The Illinois governor is considered second most powerful among the states, following New York, in formal constitutional authority.[15] An Illinois governor needs all these powers, which are described below, because he is expected to fill several roles beyond those of administering the state's business and managing his own bureaucracy.

By virtue of the governor's constitutional responsibilities to give formal state of the state and budget messages to the legislature each year, the chief executive is expected by legislators to propose comprehensive policies and a detailed budget, to which the legislature will react. In addition, his political party expects him to wear the mantle of state party leader. He is also expected to be the state's chief negotiator, who brings legislative, business, union, and civic leaders to the executive mansion or to the Thompson Center to resolve prickly conflicts such as school strikes in Chicago and legislative impasses that pit labor against management. In other words, there are great expectations for an Illinois governor.

Because the state economy struggled during the 1980s, Governor Jim Thompson took on the role—with great relish—of chief salesman, or economic developer. He set up economic development offices in eleven overseas cities, from Moscow to São Paolo, Kyoto, Tokyo, Warsaw, and Budapest, and he took two or more trips overseas each year to trumpet Illinois products and business opportunities.

To carry out these roles effectively, the governor needs powers to do things *for* people, especially for lawmakers, and powers to do, or threaten to do, things *to* people. The Illinois governor has a significant stock of such powers, though not always enough to accomplish his objectives. Among his fundamental powers are those to veto bills passed by the legislature; initiate comprehensive legislative programs and annual budgets; dispense patronage jobs, appointments, and contracts; and administer his sprawling executive agencies.

The governor has the advantage of being a single decision maker who confronts a two-house legislature characterized by divided party membership, scores of committees, and as many points of view as members. The governor can also benefit from the stature, authority, and perquisites of the office.

The president of the United States, who can sign or veto a bill in its entirety, would undoubtedly be envious of the additional veto powers granted the governor of Illinois, powers among the most extensive in the fifty states. In addition to the whole bill veto, the governor of Illinois has the authority to make substantive changes in enacted legislation (the amendatory veto), to reduce the amount of money in appropriations bills (the reduction veto), and to eliminate specific line items from these spending bills (the line-item veto).[16]

Since 1970, governors have used these powers frequently. Governor Dan Walker (1973–76) had difficult relations with the legislature. He vetoed 468 bills in entirety during his single four-year term, more than 14 percent of all bills passed. The legislature was able to override only one in fourteen of his vetoes with the required three-fifths majority in each house.[17]

Thompson used the amendatory veto more extensively than other Illinois chief executives. In 1989–90, he applied amendatory language to 140 enacted bills. The legislature was able to override, or strip away his changes, on only 8 bills.[18]

As shown in table 3, in the 1991–92 biennium the legislature enacted 1,528 bills. Governor Edgar applied one of his four veto powers to almost one-fifth (290) of them. His vetoes were overridden just sixteen times.

As Alan Rosenthal points out, however, the legislature often expects the governor to bring coherence to legislation: "An example is the crisis over Acquired Immune Deficiency Syndrome (AIDS), in which many bills have been introduced by legislators seeking to demonstrate concern and gain

Table 3: Veto Actions by Governor Jim Edgar, 1991–92

	Number	Percentage
Bills introduced	6,505	100
Sent to governor	1,528	23.5
Bills signed	1,264	19.4
Vetoed in full	174	2.7
Amenditorily vetoed	90	1.4
Appropriation (reduction) item vetoed	26	0.4
Total veto actions	290	4.5
Vetoes overridden (percentage of vetoes)	16	5.5

Source: Jack Van Der Slik, ed., *Almanac of Illinois Politics* (Springfield: Sangamon State University, 1994).

credit for action. The Illinois Legislature in 1987 passed 17 different AIDS bills, a number of which contradicted one another. Governor Thompson vetoed four, amendatorily vetoed three, and signed 10 others, trying to fashion a coherent program out of a potpourri of legislation."[19]

The extensive veto powers allow the governor to deny a lawmaker his or her cherished legislative goal or to subvert the sponsor's intent, thus providing the chief executive strong negotiating leverage. The governor's ability to award jobs, appointments, and contracts represents a more positive negotiating power. In the 1980s, just about every vacancy that occurred under Thompson's jurisdiction was scrutinized to see if a lawmaker or political party leader had a qualified candidate. If so, that patron had a good chance of seeing his candidate selected. If the patron had a candidate who was not yet qualified by examination, the position was often held open for months while the candidate tried to become qualified.

Legislators sometimes sponsor themselves for job appointments in anticipation of voluntary or involuntary retirement from their elected posts. In addition to continuing their careers in government, these persons can also add to their legislative pension benefits by holding such jobs. This interest in a postlegislative career can persuade a lawmaker to cast difficult votes on behalf of the governor's program.

The governor also fills by appointment nearly 2,100 positions on more than 329 independent boards and commissions. Many of these appointments are prestigious, such as those to the Illinois Board of Higher Education and the Illinois Arts Council. Others are highly prized for the recognition they bring within a profession, such as the forty-one boards that oversee licensure for engineers, architects, physicians, real estate agents, and other regulated occupations.

Finally, there is the award of so-called pork barrel projects and the construction contracts that go with them. Thompson's Build Illinois program melded the concept of economic development with projects that benefited lawmakers. According to Alan Rosenthal, Thompson adopted projects selected by legislators, and he agreed additionally that about one-fifth of the funding would be allocated among the Republican and Democratic caucuses of the house and senate.[20]

Each project provided for contracts that benefited contractors, financiers, and law firms. These beneficiaries were expected, some would say, to show their appreciation with large campaign contributions, and they helped Thompson raise several million dollars a year for his campaigns. In addition to financing reelection campaigns, campaign funds are used to help legislative candidates and to provide birthday, anniversary, and holiday gifts for friends and politicos.

Because of these powers, a legislator will frequently seek a governor's support and assistance. Years ago, during a closed conference of Republican members of the house, several GOP lawmakers were loudly criticizing the governor (Ogilvie, also of their party). Finally, a sage veteran silenced the bickering with this remark: "Okay, so the governor is an SOB. But just remember and appreciate this—he's *our* SOB!"[21]

The governor of Illinois has more latitude than many governors in administering the executive branch. Even though the executive is divided, the lion's share of state government functions and personnel are within the governor's domain. He appoints all his department heads and has statutory authority to terminate without cause several hundred senior civil service executives at the end of their four-year appointments.

The 1970 Constitution grants governors the power to reorganize state agencies by executive order, subject to rejection by the legislature. In 1995 Edgar used this power to merge the Departments of Conservation, Mines and Minerals and Energy and Natural Resources and units of other agencies into a single Department of Natural Resources.

A PEER OF CORPORATE EXECUTIVES

The most important informal power of the governor lies in the stature of the office itself and the perquisites that come with the job. With rare exceptions, the governor alone among state officials and lawmakers can become, by virtue of his office, a peer of corporate chief executives. The governor has the assurance that they will return his phone calls when he needs their counsel or assistance. His comments are often news on the front page and on evening television, whereas those of most legislators are relegated to the back pages, if covered at all. His personal presence often generates interest and increased participation in fund-raising events for legislators.

In Springfield the governor has at his disposal a handsome executive mansion for entertaining. Just down the street from the mansion, is an even more impressive building, an expansive, restored manse designed by Frank Lloyd Wright and owned by the state. He also has a small fleet of aircraft and, in Chicago, impressive offices atop the James R. Thompson Center in the heart of the central business district.

Although this stature and the resources of the office are real, the personal style of the governor determines how effectively they will be put to use. Governors Richard Ogilvie (1969–72), Dan Walker (1973–76), and Jim Edgar (1991–) lacked the friendly, comfortable, outgoing personality of Thompson. They used the stature and resources of office less, and less effectively, than did Thompson, who genuinely enjoyed entertaining and rubbing elbows with legislators, lobbyists, the media, and business leaders. Thompson used the mansion and funds from his campaign chest for annual as well as spur-of-the-moment parties and dinners. A Protestant, Thompson regularly celebrated certain Jewish holy days with Jewish lawmakers and friends. At the adjournment of each legislative session—often beginning at 2 A.M. or later—Thompson hosted legislators, staffers, lobbyists, and journalists for a lively predawn party on the lawn of the executive mansion.

Alan Rosenthal observes that to be effective with legislators, a governor generally needs several traits. One is to "stand tall," that is, to have a strong personality and presence and be willing to use that personality to "get tough" from time to time. The chief executive also needs to be willing to rub elbows with the lawmakers, consult with them, massage their egos, and "talk turkey," that is, be willing to use his powers of office in making deals on legislation.[22]

If a governor is selective in his proposals, makes use of blue-ribbon commissions to generate consensus, takes his case to the people (which Thompson did with enthusiasm in whirlwind fly-around press conferences throughout the state), and works the legislature from the inside, he can achieve considerable success in getting his programs enacted.[23] Thompson did all of these things with gusto. As a result, he had generally good, though not always successful, relations with the legislature.

A governor needs all the powers and skills he can muster, for powerful constraints are imposed on him. In addition to sharing his authority with other executive officers, a governor confronts a legislature that is often controlled by the opposition party. The legislature tries to live up to its textbook billing as an independent, coequal branch of government. During the fourteen years Thompson was governor, the Democratic opposition controlled both houses, with the exception of 1981–82, when Republicans had a majority in the house. Indeed, in two sessions, Thompson was unable to find a single lawmaker to introduce his unpopular proposals to increase taxes.

The role of the federal government in state government also limits and frustrates a governor. Many of the laws enacted in Washington are designed to be administered by the states and paid for with a combination of state and federal funds. Prime examples include air and water pollution programs, the Medicaid program for the poor, Aid to Families with Dependent Children, vocational rehabilitation, and transportation. Federal funds account for about one-quarter of the Illinois budget; the U.S. Congress and federal bureaucrats leverage that funding to direct the manner in which major state programs are run.

During the 1980s, there was a major difference of opinion between the federal and Illinois environmental protection agencies over how to meet federal clean air standards. The U.S. Environmental Protection Agency (EPA) insisted on an automobile inspection program; Illinois countered that it could achieve the objectives more effectively and less expensively in other ways. The EPA rejected the Illinois proposal and threatened to withhold $350 million in federal highway funds. Governor Thompson appealed personally to President Ronald Reagan, to no avail. With no other recourse, Illinois set up automobile inspection programs as required by the federal government.

The state and federal courts also tell a governor how to do his or her job. During the early 1980s, the state often reduced prisoners' sentences by more than ninety days to alleviate prison overcrowding. In 1983, the Illinois Supreme Court ruled that the executive branch lacked legislative authority to cut sentences by more than sixty days. Prison populations began rising immediately.[24] In another setback for gubernatorial authority, the U.S. Supreme Court in a major 1990 decision, *Rutan v. Republican Party of Illinois,*[25] declared unconstitutional Governor Thompson's awarding of thousands of jobs based on merit examination combined with political party sponsorship.

INSIDE THE GOVERNOR'S OFFICE

Of the governor's several roles, management of state government occupies less time and attention than might be imagined. As Thompson put it: "Governors really, especially in the latter part of their service, don't manage the state. If they're still managing the state after their first term, they ought not to be governor."[26] This opinion is understandable because most governors derive greater personal satisfaction and political rewards from the pursuit of other functions such as formulating policy, steering programs through the legislature, building popularity and support among the public, and helping develop the state's economy.[27]

Governor Richard B. Ogilvie enjoyed the management role. Yet a study of his schedule for one month, done by one of his assistants, found that he spent less than one-fifth of his time on management of state government.[28] As state government responsibilities have grown, so has the complexity and size of the governor's office. In 1993 there were 190 employees in the office itself, ranging from schedulers to Washington specialists and "ethnic assistants." This staff helps the governor make decisions—what legislation to introduce; how to resolve a policy dispute between two agencies; whom to appoint as an agency director; how to satisfy the demands of an interest group; which speaking invitations to accept.[29] In performing this role, the staff provides two important and related services: it manages the flow of information to the governor and serves as a surrogate with the groups that want the governor's attention.

Information flows in a variety of ways: memos, discussions with staff or agency personnel, staff debates within the office, contact with outside advisers, newspaper articles, and meetings with interest groups or legislators. Because it is impossible for the governor to attend to all who seek his favor, a staff member acting in the governor's stead can have a strong impact on the boss's image.

The use of staff as a go-between has some obvious tactical advantages. It tends to preserve flexibility on issues because the governor can always disavow the position taken by a subordinate. The surrogate also can sometimes say no for the governor, insulating him from that unpleasant duty.

A governor typically delegates the coordination of his staff to a deputy who has been called chief of staff, deputy governor, or chief of governmental operations. The deputy governor's job is a bit like being a secretary-general of the United Nations because the governor's office is at times not so much an organization as an alliance among nations. The reason is twofold. First, the organization of the office reflects the conflicts that are a fundamental part of state politics. Differences among staff members mirror the conflicting interests of the state's various political viewpoints. Second, it is difficult for any governor to delegate power. A governor draws his legitimacy from being the person elected to do the job. The authority of anyone acting in the governor's place can be easily undercut or become suspect unless continually supported by the governor himself. Because power is personal and not hierarchical, the notion of organization can become something of an exotic concept in the governor's office.

Ideally, the deputy governor (sometimes called the chief of staff) runs the office to accommodate the decision-making style of the governor. That style may involve open debate among staff; preparation of detailed decision memos by staff, acted upon without much discussion; advice from people outside government; or a combination of approaches. Thompson's style encouraged staff at various levels to have direct communication with the governor in policy deliberations. Edgar operates a more traditional hierarchical office, with policy recommendations flowing up to the chief of staff through a "super cabinet" of seven executive assistants, each with functional areas of responsibility.

The Bureau of the Budget is part of the executive office of the governor; yet the BOB operates apart from the rest of the governor's staff. The budget process gives the work of the BOB a much more structured focus than other staff activities. Budget analysts are hired by senior BOB staff, and there is less major staff turnover with a change in governors. For these and other reasons, the BOB tends to have an institutional life of its own.

During the budget process, conflict arises between the BOB, which sees its role as to constrain agency spending, and the agencies that want increased spending authority. Some disagreements can be resolved only by the governor. Influential interest groups also have a stake in the process. Most groups, even business groups, tend to want more spent on behalf of their constituents. All must be dealt with, and often the governor must take the lead.

The BOB plays a significant role in the governor's office because mistakes in budgeting can cost the governor dearly. There are tremendous political pressures to spend more tax dollars or to give tax relief and virtually none to control that spending. Yet the constitution requires a balanced operating budget, at least in cash terms, and a governor who allows spending to get out of control runs the risk of severe embarrassment. Thus the BOB must carefully monitor both revenues and agency spending. For example, spending for the multi-billion-dollar Medicaid program doubled during Jim Edgar's first term, growing each year far beyond BOB estimates. This created turmoil for the rest of the budget and forced the governor to cut spending in other areas and pare back growth in education appropriations.

LINKS TO AGENCIES AND THE LEGISLATURE

Executive assistants based in both Chicago and Springfield provide the governor his primary day-to-day linkages with more than 110 state agencies, including many not under his direct control such as the state boards of education and higher education. The executive assistants are also the chief executive's eyes, ears, and voices to interest groups, the legislature, and citizens. Each has an area of policy and management responsibility such as education, human services, or economic development. The executive assistant working in the area of natural resources, for example, could be responsible for serving as a liaison with agencies ranging from the Departments of Agriculture, Nuclear Safety, Transportation, and Natural Resources to the Environmental Protection Agency, Illinois Commerce Commission, and Pollution Control Board.

Executive assistants try to increase cooperation among agencies and often have to mediate disputes among them. Agencies often have narrow responsibilities that overlap with those of others. Children's services, for instance, are delivered through fifteen agencies, including the Departments of Children and Family Services and Public Aid, the Division of Crippled Children's Services, and the State Board of Education. Administration of the surface mining program is split among four agencies: agriculture, conservation, mines and minerals, and the Environmental Protection Agency. Regulation of drinking water is shared by EPA and the Department of Public Health. Public Health shares responsibility for inspecting and certifying nursing homes with the Departments of Labor, Professional Regulation, Public Aid, and Mental Health and Development Disabilities, along with the State Fire Marshal.

The governor and his staff face even stiffer challenges in maintaining effective relationships with the General Assembly. The legislature must enact substantive legislation—much of it proposed by the governor and his agencies—and pass the annual budget. It also oversees the executive branch through committee hearings, biennial audits by the auditor general, and review of agency rule-making by the Joint Committee on Administrative Rules. The legislature thus maintains a presence in virtually every area of executive branch activity, making good legislative relations crucial to the success of a governor's tenure.

Not surprisingly, a governor will often select a former legislator or legislative staff member to supervise his legislative office. For example, former legislator Jim Edgar, before serving as governor, was director of Governor Thompson's legislative office. Familiarity with the members of each house, their personalities, and the politics of their districts is essential if the head of legislative affairs is to be an effective strategist for the governor.

Generally, the legislative office lobbies for passage of the governor's budget and other initiatives and works against bills that would be politically embarrassing for the governor to sign or veto. It channels information on legislative developments back to the governor and other members of the governor's staff, serves as a contact point for legislators who wish to deal with the governor or an agency, and provides legislative advice to other gubernatorial staff and agencies.

To be effective, the office must develop a close working relationship with the leaders of the governor's party in each house of the legislature. The staff must work through the leadership in selecting sponsors for administration bills, communicating the governor's position on major legislation, scheduling legislative activity, and developing overall legislative strategies. Because much legislative work is done in committee, the staff must also work closely with the committee chairs and the minority spokespersons.

The governor maintains a traditional lawyer-client relationship with the lawyers on his staff. They advise him on the extent of his statutory and constitutional authority and explore with him the legal implications of individual decisions. Usually the governor appoints a chief counsel who supervises several other lawyers. In addition to providing assistance on specific issues, the legal staff spends a considerable amount of time working with agency lawyers on litigation—particularly cases that are politically sensitive, involve large judgments against the state, or could commit the state to new and recurring program expenditures. The attorney general is designated by the constitution as "the legal officer of the state," but with the exception of environmental issues, the bulk of the state's legal work is conducted by agency lawyers with the attorney general's concurrence.

The legal staff also engages in more routine activities. The constitution allows the governor to "grant reprieves, commutations and pardons" to convicted criminals. Four times a year the Prisoner Review Board refers fifty or so requests for commutation from prisoners to the governor's office. The legal staff reviews each one and makes a recommendation to the governor.

The lawyers also draft executive orders, which must be limited in scope to operations internal to the executive branch, and review all legislation passed by the General Assembly for adherence to the constitution and for legal consistency. The latter activity keeps the lawyers well occupied from July to September.

SHIFTING ROLE FOR PATRONAGE

With the largest bloc of jobs in the state under their control, governors have always depended on personal contacts and political recommendations when hiring employees. Patrons have been political party leaders, legislators, influential lobbyists and interest group leaders, elected officials, their staffs, and friends.

The individualistic political culture that dominates Illinois has long tolerated the practice of sponsored jobs; it was understood that elected officials would use their influence to gain employment for supporters, friends, and relatives. In return, the people assisted would provide support to the governor and his party.

Federal courts, however, have placed significant constraints on patronage.[30] In 1972, a federal court in Chicago declared that it was unconstitutional to fire an employee for political reasons. As a result, patronage activity in Illinois shifted its focus to job openings, inasmuch as it was still acceptable to hire qualified employees on the basis of patronage considerations. During the Thompson years, nearly every one of about five thousand job vacancies that occurred annually came under intense scrutiny by the governor's patronage office to see if an important patron had a candidate he or she wanted to sponsor for the opening.

In June 1990, however, the U.S. Supreme Court declared in *Rutan v. Republican Party of Illinois* that it is unconstitutional to use political party affiliation or support as a consideration in hiring, promoting, transferring, or recalling non-policy-making employees.[31] The decision appears to be narrowly focused on patronage related to political party affiliation. In other words, it is now unconstitutional to favor one job candidate over another solely because the former has a record of voting for the party of the governor and the other candidate does not. The decision does not appear to address the practice that expanded in the 1980s wherein legislators of both parties would personally recommend job candidates.

Despite these limitations, a strong expectation continues among participants in the web of Illinois government and politics that job openings should be filled after consideration of the desires of patrons. Meeting these expectations legally is the job of the governor's patronage office.

The head of the patronage office has often been a key political adviser to the governor and a major link to influential people. Virtually every employee hired by the state must meet some qualification in the form of educational credentials, experience, or test results. When two candidates meet the job requirements, the role of the patronage office is to ask, "Why not hire the person friendly to our administration, or earn a credit with a legislator who can be helpful to us later?" It is a difficult role to perform, as recalled by a former member of the staff:

> It's an impossible job in a lot of ways. On the one hand, you've got county chairmen crawling all over you thinking that all you've got to do is snap your fingers and their guy's got a job. Then you've got the agencies and the personnel system to deal with. Let's say you get an agency's okay, then you still have to make sure all the civil service requirements are met. That can take a lot of time and a lot of party people get impatient. They can't understand the delays. That's one of our biggest problems. That, and the fact that there are just not enough jobs.

Many appointments are to nonpaying positions on boards that advise agencies on such subjects as endangered species, group insurance for state employees, migrant labor camps, swine brucellosis, and beekeeping. But there are also boards with significant regulatory powers and paid commissionerships such as the Illinois Commerce Commission, the Pollution Control Board, and the Liquor Control Commission. Other appointed boards actually administer programs such as the Dangerous Drugs Commission and the Delinquency Prevention Commission. In most cases, there is a requirement that no more than a majority of members appointed to a board or commission may be of the same political party.

The existence of so many boards and commissions stems from several factors. There is the desire to provide a formal mechanism for public participation in agency programs, including that of technical specialists. They have also been created to separate sensitive quasi-legislative and quasi-judicial functions from direct executive control to promote the perception of fairness or to keep these functions out of politics, which they generally are not.

Governors Ogilvie, Walker, Thompson, and Edgar all maintained special units to receive and process citizens' complaints and to serve as outreach offices for certain programs or constituencies. Under Governor Edgar there were special assistants for Asians, Hispanics, ethnic minorities, African Americans, and women.[32]

Several other sections of the governor's office provide basic support services. The scheduling office receives hundreds of invitations each month for the governor to speak or appear at various functions. The staff processes and organizes these invitations and works with the governor, his personal aides, and senior staff to arrange the governor's schedule.

The mail-control office is the central receiving point for the governor's mail—and it is voluminous. In an average month, it is not uncommon for ten thousand or more pieces of mail to come into the office. The mail is typically sorted into "VIP" mail that the governor looks at personally, usually from senior elected officials, personal acquaintances, and prominent politicians; "negative" mail that criticizes the programs of the executive branch, which is usually answered by the agencies but reviewed by the governor's staff; and "positive" mail that compliments the governor on agency programs or raises basic questions about program operations and is usually answered by the governor's staff and goes out over the governor's signature.

AGENCIES TRY FOR LOW PROFILE

Although the governor and his staff are not involved in day-to-day management of the twenty-five code departments and thirty-three other major state agencies under the chief executive's jurisdiction, the governor's performance is often judged on how well these agencies function. This can be problematic because even here the governor does not have unfettered discretion. The major interest groups expect to have some influence over who is selected to run the programs that affect their members or constituents.[33] The unions, for example, expect to have a say in who heads the Department of Labor; at the Department of Agriculture, it is the Illinois Farm Bureau; and so it goes throughout the organization chart. Groups that object strongly to a gubernatorial appointment can attempt to stall or prevent required confirmation by the senate.

Once appointed and confirmed, directors gradually become part of a bureaucracy, with concerns and interests often different from those of a governor. Agencies and divisions within agencies have long-standing relationships with local and federal bureaucracies, old ties to legislators and legislative committees, and strong commitments to existing procedures. The directors may owe their appointments to the governor, but they are quickly exposed to new claims on their loyalties.

For these reasons, subtle tensions often develop between the governor's office and an agency director and his staff. A former social service director observes:

> The biggest burden in running an agency is that created by many people who have their fingers in our pie. For example, you have: the governor's liaison with this agency; the governor's liaison to the rate review board [which sets purchase of service rates paid by the state]; the patronage director; the legislative liaison office. And the Bureau of the Budget, which is "knee deep in what we can and can't do"; the appropriations staffs in both houses, as well as between parties . . . ; several key legislators who have an interest in the agency; Art Quern and Paula Wolff in the governor's office [former chief of staff and program office director], and the interest groups. All of which makes for a great number of people telling you how to do your job. However, the buck stops with the director. These other people are not accountable and indeed often back away very quickly when something goes wrong.[34]

Government agencies are not run like a business, nor can they be.[35] There are no profit-and-loss measures of accountability, and indeed, state agencies feel a strong need to spend all their money by the end of the fiscal year or their budgets might be cut the next year. On-the-job performance is also difficult to assess. The quality of foster care provided to an abused child is more difficult to evaluate than is the production rate of zero-defect earthmovers or cellular phones.

The lack of a clear bottom line allows a governor and agency directors to slip into fuzzy measures of success. Thus "no news is good news" is an important indicator of how well a director is doing. If the director keeps bad news about an agency from popping up on the evening news, then presumably everything is going well. Other tricks are to prevent problems from reaching the governor's desk, stay within the budget, and "keep the lid on" situations that could become volatile.

That sounds simple enough, but it has been a Herculean task for the directors of complex, demanding agencies such as the Departments of Corrections (DOC), Mental Health and Developmental Disabilities (DMHDD), and Children and Family Services (DCFS). Each of these agencies has been given responsibilities and public expectations that cannot be met with the funding provided, if at all.

Michael P. Lane began work at DOC in 1970 as a social service career trainee when there were five thousand inmates in the system. When he left in 1989, after nine years as director, there were twenty-three thousand inmates in nineteen adult prisons, seven juvenile facilities, and fifteen community correctional centers.[36] Lane supervised 11,500 employees and a budget of half a billion dollars.

The inmate numbers increased at a rate beyond the commitment of the state to build new prisons. During Lane's tenure, DOC built ten new adult prisons. Only nine had been built in Illinois history up to that time. Nevertheless, overcrowding was serious and thousands of cells built to accommodate one person had to be "double-celled" with two inmates. This is a surefire recipe for increased tension. In July 1989, an officer was murdered at Stateville Correctional Center and the prison went on lockdown for three months; there were about three hundred assaults on prison staff in that year.[37]

Lane "kept the lid on" during his tenure, in part by developing a highly detailed notebook that prescribed rules for every facility on how to operate under just about any situation. Every month he spent several days hopscotching by DOC plane (a pilot, Lane often took the controls) to every major facility. During his whirlwind inspections, Lane would review the situation with prison officials and tour the facility. He was a hands-on manager. His style would not work for everyone, but it worked for him in one of the toughest jobs in government.

If there is a more difficult job, it is running the Department of Mental Health and Developmental Disabilities.[38] The late governor Richard B. Ogilvie, respected for his tough, effective management skills, once said that he could run all of state government except mental health.

The late Ann M. Kiley was director of DMHDD from early 1986 until poor health forced her to step down in 1989. She inherited an agency of twenty-three hospitals, nearly fourteen thousand employees, and a budget of $600 million. One-third of the budget was distributed to hundreds of community-based mental health service agencies that were independent of state government.

Kiley took on a fragmented system under attack from all sides. The federal government threatened to pull Medicaid funds because of poor treatment of patients in state hospitals. The American Civil Liberties Union sued over conditions at a state facility for children. Community service providers complained that too much was spent on state facilities and not enough at the community level. Advocates for the mentally ill competed for funds with advocates for the developmentally disabled. Even the governor's inspector general found shortcomings, citing problems with the patient abuse reporting system.

"We do not have and desperately need a truly integrated system of comprehensive services for the mentally disabled," charged Governor Thompson's task force on mental health.[39] But the task force put the cost of implementing its recommendations at $300 million to $600 million annually, which was not forthcoming.

Kiley got high marks, not for solving the problems, which was impossible given the funding gap, but for confronting problems head-on, for listening to interest groups, for dealing honestly and openly with those who wanted to tell her how to do her job, for advocating within state government for more resources, and for attempting to knit together a coordinated system.

An example of what happens under less skilled agency directors—or when the problems would overwhelm even a top-notch administrator—was provided by the Department of Children and Family Services during Edgar's first administration. The agency was plagued by unrelenting media criticism of its management during those years, when the number of neglected and abused children in the care of the state doubled to more than forty thousand. A lawsuit against the state that charged inadequate care of children generated a consent decree in federal court. DCFS agreed to make improvements, and the agency's efforts were monitored and directed by the court. Edgar had four agency directors in four years.

Skilled agency directors and senior staff are crucial teammates to effective governors. Without them, the chief executives become reactive, defensive administrators and have little opportunity to become mentioned in the history books among the strong managers, great builders, or social reformers who have now and then made their mark in Illinois.

CHAPTER SEVEN

Courts and Politics Intertwined

Most citizens have only the vaguest understanding of their state's courts, having encountered their workings only now and then as a juror or perhaps to plead innocent to a speeding ticket. This is not the case for Illinois politicians, especially those in Cook County, where politics and the court system have a long and sometimes tortured history of interaction.

Judges interpret the law and thus can have a major effect on matters that might interest a politician, his or her political party, or one of the politician's friends. In 1841, when Democrats badly needed the votes of newly arrived German and Irish laborers, the opposition Whig party asked the court to block these recently arrived "aliens" from voting. It was a good strategy because the Whigs at that time dominated the Illinois Supreme Court, but they underestimated the resolve of Democrats, who controlled the legislature and knew of its constitutional authority to "pack" the supreme court. The Democrats voted to increase the court's size from three members to eight, appointed five of their own, and rested easy that the new court would protect the voting rights of "their" people.[1]

Such blatant use of power provoked the 1848 Constitutional Convention to take away the legislature's appointive power, but the decisions of the courts are so important that the judiciary remains intertwined with the state's elected leaders. Under the subsequent and still used system of popular election of judges, politicians actively promote favored judicial candidates. During Chicago's gangster days, certain judges were known for their leniency and their relationships with top mob figures. Later, Chicago's Democratic precinct workers had such intimate relations with the Cook County traffic court that they were routinely able to "take care of" parking tickets and even drunk driving charges for loyal voters. The depth of corruption was finally laid bare in the 1980s, when federal prosecutors in the Greylord and Gambat investigations brought charges against more than one hundred Cook County judges, lawyers, and court personnel. The "fix" was used widely, even for murder cases.

This is not to say that all court decisions in Illinois are partisan or tainted, only that too frequently they have been. It should come as no surprise: judges are nominated in party primaries and elected in partisan elections. Once elected with such support, some judges respond obediently to the needs of their patrons. James Touhy and Rob Warden, who documented the Greylord investigation in Cook County, put it this way: "[Richard J.] Daley treated the judiciary as just another part of the county's overall patronage system. . . . A judgeship was the grand patronage prize . . . selection was by connection. . . . Any judge who offended a Democratic politician ran the risk of being dumped at the next slating session."[2]

It is easy to see that decisions of the supreme court or a local trial court will always have some effect—negative or positive—on somebody. Court decisions, after all, resolve conflicts, enforce community norms, stigmatize people, make law, and legitimize (or deny legitimacy to) decisions made elsewhere in the government. In short, for many people, litigation can be another way of wielding political power.

Litigation falls into two general categories—civil or criminal. In civil cases, complainants seek to settle grievances involving debts, family squabbles, or disputes arising from injuries. Complainants are usually private citizens who must pay for litigation themselves. Criminal cases involve the government more directly because of its stake in preserving public order; complainants in these cases always rely on public prosecutors (state's attorneys) to handle court proceedings.

Both types of cases have the potential for political overtones, but the courts in Illinois as elsewhere in the United States are somewhat insulated by the separation of powers and a system of checks and balances. The Illinois Constitution, for instance, sets up the structure of the judiciary, the process for judicial selection, and the system for disciplining wayward judges. The executive and legislative branches have roles in court oversight and budgeting. Finally, Illinois courts must bow to federal authorities in certain circumstances, especially when the matter under review involves the judiciary itself.

The judicial branch of Illinois state government handles more than four million cases per year. On a day-to-day basis, the courts hand down decisions interpreting the constitution and legislation, make decisions and impose sentences in criminal cases, and pass judgment on appeals.

Underneath the daily bustle are controversies and unresolved issues. Should judges be elected or appointed? Are the courts capable of policing themselves? Is the ethnic, gender, and racial makeup of the judiciary appropriate? How should bad judges be removed? How far should the other branches of government be allowed to go in telling the courts how to handle criminals?

These questions have dogged political and judicial experts alike for many years and will not be cleared up in this chapter. But the framework of the court system will be explained and the major issues laid out so that the challenges facing the Illinois system might be better addressed.

UNIFIED SYSTEM WITH THREE LEVELS

The structure of the Illinois court system is neat and orderly, though it was not so before a 1962 constitutional amendment. Until then, criminal cases were handled by numerous and sometimes overlapping police magistrate courts, justice of the peace courts, and county, probate, and criminal courts.[3] Under the current unified system, there are just three layers of courts statewide with no overlapping jurisdictions: the circuit (trial) courts, appellate courts, and the supreme court, which oversees the administration of the entire system.

The supreme court has seven members elected from five judicial districts; the larger first district (Cook County) elects three judges. The justices are elected on a partisan ballot for a ten-year term. If a judge decides to serve a second (or additional term), he or she is placed on a retention ballot. The judges are nominated in party primaries. As of 1994, the Democrats had a four-to-three majority on the Illinois Supreme Court.

Illinois Supreme Court justices have historically been white males, but following developments elsewhere in the electoral process, the first black was elected to the supreme court in 1990 and the first woman in 1992.

The second-level courts are the appellate courts. The judges sitting in these courts also serve ten-year terms and are subject to a retention vote. An appellate court is located in each of the five judicial districts. In 1991 there were twenty-four appellate judges in the first district (Cook County), nine judges in the second district, six in the third district, six in the fourth, and seven in the fifth, for a total of fifty-two judges.[4]

The trial courts of general jurisdiction are the circuit courts. The state is divided into twenty-two judicial circuits. Cook, DuPage, and Will counties each consist of a single circuit. The number of judges in the other circuits is determined by the General Assembly and depends on the circuit's size and amount of business, with three judges being the minimum. Cook County has more than 186 judges, some of whom are elected countywide, some from Chicago, and some from the suburbs. Those from city and countywide districts tend to be Democrats and those from the suburbs, Republican. The term of the circuit judges is six years, and the retention ballot is also used. In 1991 there were 402 circuit judges in Illinois.[5]

Legislators in the General Assembly always hope to increase the number of judges in their districts. Despite the minimum of three judges per circuit, in reality each circuit has at least five judges. Each county also has at least one resident circuit judge, who is elected from that county alone, bringing the total number of downstate circuit judges to more than two hundred.

The constitution provides for the appointment to four-year terms of associate judges who have limited jurisdiction. They are appointed by the elected circuit court judges and, like elective judges, must be licensed attorneys. In 1991, there were 394 associate judges in Illinois.[6]

The circuit court of Cook County is much larger than those downstate; as a result, the structure is more complex. The organization chart for the Cook County circuit shows much more specialization than in the twenty-one downstate circuits. Cook County has a separate section for mechanic's liens and a whole division for domestic relations, and uses "holiday" (weekend) and evening narcotics courts to keep the wheels of justice moving seven days a week.

The Illinois Constitution places administrative authority for the entire system in the supreme court, to be exercised by the chief justice.[7] The court submits the annual judicial budget to the General Assembly. It also appoints certain support staff headed by an administrative director, makes temporary assignments of judges, appoints judges to vacancies, and creates rules to provide for the orderly flow of judicial business.

The supreme court submits an annual report to the General Assembly to suggest improvements in the administration of justice. Sensitive to the separation of the branches, the 1990 annual report said that "the Supreme Court is fully cognizant of the respective roles of the General Assembly and the courts, and does not intend to intrude upon the prerogatives of the General Assembly in determining what legislation should be enacted. It is gratifying, however, to note that the General Assembly over the years has acted to implement many of the suggestions made by the Court." In 1990, some of the supreme court's recommendations were straightforward:

> 1. The Circuit courts of Illinois are State courts and their funding should come from appropriations made by the General Assembly. . . . The Supreme Court notes that it has provided the General Assembly with a study, commissioned by the court, which details the actual cost of operating all Illinois courts, including the circuit courts, and puts the additional cost to the State at about $280 million if the State assumes the cost of fully funding the circuit courts.
>
> 2. The nonjudicial function of circuit judges appointing commissioners of boards of election commissioners in municipalities having such boards (Ill. Rev. Stat. 1987, ch. 46, par. 6–21) should be removed from the judiciary and placed in some nonjudicial body. Not only does section 6–21 of the Election Code impose a nonjudicial function on judges but it also tends to involve them in political matters that can be better addressed by nonjudicial officials.[8]

In 1994 the court further addressed the politicization of the courts when it made a controversial recommendation that elections of judges be scheduled at a different time than other state and county elections so that voters would be less distracted and make more informed decisions about judicial choices.[9] The press reaction to this proposal was negative because such separate elections would reduce voter turnout and be costly. "If the Supreme Court really wants to improve the state judiciary," editorialized the *Chicago Tribune*, "it ought to be in the vanguard of those pressing for a constitutional amendment to allow merit selection [of judges]."[10]

CONTROLLING WAYWARD JUDGES

The push for merit selection is fueled only in part by those who want to depoliticize the courts. More important is the possibility that a merit or appointive system might help reduce the unethical or criminal behavior that has cropped up throughout the history of Illinois's judicial system.

The difficulty of the judiciary policing itself was illustrated in 1969, when two supreme court justices, Roy J. Solfisburg of Aurora and Ray I. Klingbiel of East Moline, were found to hold interests in a bank whose transactions were deemed improper by a special bar commission.[11] A disciplinary body, the Illinois Court Commission, had been created in 1962 for just such cases but could not very well hear this case because it was chaired at the time by Justice Klingbiel.

Solfisburg and Klingbiel eventually resigned, but the need for oversight continued. In response, the 1970 Constitutional Convention created an additional disciplinary body, the Judicial Inquiry Board. This bipartisan board is composed of two circuit judges selected by the supreme court, three lawyers selected by the governor, and four persons who are not lawyers. The board can conduct investigations concerning judges and receive or initiate complaints. If the board so decides, it files complaints with the Court Commission, whose panel of five judges can remove accused judges from office, censure or reprimand a judge, or suspend or retire a judge.

This system has been relatively effective at addressing unethical or criminal behavior of judges. From 1972 to 1992, the Judicial Inquiry Board filed fifty-two complaints against fifty-eight judges with the Court Commission. In thirty-one of these complaints, the commission took some disciplinary action; it dismissed only a handful of complaints.

The most visible and controversial case involved Circuit Judge Samuel G. Harrod III of downstate Woodford County. The board alleged in 1976 that the judge acted illegally when he imposed sentences that included requirements that twenty-six male defendants have their hair cut, that fifteen probationers leave their driver's licenses in the custody of the court clerk in return for cards identifying them as on probation, and that three defendants, convicted of illegally transporting alcohol, collect cans and bottles along highways. The Court Commission held that the first two sentences were without legal authority and constituted judicial misconduct. Judge Harrod was suspended without pay for one month but later successfully petitioned the Illinois Supreme Court to order the commissioners to expunge his record. The judge's reinstatement raised doubt about whether the Court Commission is in fact the final action body for judicial discipline or if the supreme court holds that power.[12] The board eventually brought other charges against Harrod, but they were dismissed when he resigned from the judiciary after being sentenced to jail for shoplifting.

JUDGES FOR SALE IN COOK COUNTY

Although the disciplinary system has generally been successful downstate, it has not been in Cook County. It was federal rather than state or county action that resulted in the 1980s and early 1990s in the sentencing of sixteen judges for crimes including racketeering, bribery, mail fraud, and perjury. The judges were part of a deep-seated case-fixing network that involved crooked lawyers, bagmen, Chicago alderman Fred Roti, and Illinois senator John A. D'Arco. In the two separate investigations of Greylord and Gambat, fifty-seven attorneys were also convicted along with twenty-six criminal justice employees, including court clerks, deputy sheriffs, and police officers.[13]

Much of the evidence for the Greylord convictions was gathered by attorney Terrence Hake, who posed as a crooked lawyer, and downstate judge Brocton Lockwood, who wore a tape recorder inside his boot and played the role of a good ol' boy who needed extra cash to support his womanizing and drinking.[14] It took Hake three months to gain entry into the clandestine network that could fix cases with certain judges,[15] while Lockwood worked his way into the fraternity of opportunistic judges. Over a three-year period, the moles with the support of FBI agents and U.S. Attorney Dan Webb developed cases against dozens of individuals, whose court testimony in turn implicated dozens of others.

Judge Richard LeFevour's system was based on providing acquittals of drunk-driving and other traffic cases for $100 bribes. "The miracle workers [crooked lawyers] would leave a list of the cases they wanted fixed and in what courtrooms. Judge LeFevour would then assign bribe-taking judges to those courtrooms. Later the attorneys would drop off their payments" with the judge's cousin and bagman, Jimmy LeFevour.[16]

Judge Reginald J. Holzer worked chancery court and had a different system: he "borrowed" money from parties whose cases were before him. Ernest Worsek, a businessman who was awarded receiverships by Holzer's court, lent the judge $15,000, then $10,000 more and then another $10,000, and was never paid back. Attorney Russell Topper, who stood to earn $200,000 in fees in a damage suit before Holzer, was squeezed for $10,000. Bernard S. Neistein, a former state senator, arranged a $10,000 bank loan for Holzer. When Holzer made no payments, Neistein paid it back himself.[17]

Eleven other judges were convicted in the Greylord scandal, each with his own system and circle of accomplices. While those cases went to trial and made the Chicago headlines, a second investigation called Operation Gambat was using a corrupt lawyer-turned-informant, Robert Cooley, to infiltrate Chicago's infamous first ward organization. Long rumored to have ties to organized crime, the organization was run by Alderman Fred Roti and his party secretary Pat Marcy, who used politically connected judges to fix cases involving everything from civil matters to murder. Cooley passed $72,500 to Marcy and Roti after Judge Thomas J. Maloney acquitted four men in the murder of Lenny Chow. In another case, Marcy handed Cooley an envelope containing $7,500 to reward Judge Frank Wilson for finding accused hitman Harry Aleman not guilty. Wilson later committed suicide. In a third case, this one in the chancery court, Marcy encountered difficulties.

Judges were apprehensive because of Greylord, and a new system of random computerized case assignments made it difficult to place a case before a cooperative judge. When the computer picked Judge David Shields, Marcy thought the case was lost. But then he learned from attorney Pat DeLeo that Shields would "do whatever we want. . . . This thing is no problem."[18] The fix cost $5,000 and led to convictions of both DeLeo and Shields.

The operations had the approval of the chief judge for the U.S. district court and the U.S. Department of Justice and were groundbreaking for their use of hidden microphones in the private chambers of two judges. Some observers questioned the use of a sting operation and whether U.S. prosecutors had been too aggressive in trying to increase the number of convictions.[19] But Judge Lockwood concluded his book with a defense of the approach: "I believe the Jimmy Hoffa case, Watergate, Abscam and Operation Greylord were all necessary and appropriate steps in re-establishing the very basic principle that, in this country, no person or group regardless of power and prestige, is above the law."[20]

Leaving aside the issue of sting operations as public policy, the point for this book is that the Illinois judicial disciplinary system did not bring about the many convictions—it was federal officials who conducted the operation. This is not to say that the local powers had not looked at the courts in Cook County; they had, and complaints were filed against several Cook County judges over the years by the Judicial Inquiry Board. But the disciplinary process had clearly been inadequate to address the biggest breakdown in the history of the Illinois judicial system.

SELECTION OF BETTER JUDGES

Hand in hand with the corruption issue is the question of whether there is a better way to select judges. Judges at all three levels have been elected since 1848, and a 1962 amendment to the constitution reaffirmed the system of elective judges. The issue arose again at the 1970 Constitutional Convention, but opposition by the Democrats under Richard J. Daley, among others, forced the question out of the main document and into a separate issue, where voters chose the elective approach by a 50 percent to 43 percent margin.

The vote results masked a clear division, along geographic lines, among the voters. The suburban collar counties around Cook favored the appointive judiciary by a sixty-five-to-thirty-one margin, while downstate favored an elective system by a similar majority (fifty-eight to thirty-five). Chicago, with the urging of Mayor Daley's organization, favored elective judges by a fifty-one-to-forty margin.

The argument for appointive judges, often termed a "merit" system, is that it will bring "better" people to the bench and provide a more independent judiciary. Elections, it is argued, involve judges in political matters that can affect their independence, leading to practices such as those uncovered by Greylord.

Supporters of elective judges tend to be populists of the Andrew Jackson school. They believe that the people should pick their own judges just as they elect officials to the executive and legislative branches. Election, it is argued, provides judicial accountability by allowing voters to remove judges who have failed to maintain standards of judicial conduct or who have become incapacitated.

Proponents of the appointive system and their allies in the General Assembly have tried since 1970 to get the issue on the ballot as a constitutional amendment. No proposal has yet been voted out of the legislature. One reason is that subissues have divided the proponents. Some want local option, with each circuit or county deciding whether to have an appointive system. Others say appointments should be limited to the supreme and appellate courts. Most proponents, including the bar associations, think the governor should make the appointments after receiving nominations from a screening committee. Others in the Democratic leadership would have the supreme court, rather than the governor, make the appointments.[21]

While the debate wears on about appointive versus elective judges, the current system continues to use appointments for all associate judges and to fill vacancies for elected judges. That appointment system has weaknesses of its own, according to the Illinois Supreme Court Special Commission on the Administration of Justice, which was convened in 1992 after the Greylord and Gambat scandals. The group's final report, known as the *Solovy Report* after commission chairman and attorney Jerold S. Solovy, stated that at least some judges believe that the filling of vacancies is an "unwelcome burden" and others view it as ancillary to their chief task of deciding cases. "Moreover, in the absence of sufficient time and established procedures to select the most qualified candidates, partisan political considerations and personal relationships too often become major factors in making appointments," said the report.[22]

The commission examined the qualifications of the eighty-four judges appointed between 1981 and 1993 and found that only 43 percent had been rated "highly qualified" and that nearly one-fifth had been found "unqualified" or "not recommended" by the Chicago Bar Association, the Chicago Council of Lawyers, or both. The commission found that other judges had been appointed even though they had been defeated in judicial elections, though that practice was discontinued in 1993.

To balance such practices, the commission recommended use of nominating commissions to assist in the selection process. "The use of commissions, we believe, has several advantages over the current system: (1) it permits a thorough and systematic review of the applicants; (2) it encourages selection from a large applicant pool helping to ensure that nominees will be highly qualified and will reflect the diversity of their district; and (3) it emphasizes attributes, such as legal ability, that are essential to public confidence in the judiciary."[23]

The commission also said: "No judicial selection procedure can guarantee the integrity of the judicial system. However, judicial selection procedures that encourage scrutiny of an applicant's background and that emphasize professional ability may help reduce the problem of judicial corruption. Deterring corrupt lawyers from becoming judges is more efficient than dealing with the problem of judicial corruption through expensive and intrusive investigations."[24]

Although in 1970 the voters continued the elective process, the nominating process was changed. Judges are now nominated in party primaries rather than by political conventions. This change opened up the system somewhat to political "outsiders," allowing lawyers who are not slated by their party to get on the primary ballot by petition. In 1976, for instance, James A. Dooley and William C. Clark were nominated for the Illinois Supreme Court and subsequently elected over the Democratic party's slated candidates. Justice Clark later supported an appointive system for the judiciary.

CHOOSING FROM A FIELD OF UNKNOWNS

One enduring criticism of the elective system is that voters usually have little or no knowledge of the candidates. The bar associations over the years have issued evaluations on candidates for the judiciary,[25] as have the state's major newspapers, but these endorsements are sometimes ignored by voters. In the 1986 Cook County spring primary, three judicial candidates endorsed by Chicago mayor Harold Washington won despite being rated "unqualified" by the Chicago Bar Association. The *Chicago Sun-Times* in 1994 acknowledged the ineffectiveness of the primary system when it editorialized: "Once again, unqualified candidates in abundance are guaranteed subcircuit judge-ships by merely surviving a crowded and confusing primary election."[26]

This is not so surprising when one considers that the various bar groups cannot agree among themselves on which judges are qualified and which are not.[27] In 1986, for instance, the bar associations did not disapprove of the performance of Judge Joseph E. McDermott, who had been publicly ac-cused of taking bribes in traffic court and who was willing to go to jail rather than testify before a federal grand jury. McDermott received the largest vote in the primary and the second highest in the general election for any judicial candidate. He did not serve, however, and subsequently was convicted in federal court.

Another factor in the election of judges, particularly in Cook County, is the large number of candidates on the ballot. In 1992 in Cook County, one supreme court seat, three appellate court seats, and seventeen countywide circuit court seats were up for election. Seven circuit court seats within the city of Chicago and one in suburban Cook County were also on the ballot. Democratic and Republican candidates were on the ballot for most of the seats, and voters were asked for their opinion on whether thirty-two circuit court judges should be retained.

Even the conscientious voter who consults newspaper editorials and ad-vertisements of the bar association ratings is likely to be overwhelmed by such a list. In practice, many voters work down the list with no real knowl-edge of the candidates or skip the judicial part of the ballot entirely.

SEEKING A DEMOGRAPHIC BALANCE

Beneath the argument over "letting the voters decide" versus "merit" ap-pointments lies the fundamental political tussle over which method provides a political party or racial or ethnic group greater influence in selecting judges. When one party dominates elections, that party tends to prefer elec-tion over appointment. Minority group leaders have tended to favor election from small districts, where their group might have chances for greater repre-sentation than through appointment by a blue-ribbon group dominated by whites. In Illinois, where even the judiciary has often been viewed as a mar-ketplace in which to do business, the public arguments are often different from the motivating factors.

With the intent of providing better minority representation on the bench, and reacting to a federal Voting Rights Act suit, in 1989 the legislature adopted subdistricts in place of at-large elections for Cook County circuit and appellate courts. The legislation was backed by an unlikely coalition of blacks, Hispanics, and Republicans who sought to reduce the influence exercised by the regular Cook County Democratic organization over the nominating and elective process. It was passed only because the majority in the legislature needed the minority and Republican votes for a key revenue bill; in return the sub-district concept was voted through and signed by the governor. The Illinois Supreme Court later declared the act unconstitutional in regard to appellate courts, but the General Assembly in 1990 readopted the plan for circuit courts.[28]

New lines were drawn the following year for fifteen subdistricts with two judges elected from each (one elected three judges). Almost half of the subdistricts had no contests. Many of the no-contest candidates were "not recommended" by the Chicago Bar Association. But the purpose of the new subdistricts seemed to be accomplished because more minority judges were elected. Of 101 candidates running in thirty-one contests, 9 blacks and 2 Latinos won judgeships. Republicans were less successful, winning only three of the thirty-one seats.

The problem of unqualified candidates continued in the 1994 primary, when 163 candidates ran for forty-four subcircuit judgeships. The *Chicago Reporter* found that 43 candidates had less than twelve years of experience, the minimum recommended by the Chicago Bar Association. Twenty-two of the 40 black and Latino candidates were given qualified ratings by the bar associations. One law professor commented: "It's the last bastion of patronage for local committeemen. Judges are the only people left [for committeemen to choose] because they are not covered by *Shakman*," the court decree outlawing political hiring in Cook County.[29]

CAMPAIGNS FOR THE BENCH

Campaigns for judicial office are conducted in a lower key than those for legislative and executive offices. Generally campaigns are waged on personality and qualifications, not issues. There are exceptions such as a central Illinois race for a supreme court seat in 1984 in which the main issue was the degree of "toughness" on persons in criminal cases and the "tougher" candidate won.[30] Generally, however, campaigning is restricted to appearances at public and political affairs and to TV and newspaper political advertisements.

The amount of money spent on judicial campaigns has been increasing, as it has for other elective offices. Although the media have not given much attention to judicial campaign finances, one article in a professional journal

Table 4: Itemized Outside Contributions to Judicial Campaigns

	From Attorneys	From Unions	From Corporations	From Nonattorney Individuals
$150 to $299	381 (79%)	21 (57%)	54 (58%)	160 (70%)
$300 to $499	43 (9%)	10 (27%)	10 (11%)	23 (10%)
$500 to $999	47 (10%)	6 (16%)	23 (25%)	38 (17%)
$1,000 and over	10 (2%)	N/A	6 (6%)	8 (3%)
Total	481 (100%)	37 (100%)	93 (100%)	229 (100%)

Source: Marlene Arnold Nickolson and Bradley Scott Weiss, "Funding Judicial Campaigns in the Circuit Court of Cook County," *Judicature*, 70, no. 1 (1986): 17–25.

did analyze the 1984 campaign for the Cook County Circuit.[31] The study found that much of the money came from the candidates' own personal sources, but significant sums also come from outside sources (see table 4), including attorneys, unions, corporations, and individuals.

The authors were concerned in particular about donations from attorneys because of the potential conflict of interest if the attorney were to appear in the judge's court. For instance, one attorney provided $30,000 to a candidate in the general election, and ten others gave judges contributions of $1,000 or more. The authors also noted that many judges likely to lose their elections still managed to bring in major contributions from attorneys. They found a number of potential pitfalls in the judiciary's need to finance election campaigns:

> The use of substantial sums of personal funds by judicial candidates suggests that candidates of modest means are disadvantaged and may even be deterred from seeking judicial office. On the other hand, the large sums raised by some candidates create the potential for at least an appearance of improper influence. This appearance is reinforced by the fact that candidates who are sitting judges raise substantial funds, particularly from attorneys, even when they are sure losers. Together with the fact that some unopposed candidates raise very large sums, the data suggests that a great many contributions are given for reasons other than to assure the victory of qualified candidates. Although there are plausible explanations other than that the contributors are seeking undue influence, an aura of impropriety is difficult to dispel.[32]

Support for judges does not come just from lawyers and business interests. As noted in Chapter 10, the Illinois Education Association endorses and contributes to candidates for the Illinois appellate and supreme courts. Like other interest groups, the association wants friends on the courts that resolve issues important to the organization.

HOLES IN THE RETENTION NET

The 1962 constitutional amendment provided a new method for voters to evaluate judges after they have been elected. Judges who seek another term notify the secretary of state of their desire. A question is placed on the ballot that asks if the judge should be retained in office for another term. There is no party designation on the ballot. To be retained, the judge has to have an affirmative vote of the electors voting on the issue. This applies to judges at all three levels. The 1970 Constitution raised the retention vote to three-fifths from a simple majority, making it more difficult for a judge to be retained.[33]

Some studies suggest that voters are confused by the retention process. Voters are used to elections that pit one candidate against another, and they look for the cue of party affiliation to help them choose a candidate. As a result, fewer voters participate in these referenda than for contested elections on the same ballot. "With few exceptions, voters are ill-informed about judicial elections—the adversary type as well as the retention election. Voters rarely know much about the candidates, usually there are no issues, generally there is little media coverage, often the party identification of the candidate is unknown."[34]

Another criticism of the retention system was made by then chief justice of the supreme court William Clark when he faced retention in 1986. He said, "The process has become very political. There seems to be a feeling, projected through the media, that if a judge is assigned a case which appears to have political overtones, that judge, knowing that he has to run for retention, is going to hold for whatever side is going to help him get retained. That's an unfair inference, but there is that appearance of impropriety and it's the present system that puts a judge in that position."[35]

All judges were retained from 1962 to 1970. Under provisions of the 1970 Constitution, twenty-eight judges were not retained from 1972 to 1992. All were circuit court judges—fifteen from Cook County, eleven from downstate circuits.[36] The most notable vote was in 1978, when the chief judge of the Cook County Circuit was removed from office. Of the twenty-six judges who have not been retained, most have either received less than qualified ratings by the bar associations or have been accused of unethical or illegal practices. All supreme court and appellate judge have been retained by the voters.

In the first election after Operation Greylord, in 1984, it was feared that many "good" judges among the ninety-six judges up for retention statewide would be dropped. The bar associations for the first time were politically active in those elections. The state bar association purchased advertisements in seventy daily newspapers to alert voters to its recommendations. The media also participated, fearing a wholesale dumping of judges. The *Chicago Tribune* spoke editorially on the subject at least three times. The paper endorsed twenty-five judges for retention and did not name the judges that the paper thought were unqualified. Even the prosecutor of Operation Greylord, U.S. Attorney Dan Webb, spoke to the Chicago Bar Association and said, "Greylord should play absolutely no role in the decisions of this county in voting to retain judges running on the retention ballot."[37] The information campaign apparently worked because all ninety-six judges were retained. In Cook County, in fact, only one judge of the thirty-five facing retention votes pulled fewer than 70 percent affirmative votes.

In 1992 there was some concern that the national movement for term limits for legislative and other offices might carry over to judges under the retention system. That did not happen, however, and only two downstate circuit judges were not retained. All judges were retained in Cook County even though the bar associations found a few sitting judges not qualified.

Although voter participation is low in retention referenda, the percentage of those voters approving judges has dropped since the retention system was installed. In the first retention election in 1966, affirmative votes totaled 85.6 percent statewide. By 1982, this figure had dropped to 74.4 percent. The drop in Cook County was more dramatic—from 88.6 percent in 1964 to 73.6 percent in 1982.

THE JUDICIARY AND STATE GOVERNMENT

As a branch of state government, the judiciary has many interactions with the executive and legislative branches but strives for its independence. On this point the *Solovy Report* said: "Judicial independence is an essential feature of democracy. Yet the principle of judicial independence is seriously eroded when elected officials or other political figures are able to manipulate judicial cases and the selection of associate judges. Enhancing judicial independence by insulating the judiciary from the political system remains an urgent need."[38]

Such independence would be difficult to achieve. On some issues, the judiciary has the final word, but on others it does not. For example, the supreme court prepares its own budget, but the appropriations bills that include the court budget are subject to review and approval by both the General Assembly and the governor.

Separation of the courts from the legislative branch was tested in a ten-year running controversy between the supreme court and the auditor general, a legislative branch officer. The main issue was whether the auditor general could audit the funds of two agencies of the supreme court: the Attorney Registration and Disciplinary Commission and the Board of Law Examiners. These two funds are not appropriated by the legislature; they are collected as fees from lawyers and candidates for the bar respectively.

The auditor general nonetheless ruled that these were public funds, while the supreme court claimed that the commission and board are not state agencies under Article VIII of the constitution. The media generally were on the side of the auditor general, as were the delegates to the 1970 Constitutional Convention when they reconvened unofficially in 1987. They passed a non-binding resolution saying it had been their intent to give the auditor general the power and duty to audit these two agencies. But the supreme court considered its refusal to permit the audit a matter of constitutional principle: "The independence of the Judicial Branch of State Government is a fundamental precept of government which is grounded on the constitution's separation of powers clause and the inherent power of courts to safeguard their authority. The branches of government must cooperate with each other but such cooperation is subordinate to the doctrine of separation of power."[39]

As it turned out, personalities may have had as much to do with the battle as constitutional rights; in 1990, after a new auditor general was elected by the legislature, the court made public relations overtures to heal the division and actually requested that the new official audit the judicial agencies in question.

LOBBYING BY THE COURTS

Separation of powers seems less important to the judiciary when it is worrying about judges' pensions and salaries or the need for additional judges. Here the judges present their views to the legislature, not only by the constitutionally directed annual report but also by lobbying. Like other state agencies, the supreme court has hired lobbyists to watch out for the court's interest in the legislative process. This became an issue when the supreme court struck down the first subdistricting plan for Cook County, a plan that some charged the court had lobbied against earlier in the legislature. The court spokesman was quoted: "I have no knowledge that the court ever instructed its lawyer-lobbyist against the redistricting bill. . . . The Court will decide the case on its merits, on the laws, and on any constitutional issues."[40] But after the court's decision, the *Chicago Sun-Times,* in an editorial titled "Bench the Lobbyists for Supreme Court," said:

> Maybe this comes as no news to the political sophisticates, but it should offend the common sense of anyone yet unnumbed by the unrelentingly strange manner in which politics and government are routinely conducted in these precincts.
>
> The court has lobbied the legislature on at least two issues: in opposition to judicial redistricting and to legislation that would require the court to allow the auditor-general to audit its fee-generated high court funds. . . .
>
> Rules or no, the court ought not meddle in legislative affairs, especially in cases, such as the redistricting one, that surely will come before it. [41]

The court further complicated legislative-judicial relations when it ruled in the same year that a midterm legislative pay increase was unconstitutional.[42] A more favorable ruling from the legislators' point of view came in 1994, when the court, on a four-to-three decision, rejected petitions for a constitutional amendment that would have limited the terms of legislators. The majority said that the proposed amendment did not meet the "structural and procedural subjects" requirements of the Illinois Constitution. The decision was not on a strict party basis. Term-limit provisions have been adopted in many other states.

CRIMINAL JUSTICE AND THE COURTS

Give-and-take between the branches goes both ways. The legislature, for instance, has set the ground rules for how the court should sentence criminals for certain crimes. The Illinois Criminal Code defines nine classes of crime from first-degree murder down to Class C misdemeanors and provides parameters for sentencing for each crime (see table 5). Though not uncommon, this approach has raised some controversy in Illinois, especially because the state's "get tough" policy has resulted in longer sentences and an increase in the prison population. For so-called Class X crimes, including armed robbery, home invasion, and trafficking in controlled substances, probation is eliminated and prison terms of up to sixty years are provided. These terms were pushed through the legislature by Governor James Thompson in fulfillment of a campaign promise. In a special message to the legislature on Octo-

Table 5: Sentence Lengths for Statutory Classes of Offenses, January 1989

Crime Classification	Probation Term	Imprisonment Term		Mandatory Time Spent on Supervised Release After Prison
		Without Aggravating Circumstances	With Aggravating Circumstances	
First-degree murder	Not applicable	20–60 years	Death penalty Life imprisonment 60–100 years	Not applicable Not applicable 3 years
Habitual offender	Not applicable	Natural life	Natural life	Not applicable
Class X felony	Not applicable	6–30 years	30–60 years	3 years
Class 1 felony	4 years or less	4–15 years	15–30 years	2 years
Class 2 felony	4 years or less	2–7 years	7–14 years	2 years
Class 3 felony	30 months or less	2–5 years	5–10 years	1 year
Class 4 felony	30 months or less	1–3 years	3–6 years	1 year
Class A misdemeanor	1 year or less	Less than 1 year	Less than 1 year	1 year
Class B misdemeanor	1 year or less	6 months or less	6 months or less	Not applicable
Class C misdemeanor	1 year or less	30 days or less	30 days or less	Not applicable

Source: Illinois Revised Statutes, Chapter 38.

Figure 3. Projected Prison Population in Illinois

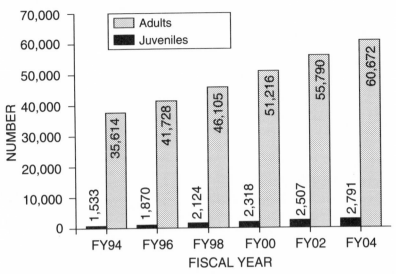

Source: Illinois Department of Corrections, 1995.

ber 25, 1977, Thompson said: "To the criminal, Class X says that if found guilty, you will go to jail for a substantial period; you will not beat the system through probation or a slap on the wrist. To the prosecutor, Class X says no more lenient sentences for violent offences. Class X is a message that everyone can understand. It says the people of Illinois will no longer tolerate violent crime. That is the message we need to make a dent in the unacceptable rate of violent crime."[43]

Earlier in 1977 Thompson signed legislation reinstating the death penalty. The first execution was on September 12, 1990. The second was in May 1994, when serial killer John Wayne Gacy was executed; at that time, 154 others were on Illinois's death row.

Both because of increasing crime and tougher sentencing, particularly in drug-related cases, Illinois has seen dramatic increases in its prison population. In 1981 there were about 12,000 prisoners in Illinois. By 1990 the population was surpassing 30,000 and is projected to reach 60,000 by the year 2004 (see figure 3). Not included in these figures are the 143,000 persons on parole at the end of 1991, including some 79,800 adults. Adult cases have increased 25 percent since 1988 and adult felony cases by 32 percent.[44]

The juvenile justice system presents its own problems. The Solovy Commission issued a separate report on this system in Cook County, documenting excessive caseloads for public defenders (some with a thousand clients per year), inadequate advocacy for youthful offenders, and excessively long separations of youth from their families. "Juvenile justice, we believe, has been treated as the 'step child' of the judicial system," reported the commission. "Juvenile justice should be a very high priority; frequently, it is our lowest."[45] Among the commission's recommendations was a call for mediation in uncontested abuse and neglect cases so that professional mediators could work with families and children and thus free judges to concentrate more fully on contested and criminal cases.[46]

COURTS SHUN PROGRESSIVE ROLE

One of the most far-reaching potential roles for a court system is to use the state constitution to implement change. There have been trends in other states, for instance, to protect citizens' liberties and individual rights more aggressively based on independent interpretation of state constitutions rather than U.S. constitutional rights. This movement has been referred to as "the new judicial federalism." In a recent article on that subject, Illinois is not listed as having an activist court, and there is no reason to challenge that assessment.[47] Nor has Illinois taken the lead in other controversial areas such as the death penalty and abortion rights. The Illinois political system and culture seem to discourage the state from being a national leader in progressive causes, and the courts are generally conservative and nonactivist.

One area in which other state courts have been aggressive in recent years has been in the revamping of school financing formulas, especially where large disparities existed between poor and well-off districts. Courts in Kentucky, Texas, Montana, and New Jersey have declared school funding provisions unconstitutional. Because Illinois has similar disparities, a lawsuit was filed by thirty-seven school districts, twenty-two children and parents, and an education rights group, asking the courts to mandate more equitable funding. The Illinois Appellate Court in September 1994 dismissed the suit, stating that doing away with the disparities "is not required under the Illinois Constitution."[48]

The courts have been more actively involved in political cases, in particular redistricting and election disputes. The Illinois Supreme Court in 1981 ruled on the disputed Illinois redistricting map, redrawing the district lines after ruling that one legislator's district was drawn unfairly. More often, however, the redistricting cases are settled in the federal courts, as in 1991, because Republicans, blacks, and Hispanics have believed they would receive a more sympathetic hearing there than in the Democrat-dominated supreme court.

A straight partisan vote is not always assured even on clearly political cases, however, as the Illinois Supreme Court proved in 1982, when the outcome of the very close gubernatorial election was challenged. After Governor Jim Thompson defeated Adlai E. Stevenson III by just five thousand votes, Democrat Stevenson asked for a recount. The court, with a four-to-three Democratic majority, voted along partisan lines with one exception: Democratic justice Seymour Simon voted with the Republicans. The bipartisan majority ruled that there was no basis for a recount, and even if there had been, the recount statute was unconstitutional. The last issue had not even been presented to the court.[49]

In another political decision, the state supreme court decided on a partisan division that the Harold Washington party was to be removed from the November 1990 ballot in Cook County. That decision was appealed to the U.S. Supreme Court and was overturned.[50]

Thus, though Illinois judges may sometimes argue strenuously that they must keep their distance from the legislative or executive branches of government, in reality the judges remain inextricably bound to the political culture of Illinois. Thanks in part to the federal Greylord and Gambat investigations—which would never have taken place under local auspices—corruption and political influence in the Cook County courts are less prevalent than a few years ago. But the elective system that ties judges to their political supporters remains in place. Expensive judicial election campaigns continue to attract contributions from attorneys and other interested parties, presenting opportunities for conflicts of interest. Rising crime and a troubled juvenile court system will keep the judiciary busy for years to come. Illinois courts are not just a part of the political structure of the state, they are an integral player in the decision-making process.

CHAPTER EIGHT

The Local Government Quagmire

Local governments in Illinois represent an extremely large number of units operating independently of each other governmentally and politically. Although most units operate under strict statutory limitations, there is a minimum of state agency control. The bewildering array of nearly sixty-seven hundred governments gives Illinois and metropolitan Chicago the distinction of being the nation's largest experiment in decentralized government.[1]

The maze of overlapping jurisdictions is so thick that most Illinois residents live under the jurisdiction of eight or more local governments. Residents of suburban Barrington Hills might live in any of four counties, depending on their street address. Those in Cook County probably do not even realize that they may pay taxes to one of four special mosquito-abatement districts.

Fairly typical are residents of Urbana, who could, if they had the time and energy, become active in the ten governments they purportedly control: the city, the county, the township, the school district, the Urbana Park District, the Champaign-Urbana Sanitary District, the Champaign-Urbana Public Health District, the mass transit district, the forest preserve district, and the community college district. Residents pay property taxes to each of these governments and contribute sales taxes as well to the city.

Illinois has more units of government than any other state. The U.S. Bureau of the Census reported in 1990 that there were 6,677 units, including 102 counties, 1,281 municipalities, 1,434 townships, 2,107 special districts, and 951 school districts.[2]

Each is either a general or special purpose government. General purpose governments include municipalities and counties and, to a lesser degree, townships. Townships are controversial, and their elimination is proposed from time to time because, with their generally narrow functions, they are considered by many reformers to be an unnecessary extra level of government. Special or limited purpose governments provide a particular service to a particular geographic area; they include school, fire protection, mosquito-abatement, and sewer districts, as well as authorities organized to operate exposition halls, convention centers, airports, ports, and mass transit systems.

The large number of government units in Illinois, some argue, provides an opportunity for many persons to participate in democracy. Indeed, one estimate is that there are sixty-five thousand elected and appointed local officials in Illinois.[3] Because power and decision making are broken down into small and distinct areas, the argument goes, citizens have more "public choice" and "local option" in the type of government they want and can pick and choose which functions their area needs or desires.

Although this may be so, the multiplicity of governments also provides a shield for weak performance, uncoordinated regional planning, and lack of accountability to citizens. The same functions that are managed in unified fashion in other states or regions are often fragmented and duplicative in Illinois. Instead of one bureaucracy, there are several; instead of one or two arenas of power, there are five or seven. In the extreme case of the six-county metropolitan Chicago area, which has twelve hundred governments with taxing powers, regionwide problems of transportation, land-use planning, and flooding are solved piecemeal or not at all.

With so many governments, public oversight is necessarily limited and lines of authority are blurred between one local government and another. As a result, featherbedding, favoritism in contract awards, and other forms of corruption have surfaced repeatedly among local governments in Illinois. As far back as 1928, officials at the Chicago-area Metropolitan Sanitary District "looted the public till through payroll padding, phony expense accounts, nepotism, mismanagement, and improper favors, among other malpractices," writes historian Robert P. Howard.[4] As recently as 1994, the daughter of a former Chicago alderman admitted to taking paychecks—without actually working—from three separate local government agencies: the Cook County clerk's office, the Cook County sheriff's office, and the city council's Finance Committee.[5] Similar stories have emerged from forest preserve districts, park districts, school districts, and other subunits of Illinois government.

Despite these difficulties, Illinois citizens in general have fiercely defended the current structure, beating back most efforts to merge or eliminate government units. The concept of local power and local accountability—however difficult it may be to wield—remains a cornerstone of Illinois's individualistic culture.

FINE-TUNING THE BEHEMOTH

It is not that Illinois residents and their leaders do not recognize the inefficiencies of the current system. Rather, they accept them as part of the state's personality and way of doing business. Instead of trying to dismantle something so integral—and in the process disrupting long-standing webs of jobs and allegiances—they develop mechanisms to fine-tune relations between the multitudes. The 1970 Constitution, for instance, encourages intergovernmental agreements, which have led, for example, to the coordination of fire and police service at major disasters. A 1980 consolidated election law helped cut down the number of elections, especially special elections for bond and tax referenda. Under the consolidated election calendar, referenda now have to be submitted at general elections. In metropolitan Chicago, periodic efforts are made to coordinate public transportation service across city-suburban lines, though "turf" is a sufficiently volatile subject that the Regional Transportation Authority remains a conglomerate, with one agency for the city, another for suburban service, and a third for the commuter railroads that link the two.

Finding ways to cooperate has been the enduring mission of the Northeastern Illinois Planning Commission, whose territory represents the densest concentration of local governments in Illinois. Encompassing the collar counties of Lake, Will, DuPage, Kane, and McHenry, along with Cook and the city of Chicago at the center, this thirty-member commission attempts to develop comprehensive plans for orderly growth and development of the region. The plans include guidelines for the development of an adequate water supply and distribution systems; storm water and sewage disposal systems; integrated air, water, rail, and highway transportation; local municipal and governmental services such as waste disposal; and improved standards of urban aesthetics and civic design.

The membership of NIPC illustrates the problem of trying to get a large number of governments to work together. Appointments are made by the governor, the mayor of Chicago, suburban mayors, the presidents of Cook County and the other county boards in the region, the Regional Transportation Authority, the Chicago Transit Authority, the Metra Board (the commuter rail authority), the Metropolitan Water Reclamation District, the Illinois Association of Park Districts, and the Chicago Park District.

NIPC has had a long and controversial history going back to its creation in 1957, when the need for planning was attacked by extreme groups, such as Save Our Suburbs (SOS), as socialistic. Resistance to coordinated planning continued into the 1990s as the diverse membership repeatedly succumbed to the natural tendency to protect one's own turf. With no one person who speaks for the metropolitan area or to the solution of its problems, NIPC has had limited success.

Lack of planning and cooperation are not peculiar to northeastern Illinois. The problem is statewide and is more intense in growing areas such as Champaign County, where uncontrolled urban growth forced a clumsy and inefficient reaction by three neighboring municipalities: Champaign, Urbana, and Savoy. Each recognized the need for an annexation agreement, but because each had its own interests, negotiations were prolonged and complex. The three cities decided to sign agreements among themselves so that they could divide up unincorporated areas just outside their boundaries. But they needed the help of a fourth entity, the Champaign-Urbana Sanitary District, so that they could withhold sewer connections to developers in areas refusing to annex to a city. What was the advantage for the sanitary district? Champaign and Urbana would assume the district's liability for the frequent flooding of Boneyard Creek, which runs through the twin cities. When the district agreed to that approach, the county of Champaign had to be convinced because it appoints sanitary district board members. It came on board and the deal went through in 1993, but only after the three cities agreed to reimburse the county for sales tax on any commercial properties they annex for an agreed number of years. All this negotiation was needed to address what would seem to be a simple matter of providing orderly growth.[6]

CROWDED BALLOTS AT ELECTION TIME

Good local leadership can help cut through the tangle of local governments, but even conscientious citizens might have trouble keeping track of candidates at the local elections. Local elections are a strange mixture of partisan and nonpartisan. In nonpartisan elections, there are no party labels on the ballot. In partisan elections, the national party labels (Republican and Democrat) or local party labels (e.g., Peoples, Citizens) appear on the ballot. The local parties in some places are "fronts" for the national parties; in other places they represent local groupings of citizens concerned with one or more issues. In still other places, local party labels are simply devices for getting candidates' names on the ballot.

There is no consistency to the partisan/nonpartisan approach. In one of Illinois's pairs of twin cities, the elections are non-partisan in Champaign and partisan in Urbana, with national party labels.

Some persons would argue that all local elections should be partisan. Such a system would create political bonds between neighboring or overlapping governments, possibly improving cooperation across regions and boosting the strength of local and, over time, state parties as well. The "good government" element, however, argues for nonpartisan local elections because "there is no Republican or Democratic way to clean the streets." With no agreement forthcoming, the strange mixture of elections continues, discouraging cooperation between governments.[7]

The large number of units of local government complicates not only local-to-local relations but also those between local governments and the state. All local governments (except those with home-rule powers, discussed below) have to look to the state statutes for their authority to function. The superior position of the state in the state-local hierarchy is clear enough on paper, but in reality the legislature and the administrative agencies of state government simply cannot police sixty-seven hundred governments directly. For instance, the state requires that local governments file either annual financial reports or audits with the Illinois comptroller, but that office lacks authority to cause a local government to change its financial practices.

A recent catalog of state assistance to local governments reports some 345 state financial and technical assistance programs, including grants for public library services for the blind and physically handicapped, soil and water conservation, housing, fire protection, museums, and drug enforcement, to name a few. The state also shares revenue with local jurisdictions. "In FY1994, $434 million was distributed to counties, municipalities and townships for road and transportation purposes. In addition, salary subsidies and bonuses are provided to many local officials, including state's attorneys, assessment officers, county clerks, police officers and probation officers."[8]

Much of the state's business on a day-to-day basis, in fact, involves serving the needs of Illinois's local governments. The Department of Children and Family Services licenses child care facilities; Commerce and Community Affairs consults with local governments on business; and corrections establishes and enforces standards for local government shelter care, detention, and correctional facilities. The Department of Public Health approves payment of state and federal funds to local health programs and services.

Most state departments must carry on regular relations with their local counterparts. But this does not mean that the state exerts a great deal of control. Local government discretionary authority in Illinois is high compared to other states. The U.S. Advisory Commission on Intergovernmental Relations (ACIR) ranked Illinois twelfth among the states overall and tenth for the relative authority of cities (because cities with more than twenty-five thousand residents are mostly home ruled in Illinois). Such rankings give credibility to the sentiment that Illinois local governments have considerable freedom from state government regulation.[9]

Governor Richard B. Ogilvie in 1969 thought the answer to improving state-local relations was a new department, the Department of Local Government Affairs (DLGA), a one-stop agency for local governments to interact with state issues. At that time, the department received much federal money that was to be distributed to local governments. The department was also interested in improving local government management, particularly in fiscal affairs.

The agency as conceived did not last. A reorganization report titled *Orderly Government,* prepared for Governor James Thompson in 1977, recommended that the department be abolished and its functions transferred to other agencies. Thompson partially implemented the recommendation when he created the Department of Commerce and Community Affairs by executive order in 1979. The community affairs section of the new department carried out some of the responsibilities of DLGA, but economic development was the main thrust.

FOR BIGGER PLAYERS, HOME RULE

True to the individualistic culture of the state, Chicago and many smaller cities had bristled under the state's authority since the nineteenth century. They wanted home rule, the ability to make their own decisions, raise their own revenues, and in general be able to make decisions without first asking the state for permission. They got what they wanted when the 1970 Constitution went into effect on July 1, 1971.

The constitution established home rule for Cook County and all municipalities with more than twenty-five thousand residents. Unlike other states, where voters have to approve a charter in a local referendum to receive such powers, the grant of home rule was automatic in Illinois. Municipalities with fewer than twenty-five thousand residents can also secure home rule, and larger cities can vote out home rule by the same referendum process.

Home-rule units in Illinois "may exercise any power and perform any function pertaining to its government and affairs including, but not limited to, the power to regulate for the protection of the public health, safety, morals and welfare; to license; to tax; and to incur debt." Some limitations are spelled out in the constitution, but the courts are admonished that the "powers and functions of home rule shall be construed liberally."[10]

The 1970 Constitution also provided that county governments with an elected chief executive automatically became home-rule units. Cook County was the only county to qualify for this power, and even though other counties can qualify by adopting the chief executive office by referendum, all such referenda have failed.[11]

James Banovetz and Thomas Kelty surveyed ninety-five Illinois municipalities and found that home rule was used in a wide variety of ways to change local conditions.[12] In descending order of importance, they were new debt (89 percent), regulations (72 percent), regulatory licensing (61 percent), intergovernmental agreements (58 percent), new taxes (57 percent), property transactions (43 percent), new sources of nontax revenues (36 percent), changes in government structure (28 percent) and consolidation of property tax levies (26 percent).

Banovetz and Kelty found that once this power is used, most municipalities prefer to keep it; when the question to retain home rule was put to the voters in twenty-five municipalities, twenty-one voted for its retention. The four municipalities abandoning home rule were Lisle, Villa Park, Lombard, and Rockford. The Illinois Supreme Court also has been "pro–home rule," according to the authors. They classify thirty-one court decisions since 1972 as favorable to home rule and twenty as unfavorable. Last, the General Assembly has reacted cautiously on bills that preempt home rule; only a handful of bills to limit home rule have been approved since 1972.

Two-thirds of the state's population is now governed by home rule because, with a few exceptions, it is in place for the state's 100 largest municipalities and its most populous county. Still, that leaves 101 downstate and suburban counties and more than 6,400 other government units that remain subject to the common law principle known as Dillon's rule, the cornerstone of municipal law since 1872, which holds that a local government has only that authority specifically granted by the state constitution and its statutes.

FROM THE TOP DOWN: MANDATES

The flip side to home rule are the mandates from the legislature that tell local governments to undertake particular functions. From the local government perspective, the problem with mandates is that the legislature often fails to provide adequate financial reimbursement to carry out the new responsibility. Mandates can be costly, intrusive, or both. Mandates can direct a school district, for instance, on how to teach a particular subject or to close its doors on a particular holiday. Mandates can also increase pension benefits for municipal and other employees.

The 1992 State Mandates Catalog of the Department of Commerce and Community Affairs estimated that 237 mandates then in effect cost local governments more than $11 million. It broke down the mandates into categories as follows: 68 organization and structure mandates, 49 due process mandates, 30 service mandates, 51 tax exemption mandates, and 128 personnel mandates.

A State Mandates Act passed by the legislature in 1980 was intended to prevent the passage of mandates that did not meet statewide policy objectives and to assist local governments in paying for enacted mandates. A study of the act in 1986 stated that "in the first few years following the passage of the State Mandates Act, it appeared to be working well."[13] But many would disagree with this conclusion. Governor Jim Edgar in 1991 vetoed four pieces of legislation that would have imposed mandates. In his remarks at the time, Edgar said that there must be a halt to such mandates on local governments. Voters in 1992 approved by an eighty-to-twenty margin a nonbinding advisory to ban unfunded mandates, and the Illinois Municipal League has campaigned in the legislature to pass a state mandates constitutional amendment, though without success.

EXPERIMENT IN DECENTRALIZATION

The wide freedom of choice in the way local government is conducted remains at the philosophical core of the decentralized approach. Like all freedoms, this one carries responsibilities, the most prominent being to create local governments that can manage themselves well. At the most prosaic level, that means creating responsible record-keeping systems, communicating well with other agencies, and remaining accountable to the taxpayer.

The very nature of the decentralized system makes it difficult to gauge how well local governments are doing these jobs. Local governments are not audited by any state agency, though they are required to have an audit by a private firm and to file that audit document with the state comptroller. The comptroller then provides a summary financial document on each type of government—municipalities, counties, townships, and special districts.

(The state board of education performs this function for school districts and has tighter control.)

The value of the reports filed with the comptroller has been questioned. A study by the Taxpayers' Federation of Illinois concluded, "As it is currently constituted, the annual financial reporting requirement set forth in Illinois law is a useless exercise because the data collected is inadequate to satisfy basic research. The reports appear to be relatively worthless for comparative tax purposes."[14]

Another indicator of local performance is the widely varying degree of professionalism in the leadership of municipalities. In suburban Cook County and the collar counties, there are many more professional administrators (usually city managers) than downstate. Suburban governments are generally free of partisan politics, whereas partisan politics can be very important in downstate municipal decision making.

Because of varying approaches to management and widely divergent agendas, it is no wonder that local governments have a difficult time presenting a common front in Springfield. Most government units in Illinois are organized into statewide lobbying groups—for cities, townships, villages—with an overall aim to improve the local governments' authority vis-à-vis the state government. But even with a strong financial base, the Illinois Municipal League has a hard time representing the needs of the rapidly growing northeastern cities along with the declining municipalities downstate. Chicago, East St. Louis, Aurora, and Naperville all have their own sets of problems. To address these differences, separate regional groupings of municipalities have developed for lobbying purposes. For example, there are strong mayors' and managers' organizations in DuPage County and South Cook County suburbs and other regional groupings throughout the suburban ring.

One of the most active of this type of professionalized intergovernmental entity is the Northwest Municipal Conference, which in 1991 included thirty-four municipalities and five townships. Pushing for the expansion of such operations, the Metropolitan Planning Council in 1991 wrote that the conference "helps members save money through joint purchasing, training programs for municipal employees, and joint testing of police and fire candidates. Special programs address issues that cross jurisdictional boundaries, including solid waste, cable franchising and stormwater management."[15]

The council's report on intergovernmental cooperation was based on interviews of fifty-seven political leaders, planners, and budget experts. Authors Deborah Stone and Joyce O'Keefe noted that many problems "leap jurisdictional boundaries" and that large-scale issues beg for regional solutions, most notably the dispersion of jobs away from areas with affordable housing, the disparity in spending by school districts, and the worsening problem of traffic congestion throughout the metropolitan area. But better relations between governments will not be easy to create. "The region is extremely fragmented, and those regional efforts that do exist are themselves fragmented either by geography or policy area. There is a serious lack of trust between municipalities and counties, local governments and the state, and the city and suburbs."[16]

THE CHICAGO APPROACH

Even if regional cooperation could be developed, the state is likely always to be affected by difficult relations between its biggest city and the state government. As by far the largest municipality in Illinois, Chicago wields a level of political power that upends the expected balance of power. Legally, Chicago is a subunit of the state, but politically, the city often appears to operate independently.[17] The disproportionate power has even spurred recommendations to make Chicago and the metropolitan area a separate state, as in 1933, when a University of Chicago study said, "There is much to be said for the separate statehood of Chicago, especially in view of the inability of the city to obtain proportional representation in the state legislature, or a degree of home-rule adequate to deal with the needs of a growing metropolis."[18] The city has since gained the home-rule powers it sought, and in any case such proposals are not taken too seriously because Illinois without its only large city would be a small state with a fraction of its current national profile.

Illustrative of the confusion on the Chicago-state relationship is the career ladder for Chicago politicians. Several former legislators (plus one former congressman) have served in the Chicago city council, but few former city alderman had sat in the state legislature until 1993. That year, in most unusual situations, three former aldermen were elected to the General Assembly. In other parts of the state, the upward mobility pattern for a local government official is to be elected to the legislature. In Chicago, the legislature has more often been a stepping-stone to more powerful local offices.

Chicago uses its home-rule powers extensively. It started the post–World War II home-rule movement in 1954, when Mayor Martin Kennelly created a Home-Rule Commission. Kennelly's successor Richard J. Daley continued to carry the home-rule banner, and his son, the current mayor, Richard M. Daley, helped create the home-rule provisions as a member of the 1970 Constitutional Convention's Local Government Committee.

Chicago in theory remains a "weak" mayor city, with much power lodged in the city council, but in practice most recent Chicago mayors have had very strong political power. Richard J. Daley was chairman of the Cook County Democratic Central Committee as well as mayor and as a result had legendary power. The mayors after his death (Michael Bilandic, Jane Byrne, Harold Washington, Eugene Sawyer, and Richard M. Daley) have not held the party office and have not been as strong leaders, but they have often been able to steer the city council.

The council is large. Aldermen are elected from each of the fifty wards on a nonpartisan ballot, although the partisan affiliations of the aldermen are well known.[19] In 1994, all fifty were Democrats, though they came from different factions of the party. The wards are the building blocks for the county political organization, and in some instances the elective ward committeeman is also the alderman. This combination makes the alderman a very potent political actor because unlike counties downstate, Chicago ward committeemen appoint precinct committeemen.[20]

The Chicago City Council has the potential for much power and used it at the start of Mayor Harold Washington's first term. The majority of the council members at the time were not supporters of Washington, the city's first black mayor. By voting as a bloc for three years straight, the aldermen were able to prevent the bulk of Washington's program from being implemented. Called the "council wars" by the media, this conflict had strong racial overtones, with blacks generally supporting Mayor Washington and most of the council's white majority opposing him.

The council-mayor stalemate was the result of the redistricting of Chicago wards after the 1980 census. New district lines drawn by veteran alderman and floor leader Thomas Keane kept the number of seats held by blacks at seventeen, the same as after the 1970 remap. In the past, minorities might have accepted the map with resignation. This time they took it to the federal district court. The judge ruled that Keane's map was discriminatory and ordered a new map drawn. The new map was appealed, but a compromise map was agreed to in November 1985. Another federal judge ruled that special elections had to be held, and the eventual result was that, with one year left in his first term, Mayor Washington had a majority on the city council and was able to get his proposals adopted.

There have been calls to "reform" the city council, most recently in a 1989 report titled "Chicago City Council Reform" by the City Club of Chicago. Some changes have been made in the council and its procedures. But the size of the council has not been changed, although it could be done using the city's home-rule powers. Apparently, the classic remark of colorful Alderman "Paddy" Bauler, uttered with gusto in 1955, still prevails: "Chicago ain't ready for reform."

A more fundamental reform, to reduce corruption within Chicago government, has also been pushed and with somewhat more success. The result has been a slow but definite movement away from the open bribery and layers of corruption within the city's departments, courts, and clerical operations. One of the most dramatic and revealing investigations of this institutionalized corruption was splashed on the front pages of the *Chicago Sun-Times* for a solid month in 1978, after the newspaper and the Better Government Association (BGA) had opened and operated a tavern, named the Mirage, less than a mile from city hall.

That Chicago's inspectors were on the take had been well known for decades, but because business owners needed licenses to operate and could cut a few corners with a fifty-dollar bribe, they rarely came forward to fight the system. Investigative reporter Pamela Zekman and the BGA's William Recktenwald decided the best way to gather hard evidence was to open a real business and let the inspectors walk in. As they prepared to open the tavern and during the four months it was in business, the would-be tavern keepers encountered repeated payoff demands. Plumbing, electrical, and fire inspectors, even a sign inspector, all looked the other way or hastened some paperwork in exchange for payoffs of ten dollars and up. The owner of a neighborhood delicatessen already knew the pattern. "The name of the game in Chicago is baksheesh. . . . That's Arabian. It means payoff, bribe. This is the city of baksheesh."[21]

It turned out that the corruption went far beyond city officials. In *Decisions for Sale,* John Gardiner and Theodore R. Lyman recounted routine skimming of income and sales taxes throughout the tavern industry, juggled records, illegal kickbacks from vending machine salesmen, and improper sales of liquor from the city's big distributors. City and state officials moved in to clean up the situation, and blatant bribe-taking, though hardly disappearing, was reduced.[22]

Under Richard J. Daley, Chicago was the last large city with an effective political machine. That is no longer true. The vote can still be delivered in some wards, but the number is declining. Among the reasons for this change, many are tied to the national trends toward less personal contact. Television has been a factor with its thirty-second news exposure for political candidates. Most important, the city can no longer force its employees to do political work because of a court decision known as the *Shakman* decree, which prohibits the firing of someone for refusing to do political work.

This discussion on Chicago politics has been almost exclusively about the Democratic party because the Republican party in the city has been notoriously weak and at times nearly nonexistent. The Republicans recently have elected one or two members of the legislature from city districts, and the Cook County state's attorney elected in 1990 was a Republican, but the party remains a marginal player in the city.

One of the only ways the Republican party has been able to pick up support, in fact, has been by converting politicians from the other side. Former sheriff James O'Grady switched from the Democratic to the Republican party when he decided to run for office. In a more dramatic conversion, the chairman of the former Cook County Democratic party, Alderman Edward "Fast Eddie" Vrdolyak, became a Republican after Harold Washington won the Democratic nomination for mayor in 1983. He even ran for mayor against Richard M. Daley in 1988, but by then he was on the Solidarity party ticket and finished a distant third.

One aspect of Chicago government is important for comparative purposes. If one looked at total spending for Chicago in comparison with other cities, the numbers for Chicago would be quite low because functions that would belong to the city elsewhere are performed by other governmental units in Chicago. These arrangements were made by the legislature and are in line with the decentralized local governments throughout Illinois. Public hospitals are a county, not city, function in Chicago. The public schools, as in other parts of the state, are a separate government unit with taxing powers. The Chicago Housing Authority has considerable independence. Public transportation is under the Chicago Transit Authority and Regional Transportation Authority. The park district, too, is fiscally independent of the city.

This decentralization helped Chicago, or at least masked its symptoms, during the 1970s, when New York City faced fiscal disaster. "Today the effect of these differences [between the two cities] is striking. Cook County, not the city of Chicago, operates the city's public hospitals and the state legislature picked up most of the city's transportation and social welfare costs. By contrast, New York is the only city in the country whose state legislature requires it to pay a substantial share of its own Medicaid and welfare bills."[23]

Although these Chicago agencies are legally independent and do not appear on the organization chart as city functions, the mayor can have considerable impact on their decision making. Recent mayors have been influential in most major administrative appointments. This is best illustrated by the

Chicago Park District for which the mayor can control the appointment of the top administrative officer. Legally, all of these separate governments are outside the jurisdiction of the mayor. In reality, their independence depends on whether the mayor has the political strength to control them.

The city has fought hard to maintain control over the city's airports. When plans were made for developing O'Hare Airport in the early 1950s, the city carefully annexed a strip of land and the ground around the airport to make sure the airport was in the city limits. More logically, the airport should have been in the suburbs. Suburban Republican legislators have since introduced legislation that would bring all regional airports under an authority appointed by the governor, taking jurisdiction away from the city and the mayor. This legislation has always provoked fierce opposition from the city and has not passed.

The importance of the airport and its job base to the city was well demonstrated in the early 1990s, when decisions were being made on whether and where to build a third airport. Mayor Daley wanted to relocate a neighborhood so as to squeeze the airport onto former industrial and landfill areas on the city's southeast side. Governor Jim Edgar wanted a south suburban site. When Daley's plan could not win legislative approval, he withdrew it, putting the burden on the governor to push forward on the suburban airport without city support.

COOK COUNTY, ANOTHER SPECIAL CASE

The other power player in local government is Cook County. With its population of five million and traditionally close working relations with Chicago, the county wields considerable leverage in the metropolitan area and in Springfield. Like Chicago, Cook County has been generally controlled by Democrats and even shares headquarters with the city, providing for relatively smooth communication between the two.

The voters elect the president of the Cook County Board of Commissioners and a seventeen-member county board. Until 1994, ten members of the board were elected at-large inside Chicago, and the other seven were elected in at-large elections from the suburbs, but now all board members are elected from single-member districts. Typically, members elected within Chicago have been Democrats while the suburban members have been Republicans. Despite the Republican presence, the county has been closely affiliated with the city Democratic organization under former Cook County Board president George Dunne, who also served many years as chairman of the Cook County Democratic Central Committee. Unlike Mayor Richard J. Daley before him, Dunne either did not want or was unable to exercise the political control that Daley had when he held the top city and political positions.

Cook County, like downstate counties, elects a "long ballot" list of administrative officials, including a sheriff, a county clerk, a circuit clerk, a recorder, a treasurer, and a state's attorney. The auditor and medical examiner (coroner) in Cook County, unlike some downstate counties, are appointive offices.

The fragmentation created by the separately elected offices and other organizational problems has led to steady criticism of the administration and management of the county. A two-month study by *Crain's Chicago Business* described a "political aversion to change in county government" and an expensive pattern of mismanagement. "Cook County Hospital and the prison system are crumbling," said the article. "Taxes are soaring, the result not only of an inequitable tax classification system, but moribund leadership at the county level." Don Haider, a professor of finance at Northwestern University's J. L. Kellogg Graduate School of Management, described it this way: "Cook County government has become a holding company for independent fiefdoms whose parts are greater than the whole. But the electorate can't find anyone accountable."[24]

The article concluded that "Cook County government enters the 1990s in need of an overhaul. The example of reform-minded officials within county government suggests that the next president of the Cook County Board of Commissioners will need to act swiftly and without hesitation to bring about changes in county government. . . . The challenges are enormous, but the opportunities to make a difference are almost limitless—restructuring the tax system, privatizing certain functions, acting as a coordinator rather than provider of key services."[25] George Dunne retired as board president in 1990 and was replaced by reform-minded Richard Phelan, who has made administrative changes, including hiring an aggressive administrator for the Cook County Hospital system.[26] But the fragmented structure, with its long list of elected officers, continues.

Even if Cook County is able to inject efficiency, the rest of the county's hundreds of units of government will remain. The problem was neatly described in *Blueprint of Chicago Government*: "The fundamental problem is that within Cook County there are more than 500 separate taxing units of local governments. Neither the mayor, city council, county board president, nor the Cook County Board of Commissioners has had the responsibility or the power to coordinate decisions of all these different governments. The end result is that intergovernmental cooperation and coordination is primitive at the metropolitan level. There is duplication, waste, and a lack of public accountability in the system."[27]

An example of the arcane complexity of local governments is the South Cook County Mosquito Abatement District. The district's state mandate is to "abate effectively and economically the mosquito problem, using modern, scientific, and practical methods of control applied in an orderly and systematic manner." The district was organized in 1953 under a 1927 state enabling statute; its jurisdiction covers both Chicago and the suburbs. (There are four Cook County mosquito abatement districts.) The governing board is appointed by the Cook County Board president, and although the district includes part of Chicago, the mayor of Chicago has no legal authority over the district.

Such specialization and independence are common in Cook County and the rest of the state.

EXCEPTION TO RULE: EAST ST. LOUIS

Although the Illinois philosophy overall is to give local governments considerable freedom, occasionally these governments have serious problems that require state intervention. One such case is poverty-stricken East St. Louis. With a predominantly black population, the city has had serious financial problems for decades, but studies and panels by state agencies and others have had little impact. The city continues to lose population and faces a chronic inability to meet its financial needs.

To provide relief, the state and others have informally taken over the city government. "The outside world has been taking over management of governments in East St. Louis. The housing authority is now run by a private company; state troopers have a regular presence in the city; legislation aimed at the East St. Louis schools will impose an outside financial oversight team; and the state has picked outside financial consultants for the city."[28]

Two recent state efforts were the creation of the East St. Louis Financial Advisory Board by the governor and the 1994 takeover of the school system's finances. The advisory board reported: "Given current revenues and obligations, the city is incapable of providing even a minimum level of services within the constraint of a [required] balanced budget. At present, services are grossly inadequate and the budget is not balanced. . . . The signs of fiscal crisis include the city's inability to meet its financial obligations;

particularly the timely payment of payroll, vendor payables, health insurance, employee retirement contributions, and retirement of debts to state agencies, federal agencies, and bondholders. . . . Property owners currently experience a high rate of taxation relative to other municipalities." "State involvement is clearly warranted," the board reported in 1990. It recommended an oversight commission and a financial adviser, and appointment by the city council of a local government manager to serve as the city's chief administrative officer. Board members said they "do not call for throwing money at the problem; they call only for the state to loan some resources, to pledge a guarantee, to help the city strengthen its administrative infrastructure and operations, and commit to cooperation."[29]

Four years later the situation had not improved markedly, especially in the schools, where problems included "overcrowded classrooms, poor building conditions, alleged diversion of federal funds for improper uses, and a $10 million deficit."[30] In response, the Illinois State Board of Education in October 1994 invoked a new state law and ordered an independent panel to run the district's finances.

It is a measure of the state's culture and of its respect for local control that the actions in East St. Louis are the exception and not the rule. Both the legislative and executive branches of the state government tend to keep a hands-off policy regarding local government issues, allowing problems to be worked out (or not worked out, as is sometimes the case) without state interference. Local governments struggle with problems every day that might be solved with a more coordinated regional or statewide approach. As long as they stay within the guidelines of state law, however, local governments in Illinois will bear the responsibility to work the problems out on their own.

CHAPTER NINE

Beyond Its Borders,
Illinois Asserts Itself

Illinois did not become what it is by being shy or isolated. Even before the state's incorporation in 1818, the territory's delegate to the U.S. Congress, Nathaniel Pope, was working hard in Washington DC. It was Pope who pushed the northern border forty-one miles up from Lake Michigan's southern tip, capturing the port of Chicago from Wisconsin and setting a precedent for aggressiveness that serves the state to this day.

Pope's advocacy beyond Illinois's borders was followed by a steady stream of leaders who went before the U.S. Congress, the federal bureaucracy, the president, and even foreign governments to assert the state's needs. The governor often played the role, but so did local politicians, legislators, business leaders, and citizen activists.

External relations are typically pursued for a simple reason: to bring back money or jobs. Chicago mayor Richard J. Daley was a master of this art, trading his ability to generate presidential votes for hundreds of millions of dollars worth of building projects and federal human service programs. Governor Jim Thompson traveled to foreign cities and helped generate thousands of jobs backed by export sales and foreign investments. Democrat Dan Rostenkowski and Republican Robert Michel brought home the bacon from the U.S. Congress with such regularity that voters kept sending them back for more: Rostenkowski had served thirty-six years by 1994 and Michel retired after thirty-eight. There were also lesser-known players such as Gail Cincotta, a rabble-rouser from Chicago's west side who helped conceive the federal Community Reinvestment Act, which coaxed Chicago banks to lend $185 million in the neighborhoods and the Boatmen's Bank of St. Louis to pledge $5 million in southern Illinois.

Table 6: Federal Payments to Illinois, 1988–93 ($ in millions)

	1988	1989	1990	1991	1992	1993
Social services*	$2,359	$2,563	$2,829	$2,869	$3,864	$4,544
Education	650	627	670	751	884	941
Transportation	548	580	562	606	700	748
Law enforcement/defense	212	212	157	274	249	267
Energy/environment	86	148	131	172	176	184
Total	$3,855	$4,130	$4,439	$4,672	$5,873	$6,684

Source: Chicago Enterprise January–February 1994, 11.

* Includes Medicaid, public health, labor, and housing costs.

A major focus for such activity has always been Washington DC, if only because that is where the laws are made and the huge federal budget is divided up. Federal payments to Illinois in 1992 totaled nearly $6 billion,[1] with major outlays for social services, education, transportation, and labor and employment (see table 6). The federal stream provided 27 percent of the state's revenues in 1994.[2] The money from Washington comes via a large number of categorical grants (for specific purposes) in addition to block grants (groupings of grant programs in a functional area such as health or community development). Other dollars flow in to the research universities, particularly the University of Chicago, Northwestern University, and the University of Illinois, via agencies such as the National Science Foundation and the Department of Defense.

Federal aid to the states has been shifting. General, unrestricted revenue sharing with the states was terminated in 1980 and then for local governments in 1986. There were reductions in numerous categorical aid programs to the states during the Carter and Reagan administrations in the late 1970s and early 1980s. But there have been massive infusions of federal dollars to Illinois since the late 1980s to match state dollars for the rapidly expanding federal-state Medicaid program, which provided health coverage for 1.4 million Illinois residents as of 1994.

Like most other states, Illinois maintains relations with the federal government through offices in Washington. It has one representing the governor, another the legislature, and a third the State Board of Education. The offices are located in the Hall of the States near Capitol Hill, serving as the state's eyes and ears and giving Illinois a Washington presence. Chicago has a Washington office as well.

FRIENDS IN HIGH PLACES

The most significant factor in external relations is the human one. Simply put, a state that provides effective political leaders will do better in Washington than one that does not. In this regard, Illinois has not been a home of presidents. Only one Illinois resident, Abraham Lincoln, has been elected president, defeating a fellow Illinoisan, Stephen A. Douglas, in 1860. Governor Frank O. Lowden was a near candidate in 1920, losing out to Warren G. Harding at the Republican convention. Another governor, Adlai E. Stevenson, was the unsuccessful Democratic candidate for president in 1952 and 1956, and John Anderson, a congressman from Rockford, ran as an independent in 1980.[3]

But if Illinois does not develop presidents, as have New York, California, and Ohio, it nonetheless plays an important role in the presidential nominating and election process. With an early primary (now March) and a large block of electoral votes, Illinois can swing an election, as proved in 1960, when John F. Kennedy narrowly defeated Richard M. Nixon in Illinois on the strength of Richard J. Daley's organization. Daley knew that the downstate vote would be sufficiently pro-Nixon that he had to deliver a surplus of four hundred thousand or more votes to put his man in the White House. That was a tall order even for Daley. "At no time . . . had the Democratic ward bosses been subject to the pressure he [Daley] applied for Jack Kennedy," wrote television commentator Len O'Connor. "There was not the slightest doubt in the minds of the ward bosses, in advance of the 1960 election, that the man who failed to deliver a massive vote was going to be permanently maimed politically."[4] Every vote counted. Daley delivered a plurality of 456,312 votes in Chicago, and Kennedy squeaked through by a margin of 8,858 votes out of 4.65 million cast. In appreciation, Kennedy was responsive when Daley called for help.

It was under a Republican president, George Bush, that Illinois had its most impressive array in top administrative posts. Four cabinet members in 1991 were from Illinois: Samuel K. Skinner as secretary of transportation, Edward Derwinski at veterans affairs, Lynn Martin at labor, and Edward Madigan as secretary of agriculture. Skinner subsequently was named President Bush's chief of staff; he had served under Governor James Thompson when Thompson was a U.S. attorney, and Thompson had been Illinois campaign manager for both Bush and President Ronald Reagan.

Richard M. Daley was less successful in placing cabinet members, despite strong relations with the Clinton administration. But David Wilhelm, who chaired the Democratic National Committee during the first two years of the Clinton presidency, cut his teeth on Illinois Democratic politics, and William Daley, brother of Richard M., played a key role as an administration lobbyist in the 1994 passage of the North American Free Trade Agreement.

CONGRESSIONAL CONNECTIONS

Probably Illinois's most enduring intergovernmental connections have been in the U.S. Congress, where a series of leaders have represented the home state in addition to taking on national roles. Joseph G. "Uncle Joe" Cannon, a Republican from Danville, was the autocratic Speaker of the U.S. House from 1903 to 1911; he served in Congress for nearly fifty years. Senator Scott Lucas, a Democrat from Havana, was majority leader in 1949–50, and Republican Senator Everett McKinley Dirksen of Pekin was minority leader from 1959 to 1969. Senator Charles H. Percy of Wilmette chaired the important Senate Foreign Relations Committee from 1981 to 1985.

An example of what a well-placed friend can produce is amply illustrated by former House minority leader Robert Michel from downstate Peoria. For nineteen terms until his retirement in 1994, he used his political skills, personal contacts, and influence to create a legacy on the prairie that his successors will have a hard time duplicating: "Residents here can cross the Bob Michel Bridge over the Illinois River, work in a new $50 million federal prison in Pekin, train in a new $50 million National Guard facility, drive a rebuilt highway to Springfield and attend classes in Bradley University's new $7 million telecommunications center." Not surprisingly, voters in 1994 were asking their congressional candidates, "What will you do to be like Congressman Michel?"[5]

The same question was being asked in another House district, the one where eighteen-term veteran Dan Rostenkowski was running for reelection despite federal grand jury charges that he broke House rules and misused public and political funds. As chairman of the powerful House Ways and Means Committee, Rostenkowski became legendary in Illinois for his bargaining prowess and his commitment to local projects. "The one great asset that Rostenkowski brings to his work is that he's a wonderful 'operator,'" wrote William Barry Furlong in a 1981 profile. "What he does in talking, cajoling, courting, and retalking is exactly what brings a man to the leadership of the Congress. . . . It is in this environment—of favors traded, of commitments made and broken, of promises as fragile as a sculpture in dust—that Rostenkowski excels."[6]

Even after stepping down from his chairmanship because of the investigation, Rostenkowski could still boast to voters of his take-home benefits. Political columnist Steve Neal reported that the congressman helped generate $292 million worth of projects in fiscal year 1995, including funds for a new science building at DePaul University (he had earlier extracted $8 million for a Loyola University building), rebuilt seawalls on Lake Michigan, a light-rail transit system in Chicago, affordable housing, and AIDS research. "In the competition with other states for federal funds, the Northwest Side Democrat is the most productive member of the 22-member Illinois congressional delegation," wrote Neal.[7] Apparently that wasn't enough to impress voters, though, because the legendary lawmaker lost his 1994 reelection bid.

INFLUENCE FROM THE OUTSIDE

One does not have to be a member of Congress or a cog in the White House to have an influence on national or even international affairs. Illinois leaders have consistently raised the state's profile with a variety of tactics, ranging from providing campaign contributions to organizing at the grass roots.

Monetary support to politicians is a time-honored approach that Dwayne Andreas, chairman and CEO of Archer Daniels Midland Company (ADM), has used with regularity. When Republican George Bush was in the White House, Andreas contributed $1.1 million to his political party, and when Democrat Bill Clinton took over, Andreas quickly shifted his allegiance and provided $270,000 to the Democratic party.[8] The payback came in June 1993, when Clinton and the U.S. Environmental Protection Agency announced that a new "clean-air" gasoline would be reformulated with a 30 percent mix of ethanol, a corn-based fuel made by Andreas's company. The deal would provide $38 million in new revenue for Illinois corn farmers and, by one analyst's estimate, about $100 million a year for Decatur-based ADM, which operates four ethanol plants in Illinois and Iowa.[9]

While Andreas's prodigious contributions have made him a regular at White House events and prompted a political column to suggest that ADM stands for "Always Delivering Money,"[10] another Illinoisan, Gail Cincotta, has made a habit of barging into Washington offices without an invitation. As director of the Chicago-based National People's Action, the former housewife and neighborhood organizer rallies activists from around the country and leads them on periodic "hits" in Washington. The target is usually a cabinet official or the director of one agency or another, depending on whether Cincotta's issue relates to housing, bank lending, or jobs. Typically Cincotta brings a couple of hundred people into the anteroom of the intended victim and demands a meeting. Based on her reputation for hard research and tough tactics, she often gets one. For several years before 1976, she was involved in the writing and passage of the Community Reinvestment Act, which required banks nationwide to expand their lending in areas where they accept deposits. By 1988, the act had prompted $1.6 billion in loan commitments by banks nationwide.[11]

Governor James Thompson went farther than Washington to bring home the goods, knocking on international doors in Asia, Europe, and Latin America. Foreign relations had never been high on the priority list in Illinois before Thompson and in fact had been shunned by a like-named (but unrelated) predecessor, Chicago Mayor "Big Bill" Thompson. An isolationist, William Thompson in 1927 said, "I wanta make the King of England keep his snoot out of America. . . . That's what I want. . . . America first, and last, and always! That's the issue of this campaign. That's what Big Bill Thompson wants."[12]

Big Jim Thompson wanted just the opposite. He wrote at the conclusion of his administration: "Expanding overseas markets and attracting foreign investment is crucial to Illinois' economy, yet some still question why a Governor participates in trade missions. But the presence of a Governor can open doors to direct contact with high level decision makers in foreign governments and corporations. Government-to-government contacts are especially important in emerging markets such as the Soviet Union, China and Eastern Europe, and the higher level of contact, the faster decisions can be made."[13]

During Thompson's tenure, the Diamond Star joint venture between Mitsubishi Motors Corporation of Japan and Chrysler Motor Corporation built an auto assembly plant in Bloomington-Normal. By 1990, total Japanese investment in Illinois was $4.7 billion, including ninety-seven manufacturing facilities employing more than twenty-five thousand workers.[14] Additional investment from Europe and elsewhere brought the number of jobs supported by international interests to more than 125,000 statewide.[15]

Thompson regularly led entourages of politicians, businessmen, and civic and union leaders on trade missions around the world. With Thompson's encouragement, the state Department of Commerce and Community Affairs established eleven foreign offices to position Illinois products in overseas markets and to pave the way for Illinois investments. The offices were located in Belgium, Hong Kong, Japan, People's Republic of China, Brazil, Russia, Mexico, Canada, Poland, and Hungary. An office was scheduled to open in Spain, but Thompson's successor, Governor Edgar, canceled that opening because of budget restraints and closed or consolidated other offices. Most states now have foreign offices, but Illinois continues to have one of the strongest networks.

GANGING UP FOR ILLINOIS

Even with the heavy hitters at work, Illinois consistently sends more money to Washington in tax dollars than it receives back in federal expenditures. A 1985 estimate was that Illinois gets back only seventy-five cents on every dollar, while South Dakota received one dollar back for every forty-eight cents sent to Washington.[16] In 1991, Illinois ranked forty-first among the states in revenue per capita from the federal government for state and local governments.[17] It ranks low for several reasons: Illinois has few major military installations and defense contractors; it is among the top ten states in per capita wealth so receives lower rates of federal matching grants than do poorer states; and Illinois provides modest levels of reimbursement to recipients of state-administered social programs and thus receives less in federal matching funds than states with higher payment levels.

The large Rock Island Arsenal has been significantly reduced in size in recent years, and two other bases, Fort Sheridan in Highland Park and Chanute Air Force Base in Rantoul, are closed. In 1993, the Glenview Naval Air Station closed, but after heavy pressure from Illinois interests, the mission of the Great Lakes Naval Training Station near Waukegan was expanded, offsetting some of the statewide reductions.

One recent development that may make the Illinois congressional delegation more united is the increased interaction among the membership. The delegation members are now meeting with some regularity thanks to the initiative of former Senator Alan J. Dixon, who in 1985 helped establish the Institute for Illinois. Composed of the congressional delegation, the institute is supported by foundation and corporate grants and has the sole purpose of looking out for the state's interests, particularly in federal grants.

The most recent effort to secure a significant federal project was the failed campaign to bring the Super Conducting Super Collider project to Illinois. In probably the largest effort to get a federal project in the state's history, Illinois spent some $4.5 million on research, lobbying, and fancy documentation to convince the federal government that the giant atom-smasher should be built adjacent to the Fermi National Accelerator Laboratory in DuPage County. The argument was that combining the new laboratory with the existing accelerator facility would substantially reduce the cost of the project and take advantage of existing expertise.

The state hired a former White House congressional liaison (an Illinois native) as a lobbyist and created a not-for-profit organization, ssc for Illinois, Inc., to coordinate and promote private sector involvement. Governor Thompson worked actively for the super collider, especially with the executive branch in Washington, and lobbied fellow Midwest governors at the 1987 National Governors' Association Conference. (The governor of Wisconsin agreed to become a partner, making the Illinois effort the only multiple-state proposal.)

The effort failed, however, and Texas was awarded the multi-billion-dollar project, only to have to shut it down because of federal budget constraints after miles of tunnels had been dug in the rock. Ironically, the director of Fermilab in Illinois was in charge of closing the Texas project.

DEFENDING AGAINST MANDATES

While trying to get funds for a fair share of new projects, Illinois and other states also fight to stop federal mandate requirements that impose new responsibilities without funds to reimburse the state or local governments. Just as local governments lobby in the state legislature against unfunded mandates, Illinois officials work against national mandates through organizations such as the National Governors' Association and National Conference of State Legislatures. State officials along with local officials even organized a National Unfunded Mandates Day in 1993 to draw the country's attention to the problems caused by mandates in the Clean Water Act, the Clean Air Act, and the Fair Labor Standards Act. Mayor Richard M. Daley of Chicago was a visible participant in the Washington demonstrations, having earlier funded a report that estimated the cost of unfunded mandates to the city at more than $200 million.[18]

Another tendency of concern to state and local governments is the federal preemption of state and local authority. Preemption is accomplished by both the Congress and the federal courts. International trade agreements such as the General Agreement on Tariffs and Trade (GATT) also may overrule state laws. A GATT panel, for instance, ruled that state laws and regulations in fourteen categories in forty states (including Illinois) discriminated against Canadian beer and wine imports.[19]

The struggle with federal preemptions, mandates, and regulations is on-going. To reduce smog-producing emissions by 60 percent by the early twenty-first century, the U.S. Environmental Protection Agency ruled that areas with severe pollution levels should reduce the number of cars on the road through commuter car pooling and other methods of discouraging single-occupant vehicles. Under the threat of losing more than $700 million in federal highway funds, Governor Edgar in 1993 reluctantly signed state legislation to implement the federal Employee Commute Options program. The state continued to fight the federal mandate nonetheless, and the legislature passed a joint resolution demanding that Congress do away with the mandatory trip-reduction program. Ultimately, as a result of both federal and state action, this mandate was rescinded in 1995.

NEIGHBORLY RELATIONS WITH OTHER STATES

Another little-noticed but important activity beyond Illinois borders is the cultivation of relations with other states, particularly those with similar needs or characteristics. Illinois has membership in a wide variety of national and regional organizations ranging from the National Governors' Association to the National Organization of State Lottery Administrators.

Several regional organizations are concerned with the problems of the Midwest and particularly the Great Lakes region. The Council of Great Lakes Governors, for instance, has worked on projects to help the huge midwestern industrial base maintain its position of relative strength while reducing its environmental impacts on the lakes and the air above them. An offshoot, the Great Lakes Protection Fund, is a grant-making organization with a $76 million endowment contributed by seven Great Lakes states including Illinois. The fund spreads money throughout the Great Lakes basin for projects that promote sustainable development in sectors such as farming, forestry, manufacturing, and tourism.

Governor Jim Thompson in 1983–84, then the senior governor in the country, served as chairman of the National Governors' Association. He held many other positions in that organization, as well as serving as a negotiator with presidential staff on President Ronald Reagan's 1982 New Federalism initiative. That effort was intended to decentralize federal programs, passing them to state and local governments, but was never adopted primarily because of lack of consensus among the governors.

In addition to the voluntary organizations, Illinois also is a member of many interstate compacts approved by the Congress. Illinois is now involved in a complicated compact pertaining to low-level nuclear waste disposal. Illinois and Kentucky are the only members of the Central Midwest Compact Commission, and because Illinois is by far the dominant generator of low-level wastes in the two-state area, a disposal site is likely to be located in Illinois. State efforts to locate a disposal site at Martinsville in southeastern Illinois generated a storm of controversy in the early 1990s and eventually proved unsuccessful. Further efforts to locate disposal sites will undoubtedly prove controversial as well.

The newest compact involving Illinois is the Midwestern Higher Education Compact, which Illinois joined in 1991. The compact's purpose is to let member states share equipment, expertise, and funding. The compact would allow university students in a state with no optometry school, for example, to attend a neighboring state's school at in-state tuition costs. Like other such compacts around the country, the purpose is to eliminate duplication and allow more efficient use of resources.

Not all interstate relations are without problems. An example is the competition between different states' economic development agencies for new industry. This has caused considerable tension between states as they try to outbid each other with special inducements. Governor Edgar urged his fellow governors at a National Governors' Conference to stop using special inducements such as tax breaks, which pit one state against another. But in 1994 he competed with Wisconsin for the location of a new three-thousand-employee Motorola cellular phone plant and won the battle when the company chose the town of Harvard, just south of the Wisconsin border.

To Edgar's credit, no big incentives were bargained away to land the Motorola plant, as has often been done in recent years to keep big companies like Sears, Roebuck in Illinois. Similar low-cost victories will become more important in coming years because relatively wealthy Illinois will probably never retrieve a dollar in federal revenues for each dollar state taxpayers send to Washington. But the state's political culture will likely help keep the state's portion from shrinking because voters will tend to elect officials who consider the nation's capital another marketplace in which to scrap for the state's fair share of federal largesse.

CHAPTER TEN

As Schools Struggle, Leaders Respond Slowly

Education is the foundation of the state's future health, preparing both children and adults for the increasingly knowledge-centered demands of the modern workplace. It is also a major state investment, absorbing almost one-fourth of all appropriated state funds, more than any other spending category. Yet Illinois lags behind most other wealthy states in the amount it provides for public education.

The state's modest support of education is rooted in both the politics of regional wealth differences and the individualistic culture of Illinois. Elected officials in the generally wealthier collar counties chafe at appeals that more of their taxpayer dollars be distributed to Chicago and to downstate schools to reduce disparities in per pupil spending. Downstate and Chicago leaders, resistant to further increases in their property taxes (which are often less burdensome than in the collar counties), are envious of the rich educational offerings in the suburbs. And the standoff continues.

The culture of individualism means taking care of your own. In Illinois, the education power structures have done that. The Chicago Teachers Union and its counterpart in the collar counties and downstate, the Illinois Education Association, are proven champions of better benefits, good pay, and protection of seniority. The universities have grown impressively thanks to flush times in the post–World War II decades and a shrewd bargaining approach that awarded each institution a share of the growing education pie. Even some politicians have staked their claims in the rugged terrain of education, rising in the process to expert status through the often indecipherable haze that blankets educational budgets and statutes.

For all this, taking care of your own has not always served the students well. New Trier High School in suburban Winnetka is a great school, as is

Lake Forest High School farther north. Many departments at the University of Illinois are nationally respected. But for every strong player there are weaker brethren. The largest public school system in the state is also one of the worst. Whereas New Trier showers its students with enrichment classes and computers, the East St. Louis schools were in such fiscal disarray in 1994 that their finances were taken over by the state. Lawsuits have been pursued, without success, to strike down the current system of school finance, and elaborate mechanisms have been developed to reform education. Yet the status quo has been protected for the most part by the powerful players who created the situation. Change is coming, albeit slowly, only because of relentless pressure from community and business groups, the public, and elected officials.

This chapter provides an overview of the state's education system and profiles some of the major players, showing how their work, though highly effective in some areas, has been inadequate to resolve fundamental problems. It begins with an overview of the system, then looks at the political tugs-of-war that characterize the state's education community at both the elementary-secondary and higher education levels.

"FOURTH BRANCH" COMPETES FOR DOLLARS

Many educators like to think of education as an independent fourth branch of government, and in many ways it is. In 1941 public university employees were placed in their own civil service system, and job openings have been mostly exempt from political patronage. University and school employees have their own separate retirement systems, and on the organization charts, education is distinctly separated from other state agencies.

Governors and lawmakers traditionally viewed education as a major responsibility, but they did not consider it as important politically as transportation, regulation, criminal justice, and capital spending for a lawmaker's district. Since the 1970s, education has become more important politically because it has been linked to economic development and workforce quality. Also, the post–World War II growth of the twelve public universities and forty-nine public community colleges has made higher education a part of pork barrel politics because a lawmaker seeking reelection can pick up votes by delivering an auditorium or law school to the district. The trend toward full-time service by lawmakers has played a role as well. It increased the amount of time legislators and their staffs could devote to education and encouraged a tendency to keep constituents happy by addressing parochial needs rather than trying to institute comprehensive statewide change.

The Illinois Constitution of 1970 devotes only three short sections to education, but a few clauses are often quoted and debated hotly. "The State shall provide for an efficient system of high quality public educational institutions and services," the constitution says, and the state "has primary responsibility for financing the system of public education."[1] The suggestion has been made, again and again, that the state does not meet these two constitutional mandates.

If politics is defined as who gets what, why, and how, then education is of course political. Every year, schools and universities, including private ones, compete with other government programs and among themselves for scarce state dollars. There is even continuing, if usually civil, competition among the boards for higher education and those for kindergarten through twelfth grade (though generally the "little kids" get about two dollars for every state dollar allocated to the "big kids"). In 1992 about $19 billion was spent on education in Illinois by government, the business sector, private schools, and universities.[2] Nevertheless, relative to the other forty-nine states, Illinois displayed less than average financial effort to support its schools, both in per pupil expenditures for public schools and for higher education (see table 7). On a per capita basis, Illinois in 1991 ranked forty-first among the states in support for elementary and secondary education and forty-eighth on a per $1,000 income basis.[3]

Public school enrollment declined from a high of 2.37 million pupils in 1972 and stood at 1.93 million in 1994;[4] only one in four households has a child enrolled in the public schools. Minorities represented 34.4 percent of public school students in 1990–91, up from 28.8 percent a decade earlier and expected to reach 40 percent by the year 2000. Nearly three of every ten public school students came from low-income families in 1991, and this figure too is projected to top 40 percent by the end of the decade.

Many families do not use the public system. Private schools play a larger role in Illinois than in the nation, enrolling 14 percent of all elementary-secondary students in 1994 compared with an estimated 10 to 13 percent nationwide. The private sector is especially large in Chicago, where 22 percent of students are enrolled in nearly 430 private schools. About half the schools are Roman Catholic, 13 percent are Lutheran, and the remainder include Protestant denominations, Jewish, Greek Orthodox, Islamic/Moslem, Montessori, and other affiliations.

Table 7: Expenditures for Education in Selected States

Rank	State	Amount
School District Expenditures for Elementary and Secondary Education Schools, per pupil, 1993–94		
1	New Jersey	$10,112
2	Alaska	9,811
3	New York	8,899
	U.S. Average	*5,730*
23	Illinois	5,520
48	Arkansas	3,949
49	Mississippi	3,512
50	Utah	3,419

Rank	State	Amount
Expenditures for Higher Education, per Pupil, 1992		
1	Alaska	$ 9,872
2	Hawaii	7,458
3	Wyoming	5,574
	U.S. Average	*4,041*
38	Illinois	3,483
48	Massachusetts	2,503
49	Vermont	2,081
50	New Hampshire	1,720

Source: States in Profile (McConnellsburg PA: U.S. Data on Demand, Inc., and State Policy Research, Inc., 1995).

As in public schools, private school enrollments have declined, from 480,000 in 1969 to 317,500 in 1994. Rising costs forced the nation's largest Catholic archdiocese to close fifty schools in Chicago between 1977 and 1988.[5] The 239 remaining schools enrolled about 99,000 students in 1990, when the archdiocese announced the closing of eighteen additional schools.

Illinois public schools are organized into a tangle of central, intermediate, and local administrative units. The governor appoints the seventeen-member Illinois State Board of Education (ISBE) from the state's five appellate court districts; the ISBE in turn appoints a state superintendent of education who oversees a staff of 935 in Springfield, Chicago, Mt. Vernon, and regional offices throughout the state.

In 1942 there were 12,000 elementary school districts in Illinois, mostly with one one-room schoolhouse per district.[6] Some counties had more

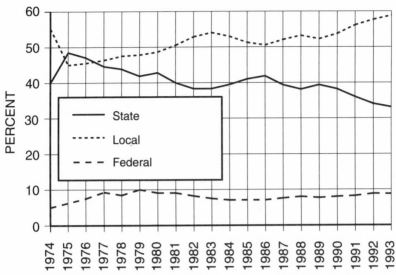

Figure 4. Percent of School Funding from Each Source, 1974–93

Source: Illinois State Board of Education, March 1994. (State and federal fiscal years may not coincide directly with school years and local tax years)

school board members than teachers. Increased state aid and persistent efforts by groups including the Illinois Farm Bureau cut the number of districts in half by 1948. Consolidation continued in the 1950s with the total falling to 2,000 districts, and further decline reduced the number to 922 by 1993, which is still far more districts than in most states.

AGAINST TIDE, STATE REDUCES SHARE OF AID

A total of $10.35 billion was spent in 1993 on public schools in Illinois.[7] Property taxes and other local sources provided 58 percent; state government contributed 33.6 percent, and 8.3 percent came from the federal government. As figure 4 illustrates, the state share of support has been declining since 1975–76. This is the opposite of the trend nationally.

Paradoxically, as the local financial burden increased, control over policymaking and administration shifted in the other direction to the state and federal governments. The trend began in the late 1930s, when the legislature gave the state superintendent power to determine the standards for recognition of elementary schools.[8] The erosion accelerated in the past two decades because of increased policy activism by the federal and state governments and an intensified focus on state legislative action by the powerful teachers' unions. On behalf of both federal and state agencies, the ISBE staff has generated new rules, guidelines, and reporting requirements that increased state influence. By one superintendent's count, school administrators are required to file forty reports annually with the ISBE.

Also limiting the power of local school boards and administrators are the teachers' unions. A statewide collective bargaining law, seniority protection for nonteaching as well as teaching personnel, and union dominance of the teacher certification process all tend to limit local flexibility.

Finally, there are scores of mandates in the six-hundred-page Illinois School Code that tell what must be taught and how schools must be run. Instruction must be provided in patriotism, honesty, and kindness, consumer education, the Holocaust, prevention of steroid abuse, and the avoidance of abduction.[9] The state mandates that driver training be made available to public and nearby nonpublic students and that precisely "thirty clock-hours of classroom instruction and six clock-hours of behind the wheel instruction" be provided, including instruction on how the Litter Control Act pertains to auto use.[10] Legislative efforts to remove instructional mandates, such as the requirement for four years of physical education in high school, are quickly buried as the unions rally teachers to the cause. Even efforts to reform education tend to create new mandates; the 1985 requirement for "learning assessments" and school improvement plans created lengthy exercises in paperwork that may or may not translate into better schools.

Federal policymakers play a larger role in local education than is represented by the small federal share of school funding, as illustrated by Public Law 94–142, the Education of All Handicapped Act, enacted in 1976. In return for federal grants that amount to a fraction of the cost of the act, state and local education agencies are required to meet highly detailed federal standards such as mainstreaming of handicapped children into regular classrooms and creation of detailed individual education plans for each child with a disability. In 1990 Illinois received $64 million in federal funds to implement Public Law 94–142; the state's share for the same programs was $354 million.[11]

Increased external control has diminished the role and effectiveness of local school management. Referring to the 1985 Illinois reforms, education professor Fred Coombs said at the time, "The reforms sharply reduced local discretion, so that citizens' sense of owning their own schools is most likely gone, even though polls show that they strongly approve of that control."[12] A rural school board member lamented, "The only thing that we control anymore is our school district boundary lines, and the state keeps trying to take away that authority as well."[13]

By 1995, however, the tide appeared to be turning back toward increased local school authority. That year the General Assembly enacted Governor Edgar's recommendation that authorized school districts to request waivers from most state mandates.

AN EXCUSE FOR INACTION

Just as the states have been willing accomplices to the increased role of the federal government in setting policy, local boards and administrators have often found it comfortable to quote state statutes and rules as justification for taking—or not taking—action. School boards and administrators have been known to cite the difficult procedures for dismissing a tenured teacher as a rationale for not firing an underperforming employee. Administrators have complained that their hands are tied by state statutes and court decisions on everything from smoking on school grounds to length of haircuts and appropriate attire.

Despite these complaints, the strongest state government sanction against local schools has never been used—that of non-recognition of a school. In 1990, however, in collaboration with and under pressure from business leaders, the ISBE overhauled the school recognition statutes, shifting from a long-standing focus on school processes and "bean counting" to school performance and student outcomes. The new concept was intended to increase state monitoring of and involvement with school districts that are in financial difficulty or performing poorly. It empowered the state to decertify poorly performing school districts and to reassign the pupils to other schools. The consequences would appear to be greater state involvement in troubled schools—as when the state took over the finances of the East St. Louis system—and possibly less oversight of schools that are performing well.[14]

FORCES THAT SHAPE POLICY

Education policymaking is embedded in a larger social system. Frederick Wirt and Samuel Gove suggest that the modest investment in education in Illinois is a reflection of a statewide political culture that accords less trust and responsibility to government than in many other states.[15] In Illinois, fundamental change in education policy tends to be initiated outside the state and local education community.

National leaders and the media have often been catalysts for change. Test scores had been declining for a decade before the alarms sounded in *A Nation at Risk,* published by the U.S. Department of Education in 1983, and a spate of other national reports that decried deteriorating educational performance. Yet it took those reports, combined with massive and sustained attention by the national media, to spur the governor and legislators in Illinois to address education reform, even though state officials had been aware of the problems for years.

In the 1980s, business leaders across the country, including those in Illinois, became deeply involved in school improvement. Corporate chief executives have more potential to cause fundamental change in education than any other groups, including school leaders and elected officials. When aroused, they can raise the necessary funds and organize to generate pressure for change, as they did in the case of Chicago school reform in the late 1980s. Typically, however, the public schools community in Illinois has been insular and detached from the business and political elites of the state. State superintendents and ISBE board members have not generally been professional intimates of CEOs and governors. Thus business pressure for reform came late to Illinois and its effects have been less pronounced than elsewhere.

The education community in Illinois tends also to be inherently cautious, protective, and resistant to change in part because statewide associations of teachers, administrators, and school board members encompass the state's regional differences. Each region—indeed, each school district—is affected differently by changes in the school aid formula, making it difficult to forge statewide consensus on change.

The issue of choice in school attendance illustrates the resistance to change. Although there is a serious scholarly debate over the merits and shortcomings of choice, a 1989 Gallup survey found that the public favored choice by a proportion of two to one.[16] The ISBE spent 1988–89 developing a statewide policy on choice, but it was not much of a policy; it recommended that any choice in Illinois be limited to choice within a school district, which limits the concept dramatically.[17] The recommendation produced no significant change, but it served its purpose by allaying the fears of teachers' unions and the associations of administrators and school board members. The issue surfaced again in 1994, when Governor Jim Edgar proposed creating fifteen public charter schools that would be exempt from most state regulations. This modest proposal was defeated in the legislature by the teachers' unions, but forty-five charter schools were authorized the following year when Republicans gained control of the legislature for the first time in more than two decades and the influence of teachers' unions was trimmed.

UNIONS SHOW THEIR MUSCLE

The strength of the unions in a state with strong union traditions should not come as a surprise, but it was not always so. Up to the 1970s, Illinois education policy tended to be shaped by small groups of education elites and legislators.[18] Teacher organizations were passive. Governors were not much involved, except in setting overall budget limits, nor was the federal government active. Most funding came from the local taxes. Those days are over. Today the state and national governments have greater funding at risk, and the U.S. Congress and the Illinois legislature have large and active education staffs. Governors now see education as central to economic prosperity. Most important, the teachers' unions have become assertive and highly protective of their gains.

The Illinois Education Association is a teachers' union with eighty-one thousand members in suburban and downstate school districts, dominating the politics of education outside of Chicago. The other major union is the Illinois Federation of Teachers (IFT), with seventy thousand members in Chicago and several downstate cities, including Champaign and East St. Louis.

Beginning in the late 1960s, the IEA transformed itself from an apolitical, milquetoast group of teachers and administrators into a political powerhouse that can strike terror into a lawmaker. Ken Bruce served as director of government relations for the IEA for more than two decades, until 1993. "When I started, we would not take a stand on any—not any—piece of legislation," recalls Bruce. "In 1989, we tracked seven hundred bills, and not just education bills, but bills on pension issues and school bonding and other matters, and we took positions on most of those bills."[19]

The IEA contributes to favored candidates, sends staff professionals to help manage campaigns, and organizes teachers to get involved in local races. The IEA endorsed Governor James R. Thompson early in his first campaign in 1976 and contributed $80,000, more money than any other group that year. IEA teachers were active in each of Thompson's four successful campaigns. Not surprisingly, Thompson's first assistant for education reported that he consulted with the IEA on education issues as a matter of standard operating procedure.[20] The IEA received gubernatorial appointments of its friends to the ISBE, the teachers certification board, and the Illinois Educational Labor Relations Board, which oversees collective bargaining. The IEA became involved in judicial contests as well, endorsing and providing contributions to candidates for the appellate and supreme courts. It makes sense to see friends of the IEA succeed to the state's high courts, notes Bruce, because many issues of importance to teachers are resolved by lawsuits.

The IEA has had more influence than other education interests because the union has invested heavily in Illinois elections. During 1991–92, the IEA political action committee (IPACE) spent $1,426,000 in political and campaign activity.[21] In contrast, the IFT made the second largest expenditures among education interests, at $81,000.

In 1992 primaries, the IEA contributed an average of $1,275 to 87 candidates, and one candidate received $17,100. In that year's general elections, the union contributed $3,575 on average to 139 candidates; one received $36,600. Nonmonetary contributions were made as well, typically by local affiliates for rallies and other campaign activities. Bruce points out that these efforts can be valuable. Attracting eight hundred teachers to a rally generates media coverage, increases enthusiasm among teachers to go out and do telephoning and other campaign work, and increases credibility for the candidate, spurring support and contributions from elsewhere.

The IEA has long linked contribution decisions to legislative performance, according to analyst Kent D. Redfield.[22] Even legislators who are confident they could beat an election challenge from the IEA would just as soon avoid the increased time, effort, and money needed to do so. So whenever a legislator can give the IEA a vote in committee or on the floor, he or she generally tries to do so. As a result, the IEA has dominated education action in the house and senate. Its four full-time lobbyists meet with committee members before every hearing, testify in committee, and organize teachers and specialists to provide testimony. Several observers of the legislative process say they have watched IEA lobbyists give "thumbs up" and "thumbs down" signals from the committee hearing room audience and house and senate galleries as cues to legislators about to cast votes. The IEA has even provided written colloquies for legislators to read into the record on the house or senate floor, thus establishing a record of legislative intent for use later when the resulting statute is being interpreted by lawyers and judges in court cases.

On the two hundred or more bills introduced each session that are specifically on school matters, the IEA generally—but not always—gets what it wants. The IEA beats back with apparent ease efforts to reduce instructional mandates. The union has progressively restricted the authority of local boards. In 1987, for instance, it was successful in extending seniority protection to all nonteaching personnel, including bus drivers, food service workers, aides, and secretaries.

There are, nonetheless, limits to the union's power. On the one issue that all seem to agree is the most important facing the education community—finance—the IEA has had little effect. Throughout the 1980s, state spending per pupil declined when adjusted for inflation, and the share of state general revenue funds going to elementary-secondary education declined as well. The IEA's lack of aggressiveness may be the result of its internal dominance by teachers from the collar counties, where schools generally have strong property tax bases and thus need relatively little state funding. The IEA also has shown more influence over narrow education issues than on broader questions such as school funding, which involves taxes and thus transcends the education arena.

MANAGEMENT FIGHTS BACK

School management interests have had much less influence than the IEA, in part because of the fragmentation created by regional differences—primarily differences in wealth—across the 922 school districts. The Illinois Association of School Boards (IASB) and Illinois Association of School Administrators (IASA) find it difficult to represent all their members satisfactorily on contentious issues such as funding and school consolidation. Thus many sub-state organizations have been created to represent categories of interests. These include the Large Unit District Association (LUDA); Education Research and Development (ED-RED), an organization of 135 north suburban school districts; South Cook Public Education (SCOPE), 35 districts in south Cook County; Local Education Network of DuPage (LEND), an affiliate of the IASB for DuPage County; LO-CON, for local control of schools, which represents smaller downstate and suburban elementary and high school districts that oppose consolidation; and FAIRCOM, an organization of school districts that have utility power plants in their boundaries and thus great property wealth coveted by other districts.

School management groups appear to have more potential than they have realized. Each district elects seven board members so more than six thousand individuals could be rallied around issues. But this has not happened, perhaps because the board members serve as volunteers and thus lack the vested interests that spur teachers to action. In addition, the school board members often devote long hours to their local schools, leaving little time or energy for state lobbying.

In years past, the IASB staff nonetheless presented well-developed testimony in legislative committees and in other communications with lawmakers. The legislators and their staff listened respectfully and sometimes acted on the basis of a case well made. But because the group had not produced votes at the polling place, lawmakers did not fret much when they cast a vote against the IASB or the IASA.

In 1994 school management groups began to play political hardball. They forged the Illinois School Management Alliance, a single lobby representing the statewide organizations of board members, administrators, principals, and school business officials. They developed unified positions on bills, coordinated their lobbying efforts, and created a political action committee to raise money for contributions to legislative candidates. Early in the 1994 election campaign, they endorsed Governor Edgar's re-election bid. This endorsement was unprecedented and was doubly appreciated by Edgar, who had just lost the endorsement of his previous ally, the IEA.

During the campaign, volunteers for the alliance walked precincts for Edgar and fourteen legislative candidates who were locked in contests with IEA-backed opponents. Thirteen of the fourteen and Governor Edgar won their races. Clearly the statewide school management groups had learned the lesson that if they wanted a seat at the table where education policy was shaped, they had to get into the trenches of electoral politics.

Several other players sometimes influence legislators. The Catholic church has worked effectively to extend transportation, driver training, textbook, and other services to nonpublic schools. Small school districts are another force. In 1985, when legislation was introduced that would have required the smallest districts to consolidate, a group called Save Our Schools was organized literally overnight. SOS joined with LO-CON to fill the Capitol with emotional adults and children opposed to the plan. Legislators and the governor quickly backed off.

FINANCE IS TOUGHEST CHALLENGE

The most intransigent education issue in Illinois is that of finance. State support for local schools is provided through a general state aid (GSA) formula and via categorical grants for specific programs in special education, transportation, vocational education, preschool, reading, and others. Three-fifths of total state dollars for education are allocated as GSA through a complex formula that mystifies most policymakers. In principle, the formula aims to reduce disparities in per pupil expenditures between property-wealthy and property-poor districts. The formula allocation is based primarily on a district's property valuation, the number of pupils, and the proportion of pupils who come from low-income families.

The collar counties pay more of local school funding from local property taxes than do the other two primary regions of Illinois.[23] The GSA directs more money toward Chicago and downstate Illinois districts to reduce spending disparities, but the formula falls far short of equalizing financial resources for all children. As of 1994, the formula "guaranteed" that each district would have no less than $2,741 per pupil in total state and local general operating expenditures, exclusive of spending for categorical programs. This is less than one-third the amount spent by many districts with high property wealth. Those with shopping centers, nuclear power plants, or luxury housing in their bounds were able to spend $9,000 and more per pupil, even though they received very little from the GSA formula.

The formula is a political instrument. Seemingly minor tinkering can create winners and losers. In the early 1970s, there was a battle between the teachers' unions over whether the formula should count pupils on the basis of average daily attendance or daily enrollment. The Illinois Education Association favored attendance, while the Illinois Federation of Teachers and the Chicago Teachers Union favored enrollment. The reason was simple: suburban and downstate schools tend to have higher daily attendance rates than do Chicago's public schools. Similarly, because wealthy school districts receive little formula aid, they prefer to see increases in funding for categorical programs, where funds are generally allocated on a per pupil rather than a wealth basis.

GEOGRAPHY LEADS TO INEQUITIES

The principal reason for the inequities is that Illinois relies more heavily on the local property tax to fund schools than do most states. This system would work acceptably if property wealth were spread somewhat evenly across the state, but it is not. Because of economic change, rural school districts lost much of their assessed valuation in the 1980s, while property valuations were increasing rapidly in the suburban collar around Chicago.

The resulting variance in spending per pupil can be dramatic. In 1992–93, per pupil spending ranged from $2,470 for the Aviston School District in downstate Clinton County to $13,877 at Lake Forest High School in Lake County.[24] Speaking at a meeting of poor school districts, University of Illinois education professor James Ward declared, "If you folks spent a couple of days in a top flight school in DuPage or Lake counties and saw what they had that you don't, there would be a revolution."[25]

There are inequities in suburban areas as well. Both the Salt Creek and Queen Bee school districts are in DuPage County. The huge Oak Brook shopping center is located in the Salt Creek district. Queen Bee has no such sugar plum, so even though it taxes property at almost three times the Salt Creek rate, in 1991–92 the Queen Bee district could spend only $4,671 per student while Salt Creek spent $7,603.

No revolution occurred during the 1980s when the per pupil spending gap was widening, for two basic reasons. First, the fragmented education community could not agree on a course of action. Second, huge infusions of state funding for local schools would have been required to reduce the variance unless local funding were taken away from wealthier school districts, which was politically unacceptable. State lawmakers have appeared paralyzed by the magnitude of the action needed to reduce the variance—a shift in primary reliance for funding schools from the local property tax to state sources such as the income tax, which would require a major statewide tax increase.

Efforts have been mounted to reverse the inequities, but none has been successful. The legislature in 1985 tried to institute a no-pain approach by passing a law that all profits from the Illinois lottery would go to education. The law turned out to be the equivalent of a shell game: the lottery profits replaced general revenue funds rather than supplementing them. No additional money was generated.

Poor school districts organized in 1990 to mount a legal challenge to the school funding system. Thirty-six downstate, generally poor school districts, joined by the Chicago Board of Education, organized the Committee for Educational Rights. They filed suit against the state of Illinois, alleging that the per pupil expenditure variances violated the Illinois Constitution's mandate for "an efficient system of high quality public educational institutions and services." The suit was rejected at the circuit court level in 1992, and when the school districts appealed, the group was rebuffed again in a 1994 appellate court decision.

Another approach was tried in 1992, when the legislature put to referendum a constitutional amendment that would have assigned the state "preponderant responsibility," as opposed to the current "primary" responsibility, for financing local schools. Opponents led by the Illinois Manufacturers Association and the Illinois State Chamber of Commerce targeted the collar counties and declared that adoption would require a doubling of the individual and corporate income taxes. The proposal garnered strong support in Chicago and downstate because those areas include the underfunded districts, but only 46 percent of voters in the collar counties were in favor of the change. Statewide the amendment received 57 percent of those voting, shy of the 60 percent required to ratify an amendment.

THE EXPERIMENT IN CHICAGO

As in the rest of the state, change came slowly to the Chicago public school system even though its problems were evident to any who cared to look. But after years of teacher strikes, crumbling buildings, and declining performance, a major reform effort was mounted in the late 1980s.

The Chicago system is the third largest in the United States, with four hundred thousand pupils in 540 schools. Many of the city's white residents and those with the means to afford private schools have fled the system, so by 1993 its student body was 56 percent African American, 30 percent Hispanic, 12 percent white, and 3 percent Asian and others. Nearly half the pupils lived in poverty, the majority of this half without fathers at home.

Traditionally Chicago Democratic political leaders have declared this huge system and its forty-two thousand employees to be out of bounds for education policymakers. The schools have been the province of local politicians, the Chicago Teachers Union, other AFL-CIO unions that represent nonteacher employees, and the central bureaucracy of the Chicago Board of Education.

In 1988, state policymakers were forced to deal with the Chicago public schools in response to intense local and national pressure and to an energized—and anxious—business community.[26] In a scathing multipart series on the schools, the *Chicago Tribune* declared: "Chicago public schools are hardly more than daytime warehouses for inferior students, taught by disillusioned and inadequate teachers, presided over by a bloated bureaucracy, and constantly undercut by a selfish, single-minded teachers union."[27] U.S. secretary of education William Bennett spread the stain nationally by repeatedly calling Chicago's schools the "worst in the nation."

There was reason for concern. Thirty-five of the sixty-five Chicago high schools ranked in the bottom 1 percent of all high schools in the United States in achievement test scores. Fewer than half who entered high school graduated; in several schools only 10 percent made it. In 1984 the system graduated only ninety-five hundred African American and Hispanic young people out of twenty-five thousand originally enrolled as ninth graders. Only two thousand of those who did graduate could read at or above twelfth grade level.

Until then few Illinois leaders and elected officials cared about the Chicago public schools. Their children for the most part did not attend them; only one of Chicago's eighteen state senators had a child enrolled in a Chicago public school in 1988. The segregated ghettoes in which the worst schools are located were outside the field of vision of most Illinois business and political leaders.

Money was not the most obvious problem. The Chicago Board of Education spent more money per pupil than the average school in Illinois (about $6,031 in 1991–92 compared to a statewide average of $5,327), but it was getting no results. The system's bureaucracy was partly to blame—a great deal of waste was suspected at the central office—but the fundamental problem was a feeling of defeatism. Many of the schools were embedded in the social pathologies of the areas they served—poverty of money and spirit and an absence of family, parenting skills, and good role models. Children with signs of potential were often "creamed off" to private or public magnet schools, and in the city's worst neighborhoods, many stronger families moved out when they were financially able to do so.

The bureaucracy and teachers responded exactly as organizational theorists would have predicted. Because problems seemed beyond fixing, the teachers and staff often displaced the goal of good performance with the pragmatic objective of protecting themselves with good pay and the privileges of seniority. The catalyst for almost every negotiation over these matters was a strike, one every other year, on average, for two decades.

By 1987, when the walkout extended to nineteen days, Chicago parents and the business community had had enough. In addition to the embarrassing national attention, businesses were having increasing difficulty finding qualified entry-level employees. In a major effort to generate school reform, chief executive officers of leading companies joined forces with education activists and school reform groups such as the Chicago Panel on Public School Policy and Finance. They soon made history.

It was a remarkable period of civic involvement in Chicago as community interests gained strength and found common ground with the business leaders. After Mayor Harold Washington convened an education "summit" in the fall of 1987, bank presidents and corporate executives sat down to hash out a plan with community activists, young mothers, and university professors. More than half a dozen groups and coalitions developed various reform structures, most of them similar in their emphasis on shifting power from the central bureaucracy to school-based councils. In the spring of 1988, the reformers went to Springfield. Mary O'Connell, a journalist and mother of two students in the system, documented the process in *School Reform Chicago Style*:

> [The legislative campaign] featured continual assault waves of reformers, parents and community members, business leaders, and other "interested par-

ties" descending on Springfield. They didn't just come on one designated day; they came day after day, week after week throughout June, forming what one experienced legislative observer calls "a consistent vigil" for school reform. UNO [United Neighborhood Organization] organized "five to ten" busloads of people; the People's Coalition sent six busloads. . . . The Campaign for School Reform . . . organized car pools and four busloads of people. The PTA estimates it sent "300 to 400" people. . . . At the same time, the business leaders organized by Chicago United came down by corporate jet and met with every legislator who would see them.[28]

The constant pressure by so many parties triggered an unprecedented collaborative process to hammer out reform legislation. In Speaker of the house Michael Madigan's office, Representative John Cullerton and an ad hoc committee consisting of Senator Arthur Berman and Representative Anthony Young led a series of meetings that spanned, as Cullerton remembers it, "sixty hours, the last two weeks of the session, twelve hours a day."[29] In the room were parents, business leaders, union leaders, principals, and representatives of reform groups and community organizations.

The product of these efforts was the Chicago School Reform Act of 1988, whose reforms were called revolutionary for their scale and the level of control given to parents and local communities. The act mandated a 25 percent cut in the central school bureaucracy and set elections to establish 540 decentralized local school councils.[30] These councils, each consisting of six parents, two community members, two teachers, and the principal, were charged with hiring the principal, approving the school budget, and creating a school improvement plan. Corporations encouraged their employees to run for the councils and provided training for the candidates. In the October 1989 elections, there were 17,000 candidates for the 5,400 council positions and 312,000 voters; Senator Berman called it "the most democratic election in the history of this country."[31]

The first dose of reality for the new councils came from the building engineers' union. The engineers, not the principals, controlled the school buildings. The councils were told that under union rules no one could use a school in the evening unless a building engineer was present—at a cost of $162 a night in overtime pay. The central board of education had little money for such payments. Incredibly, therefore, some school councils were forced to hold meetings outside their schools. This glitch was overcome, and in a few months the councils were meeting inside their school buildings.

There were other frustrations for the councils as they jousted with statutes, rules, and central office officials to carve out some authority over their schools. But as education writer John Camper noted, reform was not to be discouraged easily: "In the struggle between the amateurs on the local councils and the 'experts' on Pershing Road [central school system headquarters], most of the public is likely to sympathize with the amateurs."[32]

By 1994, five years into reform, no clear verdict had been rendered on the process. Anecdotal information and several surveys by reform organizations showed that many schools had gained ground through addition of new programs, intensive teacher training, and more flexible use of some school funding. A 1993 report concluded that school reform had brought "strong democratic participation . . . focused on a systematic approach to whole school improvement"[33] in one-third of the schools, with another third showing some of the same characteristics. But test scores showed only marginal or no improvements in many schools, and the Board of Education faced a potential deficit of $300 million going into the 1995–96 school year.

Out of exasperation with the continuing problems in the Chicago public school system, in 1995 the suburban-dominated Republican legislature and Governor Edgar enacted a sweeping reorganization of the system. The legislation gave the Chicago mayor power to appoint a five-person board and chief executive officer, prohibited Chicago teachers from striking, and provided local budgetary and regulatory flexibility. In other words, it's your problem, Mr. Mayor; you fix it. With lightning speed—and to everyone's amazement—Mayor Daley and his appointed team balanced the budget, negotiated a multiyear contract with teachers before school opened, and infused the system with newfound enthusiasm and hope. Ironically, because of political fiefdoms in Chicago, these changes could have been imposed only by outsiders, that is, the suburban Republican legislative leadership and a Republican governor from downstate.

FAIR SHARES FOR HIGHER EDUCATION

While the state's political culture helped hold back improvements at the elementary and secondary level, it contributed to the rapid expansion of Illinois's system of colleges and universities in the decades of economic growth after World War II. "While the schools are in some difficulty," observes Harold Hodgkinson, a leading student of education demographics, "there is no doubt that Illinois has, over the years, built a major system of higher education, diverse and of high quality, including both public and private institutions."[34]

More than 740,000 students were enrolled in 1993 in 12 public universities, 40 community college campuses, and more than 125 private colleges and universities.[35] Almost half the total were enrolled in the two-year community college system, two-thirds of them attending part-time. The public and private four-year institutions roughly divided up the other half of enrollment. In full-time equivalent enrollments, each of the three sectors—public universities, private colleges and universities, and community colleges—enrolled roughly one-third of the total.

The dramatic growth of the community college system in the past generation is but one element of rapid change in higher education in Illinois. The age of the student body is another. In the community colleges, more than half of all students are twenty-five or older, and almost 30 percent are over age thirty-four. There has also been a major shift in enrollment toward public institutions. In 1947, before expansion of the public system, two-thirds of Illinois students attended private institutions. By 1992, they were just 29 percent of the total.

Politics has played a part in the development of higher education in Illinois since 1863, when the Illinois General Assembly accepted 480,000 acres of land from the federal government through the Morrill Land Grant Act for the establishment of programs of higher learning.[36] Presidents of the sectarian colleges immediately lobbied to seek division of the proceeds among a select number of private institutions. This approach was resisted by legislators, however, and the communities of Lincoln, Bloomington, Kankakee, Jacksonville, and Urbana entered into competition as prospective sites for the new institution, each city bidding for the prize. Urbana's $285,000 was a low bid, but through political manipulation, it garnered the campus, which would become the University of Illinois.

From 1867 until World War II, the University of Illinois was the sole state university. There were five teacher education "normal" schools that struggled with whatever appropriations were left after the university had been funded. After World War II, public higher education in Illinois blossomed into five multi-campus systems coordinated at the top by a statewide Illinois Board of Higher Education (IBHE).

Since the great European universities were established in the Middle Ages, higher education has, above all else, valued autonomy, or at least relative independence, from the outside world. This status has become increasingly difficult to sustain in recent decades as state lawmakers have more actively demanded accountability for their appropriations. In 1961 the legislature created the Illinois Board of Higher Education to provide comprehensive planning and to reduce what had become blatant political logrolling by the legislative patrons of the two dominant universities, the University of Illinois and Southern Illinois University. Conceived to be independent of both elected officials and higher education institutions, the IBHE quickly came to be seen as a fair and relatively impartial advocate for higher education.

Executive directors of the IBHE sought unity among the five higher education systems in support of its budgetary recommendations to the governor and legislature. They maintained a strategy of recommending annual budget growth, which was relatively balanced among the public systems as well as the private college sector. That is, if the governor's annual budget proposed a 4 percent increase for higher education, the IBHE staff would allocate increases of around 4 percent to each of the five systems as well as the private college sector. (Private colleges and universities have consistently received about 8 percent of state spending for higher education, primarily through tuition assistance and direct state grants based on the number of Illinois residents enrolled.) Under this approach, although no system gets everything it wants, all systems—certainly the less prestigious ones—are better off than they would be with a return to raw political bargaining.

Through the 1960s, the fair share system worked rather well. Public enthusiasm for higher education was strong and money was plentiful; the universities' program and budget recommendations were usually accepted by the IBHE, and in turn by the governor and legislature, with little change.

When revenues for higher education tightened during the 1980s, cracks appeared in the wall of solidarity. Northern Illinois University went directly to the legislature to request a new law school. Over the strong objections of the IBHE and expressions of concern from the other systems, the legislature and governor agreed to establish the new school. In a similar move, University of Illinois president Stanley Ikenberry negotiated directly with Governor Thompson on establishment of new research facilities. These projects required funding that was outside the capital construction priorities established by the IBHE; nevertheless, the university received the governor's blessing and garnered the funding.

In 1995 the community college sector successfully advocated legislation that would take their system out from under the umbrella of the IBHE, but Governor Edgar vetoed the legislation at the urging of IBHE leadership. The IBHE has been put in an uncomfortable position. Its executive director holds a position that lacks the visibility and institutional prestige that comes with presiding over a flagship public university system, and the organization has no built-in constituency of faculty and alumni. As IBHE executive director

Richard Wagner has commented, "I'm a general without an army, and that makes leadership difficult, to say the least."[37]

FACING STAGNATION. NEW MARKETS

When enrollment demand is strong, growth comes easily and all can benefit, as happened in Illinois between 1951 and 1967, when total college enrollment grew from 127,000 to 344,000 students.[38] During the 1980s, full-time-equivalent enrollments were basically flat for public universities, community colleges, and private colleges, and state appropriations grew at less than the rate of inflation. This combination created understandable concern within all of higher education and forced private colleges and public universities to seek additional markets to ensure stability or growth.

Lawmakers representing NIU pushed legislation that would create an independent board for NIU and free it from the perceived constraints imposed by the regents system. Albert Somit, retired president of the Southern Illinois University (SIU) system, proposed compressing the present five systems into two, with SIU to become a part of the University of Illinois system. The IBHE has vigorously opposed such changes, defending the "system of systems" as working well for Illinois. But in 1992, Governor Edgar proposed the abolition of the boards of regents and governors and the creation of separate appointed boards for each of their universities. (This would include Eastern Illinois University, the governor's alma mater, which Edgar felt suffered within the constraints of the Board of Governors system.) The legislature adopted the proposal in 1995, also merging Sangamon State University in Springfield with the University of Illinois.

The old system had been slow to respond to rapid growth in the largest, richest, and best-educated region in Illinois. Other than Governors State University in the south suburbs, there is no major public university campus in the collar counties. With bureaucratic and political hurdles slowing public expansion into the student-rich collar, the private universities rushed ahead of their competitors into the new market. In the 1990s, Roosevelt University and Illinois Institute of Technology (IIT) both headquartered in Chicago, opened suburban campuses. Northern Illinois University, located in DeKalb at the far western metropolitan fringe, sought IBHE approval to open a satellite campus in Hoffman Estates, on the grounds of the new Sears corporate headquarters. This move was opposed, unsuccessfully, by the private college federation, on the ground that its member institutions could fill the need without constructing expensive new public facilities.

In 1990, the IBHE recommended an appropriation of $27 million to construct a University of Illinois–DuPage County Center that would offer courses primarily at the graduate level and in high technology. IIT saw this as unnecessary duplication of its own $15 million campus in the county, then under construction. IIT hired a lobbyist and, joined by the private college federation, mounted opposition to the appropriation. State senator Patrick Welch (D-Peru), whose district included NIU in DeKalb, killed the plan by amending the appropriation out of the bill.

Similar conflicts are being waged elsewhere. After two decades of on-and-off agitation, legislators in Rockford in 1989 won an appropriation of $500,000 to establish a branch of NIU in their city. This was achieved with the encouragement of NIU but over the objections of the Federation of Independent Illinois Colleges and Universities, which counts Rockford College among its members.

In 1990, Sangamon State University (now the University of Illinois-Springfield) sought to expand its offerings in Peoria. Bradley, a private university in Peoria, countered by proposing degree-completion courses for part-time students at public university tuition rates subsidized by the state and by Bradley. The IBHE staff approved the experiment, and, over the objections of the four board members who represented the public university systems, the IBHE board gave it the go-ahead.

The increasing competition between the public and private institutions comes as the two sides become more like each other. Corporate grants to public universities have been growing so that by 1989 public and private institutions received roughly equal shares of corporate donations.[39] Public institutions have become more aggressive in generating support from alumni, as the private colleges have done since their origins. This makes up somewhat for the recent decline of state funding, which dropped from 49 percent of total 1979 revenues at the University of Illinois to 39 percent in 1989.

Tuition charges have been outpacing inflation at both public and private institutions since the 1980s, striking fear in the hearts of parents and students alike. For competitive reasons, the public universities fight to keep their tuition low. The private colleges counter by seeking increased state financial assistance for their students. When admissions officers at the private Knox College in Galesburg find that students are considering both Knox and the University of Illinois at Urbana, they build packages of federal, state, and Knox financial assistance to bring costs for Knox prospects close to those for students at the state school.

The struggle for funding between the public and private sectors has been civil but intense. In the 1980s, the private sector received total state revenues (primarily in financial aid to students) of about 8 percent of general revenue appropriations for all of higher education. In an effort to increase that amount in 1989, the Federation of Independent Illinois Colleges and Universities convinced a legislator to introduce a bill that would require the IBHE to fund the monetary award program of the Illinois Student Assistance Commission. This program helps needy students pay tuition at either private or public institutions, but it does not meet all the financial needs of its applicants. To do so in 1990 would have required about $90 million in additional state funding.

The bill was opposed vigorously behind the scenes by IBHE, which tried without success to get the federation to withdraw the proposal. IBHE staff did not fear the bill would pass, only that the effort represented a serious breach in the agreement among sectors to support the fair-share allocation approach. Indeed, the bill generated open conflict between the public and private sectors, and though ultimately defeated easily on the house floor, it violated two of the norms of higher education politics in Illinois: do not propose anything that would take funding away from another sector within higher education, and do not impose on legislators the task of resolving conflict that higher education ought to resolve within its own community.

SHAKEOUT AS FORCES COLLIDE

By the 1990s, the old system was breaking apart at both the elementary-secondary and the higher education levels. Clearly, the education systems in Illinois faced tough times; yet in a backward sort of way, the political context that shapes them and determines their fortunes showed a vitality that could lead to higher-quality education. It is the rough-and-tumble marketplace, after all, that divides resources in Illinois, and there had not been so much jostling in that marketplace for years. Where the unions and school district bureaucracies had become well-fed and complacent, hungry reform forces have edged in, forcing everyone to tighten up operations and improve performance. Within the carefully nurtured comity of higher education, the emerging suburban market and stagnant financial support have turned once-amiable players into sly competitors. In the Illinois education community, a shakeout is under way.

This is an important and probably favorable dynamic because in the last years of the century, education at all levels will come under increasing pressures. If Illinois is to remain economically competitive, school buildings and campuses will have to be busier than ever as centers of lifelong workforce education, training and retraining. Somehow this will have to be engineered within a political context of public resistance to increased taxation and skepticism that increased funding will improve achievement.

Education thus has been pushed to the heart of the political agenda. Voters want better education and more job training at low cost. Education interests, much as they prize independence from politics, have decided they must become politically savvy and fully engaged in the political thicket if they are to be assured their fair share of state spending. As a result, governors and lawmakers have been feeling the heat. They will have to give more than lip service to the almost universal campaign pledge that "education is the number one priority."

CHAPTER ELEVEN

Modest Tax Effort
from a Wealthy State

Budgets are the scorecards of politics. The ponderous documents tally in dollars the winners and losers in the game of who gets what.[1] The politics of budgeting revolve not only around who gets what but also who pays, and how much.

Elected officials have strong political incentives to do things *for* their voters (e.g., more program spending) and to avoid doing things *to* them (e.g., imposing more taxes). As a result, budgets have a natural tendency to increase over time, often faster than revenues to pay the bills.

The only way to make up the difference, besides cutting back on spending, is to increase taxes. This is a tricky proposition that might be likened to the ritual mating dance of the wild turkey. The governor, who often must initiate the revenue search, preens and struts throughout the state, trying to make his tax package attractive. The legislature reacts coyly, waiting to see how well this statewide dance plays with their voters. All the major players in state politics join in the ceremony. Educators, as major beneficiaries, orchestrate marketing efforts among their constituents. Business groups often, but not always, rally the opposition. Government and university economists weigh in with projections of the consequences good and bad for the state's business climate. The Taxpayers' Federation of Illinois, a moderate business group, is watched closely for its analyses and recommendations.

Sometimes the ritual is never consummated. A scaled-back budget is contrived, cuts are made in programs, revenue projections are inflated, the payment of bills is delayed, and the tax dance is put on hold for another year or two.

The Illinois state budget is a plan for spending scarce financial resources, including taxes, fees, lottery profits, interest income, and borrowed money.

It reflects an allocation of public values. Each spending item competes with all others because the dollars available are always scarce relative to demand. Aid to college students competes not only with spending for prisons and county fairs but also with programs for mentally retarded adults and poor children. (See figure 5 for the allocation of state spending proposed by the governor for fiscal year 1996.)

An appropriation adopted by the legislature and approved by the governor represents spending authority for the fiscal year (FY), which for Illinois begins July 1 and ends June 30. The state spends money from almost five hundred funds, such as the Cycle Rider Safety Training Fund (total resources in FY 1993 of about $3.4 million), the Hazardous Waste Research Fund ($1.1 million), and the Wildlife and Fish Fund ($23.8 million). But slightly more than half of all spending is allocated through four general funds known as General Revenue, Common School, Common School Special Accounts, and Education Assistance. Budget problems tend to occur in this area.

Demand for state spending is driven in large part by the federal government, demographic change, society's preferences, and the health of the economy. State budgeteers have little control over any of these "drivers."

The federal government sets eligibility standards for the federal-state Medicaid program, which provides health care for 1.4 million Illinois residents. In the 1980s and early 1990s, the federal government expanded eligibility to encompass more children and disabled persons. As a result, the number of persons certified as disabled, and thus eligible for Medicaid, almost doubled from 123,000 in 1983 to 229,000 in 1993. During that period, Medicaid expenditures for that group more than tripled, from $595 million to $2.1 billion. As American society ages, there have also been inexorable increases in the number of Illinois residents over age eighty-five. The result has been an increase in the number of persons in Illinois nursing homes who are paid for by Medicaid, at more than $20,000 per person per year.

Change in the structure of society also affects the budget. The number of children placed by the state in foster or substitute care has increased from fewer than fifteen thousand in 1986 to more than forty-five thousand in 1995. The state, with federal government matching fund support, spends about $10,000 per child in foster care support, plus additional amounts for health care and other services.

Society is also demanding that the state get tougher on criminals. As a result, the number of prison inmates—and prisons—has increased dramatically in the past generation, from five thousand in 1970 to thirty-five thou-

Figure 5. Proposed Illinois State Appropriations and Revenue,
Fiscal Year 1996, all Appropriated Funds

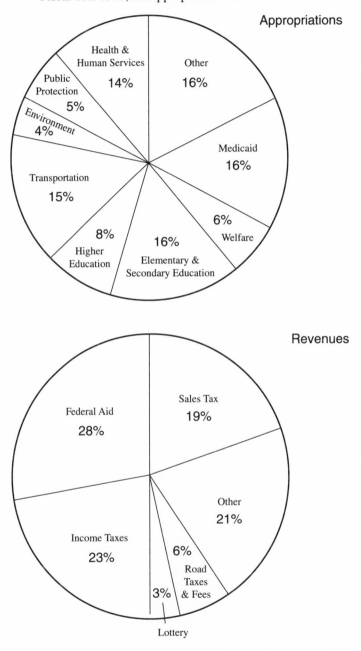

Source: Illinois State Budget, Fiscal Year 1996, Illinois Bureau of the Budget, Springfield, 1995.

sand in 1994, and numbers are expected to continue upward. Illinois spends about $19,000 per prison inmate per year.

State budget demands tend to be countercyclical to the economy, that is, when the economy declines, demand for public assistance, health care, and other services increases. For instance, when the number of persons employed falls, enrollment in higher education tends to increase as people return to community colleges and other campuses to improve their skills and employability. The countercyclical nature of budgeting creates problems for budgeteers because as demand for state dollars goes up, tax revenues decline. Several states maintain a "rainy day" fund that can be used during economic recessions to avoid raising taxes, but Illinois has no such fund.

Some budget categories may require only modest spending increases in coming years. The state's school-age population is expected to increase only marginally, and participation in Aid to Families with Dependent Children may not grow much because the predominant population served by that program, women aged fifteen to twenty-nine, is expected to decrease. But other areas show every sign of demanding heavy additional spending that will far outstrip inflation. In a state that has limped along on tight budgets for years, this is not a good sign.

PRIORITIES OVERWHELMED BY NEEDS

At a 1992 workshop on the state budget for legislative candidates, each was asked where he or she would like to spend more, or fewer, state dollars. Almost to a candidate, they wanted to spend more on education and less on welfare and prisons. But Illinois has been doing just about the opposite. What people want to do has been overwhelmed by what they must do.

From FY 1990–95, general funds spending for the Illinois Department of Public Aid doubled. Spending for prisons increased by 41 percent. The greatest increase was recorded by the Department of Children and Family Services, which more than doubled its budget. State spending for elementary and secondary education was up a stingy 20 percent, approximately equal to the rate of inflation for the period, while state general fund spending for higher education actually declined.

During the past two decades, spending for health care has been transforming the social compact in Illinois, primarily because of Medicaid. Spending for Medicaid increased from 6 percent of the state budget in FY 1972 to 16 percent projected for FY 1995. As a result, inflation-adjusted spending for Medicaid went from less than half of what the state spends for public schools to slightly exceeding funds spent for public schools.

Medicaid is the federal-state program of health care for low-income families and also for many nursing home residents originally from middle-class circumstances. The federal government sets the eligibility standards and gives state governments some latitude to determine what services they will provide. The state government administers the program and negotiates reimbursement rates with health care provider interest groups. The federal government and Illinois share program costs on a 50-50 matching basis.

The federal government has expanded eligibility significantly in recent years, to 1.4 million Illinois residents in 1994, and the number will continue to increase because the federal government has required that additional children be enrolled on a phased-in basis throughout the 1990s. The program is an entitlement. All who are eligible, or entitled, will be served and the bills paid, no matter what the total cost.

Because of a federal court suit that charged inadequate care, the federal court is monitoring the administration of the state children's welfare agency. The settlement of this suit dictated the increased funding that has occurred for the agency. Illinois spends less per prison inmate in constant dollars than it did two decades ago. Unfortunately, the correctional facilities are being overwhelmed with new inmates, hence costs are increasing irrepressibly.

Education, unlike these other programs, is funded at the discretion of state government. Naturally, then, budget makers fund first what they are required to pay for and then provide what is left for education. Per pupil state spending for public schools, adjusted for inflation, is lower in 1994 than the high-water mark of 1976. Inflation-adjusted state spending for higher education on a per full-time equivalent basis was down from $1,900 in 1972 to $1,620 in 1991. Spending for Aid to Families with Dependent Children is down dramatically on a per case, inflation-adjusted basis.

Though among the top ten states in per capita income, Illinois is consistently below the national average in most expenditure categories. Figure 6 illustrates that for 1991, state and local expenditures for elementary-secondary education, welfare, and higher education were only about 90 percent of the national averages. Only in highway spending did Illinois exceed the national average.

SIMPLE MATH, DIFFICULT DECISIONS

The dean of budgeteers in Illinois, Robert L. Mandeville, says that budgeting is a simple five-step process: find out what you have in the bank; estimate

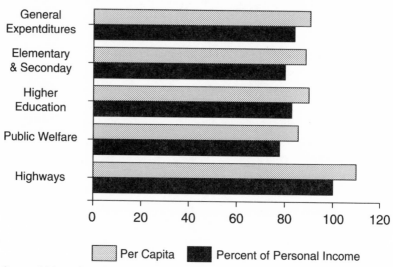

Figure 6. Illinois State and Local Expenditures as a Percentage of National Averages, 1991

Source: Advisory Commission on Intergovernmental Relations, *Significant Features of Fiscal Federalism,* 1994.

your receipts for the budget period; decide what you want to have in the bank at the end of the budget period; subtract item 3 from the first two items; and allocate that amount among programs.

"That's all there is to it. That's the truth," says Mandeville, who served as director of the Bureau of the Budget from 1977 to 1990.[2] Simple, perhaps, but never easy because of Step 5.

There are several fundamental points to keep in mind about budgeting in Illinois. Major changes are difficult because most funding is already committed. Demands will always outstrip resources, and the growth generated primarily by inflation will not be enough to cover new programs.

The balanced budget is required by the Illinois Constitution, which says that "proposed expenditures shall not exceed funds estimated to be available for the fiscal year as shown in the budget."[3] This means that unless some new revenue stream is available, most of the spending for the coming year's budget will mirror that of the previous year. Education, transportation, health care, assistance to the poor and abused, and state agencies consume most of the budget every year, leaving little room for dramatic changes.

Within the budget there is little room for flexibility because it is either impossible or difficult to transfer funds from one dedicated fund to another. For example, the road-building lobby guards against diversion of revenues from the Motor Fuel Tax Fund, and the medical and dental societies protect the funds the state receives from professional license fees, which are dedicated to oversight of their professions. In addition, appropriations of state monies are made for specific line items such as printing and telecommunications, rather than for general program objectives such as prisoner care and rehabilitation. Transfer of funds from one line to another is limited to no more than 2 percent of the line's total; greater amounts require legislative approval.

Budgeting frustrates a new governor, who wants to do for his constituents all the good things he might have promised in his campaign. A participant recalls a scene from the transition to office in 1976 of James R. Thompson, who had been holding sessions with his budget director, Robert Mandeville. As they prepared to review the education budget, Thompson looked at Mandeville and said, with some exasperation, "Okay, Bob, how much can't I spend today?"[4]

There are always more demands than available resources can satisfy. As Mandeville explains:

Working on the budget is like spending an afternoon watching "Poltergeist II" and the "Attack of the Killer Bees." Just as Carol Anne yelled, "They're Baaack!!" so lobbyists and advocates will soon descend upon Springfield arguing for a bigger piece of the budget pie. . . . Killer bees have not yet reached Illinois, but the KILLER P's have. Pensions, Public Aid, and Prisons have all made their assaults on the state's programs. These programs are not killers in themselves. They are legitimate program needs that deserve as high a level of funding as possible. They can be budget killers because they require large increments to make changes. . . . Full funding of the pension systems is a noble goal. Cutting the funding from the poor to pay for state pensions is not. Restructuring medicaid to make poor children healthier is a noble goal. Cutting the funding for poor children's education to fund medicaid restructuring is not. If passing tough sentencing laws to put criminals behind bars is a noble thing to do, providing taxes to build the prisons and pay the guards is a noble thing.[5]

Under this pressure from areas of growing need, lawmakers must seek other ways to fund their pet projects, and they often latch onto inflation-induced growth in revenue. This growth is the revenue increase that occurs even when there is no change in the tax rates. It is generated primarily by inflation and generally does not represent a windfall, for the costs of salaries and goods purchased by state government also increase with inflation.

Although it might seem self-evident that such growth is not a dependable source of new money, Governor Thompson in his FY 1989 budget book listed twenty-one new initiatives adopted either by the legislature or by administrative action of the governor since 1985. They included education reforms, expanded probation services, expanded circuit breaker (property tax) relief for the elderly, searches for missing children, AIDS research, and asbestos removal in schools.[6] There had been little change in the state's tax structure during this period; Thompson and the legislature were counting on inflation-induced growth to carry the budget forward.

This approach might work more often if minor cutbacks in various program areas were considered a normal part of budgeting, but in reality the opposite is true: the tendency is for programs to cost a little bit more each year. Governors, budget staff, and lawmakers basically accept what was spent during the preceding year, on the assumption that it was reasonable—after all, they voted for it. Then they focus on how much of an increase, or increment, is proposed for the coming year. Specialists in public management have criticized this approach as less than rational, saying it lacks comprehensiveness and leaves most of the budget outside review. Yet the time pressures of an annual budgeting cycle and the size and complexity of the budget induce this focus. As budget analyst Raymond F. Coyne points out, incremental budgeting has the consequence of limiting political conflict.[7] If the whole budget were opened up and budgeteers allowed to start from scratch each year, the executive branch, legislature, interest groups, Democrats and Republicans, and the media might feel compelled to joust over the whole pie rather than just the small slice represented by the increment. It would be politically treacherous and thus is almost never done.

THE OTHER BUDGET: CAPITAL PROJECTS

In addition to expenditures for immediate purposes, the state makes long-term investments in highways, university laboratories, wastewater treatment plants, prisons, and other projects that will last many years. In the three-hundred-page 1991 capital budget, the Illinois Bureau of the Budget noted that almost one-quarter of FY 1991 appropriations, about $6.5 billion, went to capital projects.[8] Not all the money was actually spent in FY 1991, however, because the work on most projects stretches across several years.

Just as individuals pay for a home with a mortgage, the state borrows money and retires the debt by paying off principal and interest over ten to thirty years. Illinois has authorized twenty-two agencies to borrow money by issuing bonds. The primary authorities are the Capital Development Bond Fund and the Build Illinois Fund. Others include the Metropolitan Pier and Exposition Authority (for Chicago's McCormick Place and Navy Pier) and the Sports Facilities Authority (which built the White Sox stadium).

The politics of who gets which capital projects are intense because big money, political credits, and local boosterism are involved in the competition. The Build Illinois funding, discussed in Chapters 5 and 6, provides a classic illustration. Local swimming pools, parks, and golf courses were among projects constructed or improved with Build Illinois funds. Although many important projects were funded, a report by the Taxpayers' Federation of Illinois concluded that "the Build Illinois program lacks a sense of continuity and definitive priorities."[9]

Although capital spending differs from operating expenses, the two budgets are nevertheless in competition. A special tax on used cars was to be a primary source of revenue for the Build Illinois bonds, but in FY 1990 that source generated only $41 million of the $83 million needed. As a result, an additional $42 million in general revenues was deposited in the Build Illinois account, money that might otherwise have been available for education or child care services.[10]

Pension funding provides another illustration of the competition between current expenditures and long-term deferred obligations. Each year the state appropriates funds into five retirement systems for state employees, judges, legislators, schoolteachers, and university faculty and staff. But the pension funds already have balances large enough to pay for the current year's obligations, so it is possible to reduce the annual appropriation for pensions without shorting anyone *at the moment*. This often happens when money is tight, as in the FY 1991 budget, when the legislature authorized the Chicago Board of Education to take $66 million that was to be invested in the Chicago teachers' pension system and appropriate it instead for teachers' salaries. The practice had become so widespread across the system that by 1994, the state pension systems had unfunded future liabilities of $14 billion. The General Assembly enacted a "continuing appropriation" law in 1994 that requires increased pension appropriations and full funding of the systems over forty years.

SEARCHING FOR NO-PAIN REVENUES

Elected officials enjoy doing things for people like appropriating money for programs that benefit the voters. They do not like to do things to people, in particular to levy taxes on them. But the bills have to be paid and the operating budget balanced. To meet this responsibility, public officials search for revenues that are least painful (for example, a quarter-percent increase in the

Table 8: Twenty-Six Illinois Taxes, 1994

1. Automobile renting occupation and use tax	13. Income tax (individual)
2. Bingo tax and fees	14. Insurance taxes and fees
3. Cannabis and controlled substance tax	15. Liquor taxes and fees
4. Charitable games tax and license fees	16. Lottery
5. Cigarette and other tobacco taxes	17. Motor fuel tax
7. Corporation franchise tax	18. Personal property replacement tax
8. Driver's license and vehicle fees	19. Public utility tax
9. Estate and generation-skipping transfer taxes (death taxes)	20. Pull tab and jar games tax and fees
10. Health care assessments	21. Racing privilege tax
11. Hotel operators' tax	22. Real estate transfer tax
12. Income tax (corporate)	23. Riverboat gambling tax
	24. Sales and use tax
	25. Vehicle-replacement tax
	26. Vehicle use tax

Source: Illinois Tax Handbook for Legislators (Springfield: Legislative Research Unit, Illinois General Assembly, 1994).

sales tax would add only a small amount to each purchase); tied to use of a product (such as the motor fuel tax); or voluntary, nontax revenue, such as buying a state lottery ticket, of which thirty-seven cents of each dollar becomes net profit to the state.

The issue of who pays becomes complicated. Should governments impose taxes on property, income, goods, services, gasoline, utilities, or the "sins" of consuming tobacco and alcohol? If it is to be property, should farmland, residential, and business property be treated the same? Who bears the greater burden—individuals or corporations, the wealthy, middle class, or poor? These are tough questions for governors and lawmakers who want to be reelected.

Twenty-six categories of revenue are listed in the 1994 edition of the *Illinois Tax Handbook for Legislators* (see table 8), including taxes for car rentals, pinball machines, and carnival games.[11] Fees for services and for the privilege of doing business are a significant category, including drivers' licenses, carnival amusement ride inspection fees, fishing and hunting licenses, and professional licenses for physicians, architects, and beauticians. As shown in figure 5, however, the income and sales taxes represent by far the largest sources of state revenues, at 42 percent.

Governors and lawmakers try to be sensitive to the impact that taxes might have on politically important groups, such as senior citizens, and on the state economy. Pension income of retirees was exempted from the state income tax, for example, even though it is taxed by the federal government. In efforts to boost the economy, the sales tax on the purchase of manufacturing machinery was phased out in 1985, and farm machinery sales were exempted as well. The tax handbook lists sixty-seven types of sales exempted from the sales tax, including newsprint and ink, coal gasification machinery, and sales to not-for-profit music or dramatic arts organizations.[12] In addition, utility taxes may be abated (reduced) in a given year if a business has made investments that created two hundred full-time jobs or retained at least a thousand jobs in Illinois. All told, the General Assembly provided tax relief on seventeen occasions during the 1980s, amounting to more than $1.2 billion in FY 1991 alone—a sizable amount of revenue lost to the state treasury.[13]

During the same period, other taxes went up. To build and maintain the state's 137,000 miles of roads and 25,000 highway bridges, the state motor fuel tax on gasoline rose from eleven cents a gallon in 1984 to nineteen cents in 1990.[14] The flat-rate income tax on individuals and corporations was increased in 1989 from 2.5 percent to 3 percent for individuals and from 4 percent to 4.8 percent for corporations.

In the quest for relatively painless revenue sources, policymakers in Illinois have been attracted by sin and gambling. The state tax on cigarettes went from twenty to thirty cents a pack in 1990 and then to forty-four cents in 1993. The lottery was the big revenue success story of the 1980s. Created in 1974, it got off to a slow start, generating net revenue of only $28 million in 1979, but by 1993, with steady promotion and regular introduction of new types of game cards, the lottery was netting $650 million on sales of $1.6 billion. This was more net revenue than from the income tax on corporations and represented $140 in yearly ticket sales for every man, woman, and child in Illinois.

Riverboat gambling was approved in 1989, and by FY 1996 the popular boats were generating about $230 million for the state, plus additional revenues for the municipalities where the boats were docked.

Legal gambling does not come without other costs to the state. It is widely assumed that poor families spend higher percentages of their income than the wealthy on the lottery and other state-sanctioned games. Jack R. Van Der Slik contends that the biggest negative is that the state legitimizes the making of new gamblers: "The state's slick television ads sustain hope among many, especially the poor, of a big hit, a jackpot, and then let the good times roll. Forget hard work. Saving is for suckers. Why sacrifice for the future when the future is now? And, like alcohol, widespread gambling reveals more and more people for whom it is an addiction. What a regressive way to serve the public."[15]

Indeed, state-operated and authorized gambling is the only function of state government in which its citizens must lose overall for the state to be a winner.

POLITICS OF "SHIFT AND SHAFT"

The politics of federalism can be seen in large part as a serious game in which each government—federal, state, and local—tries to expand its authority over programs while inducing the others to pay for the changes. The chapter on education showed how the federal government imposed extensive authority over programs for educating the handicapped while paying only part of the bill and how the state of Illinois has increased mandates on the way its local schools must operate while shifting the cost from state taxes to local property taxes. Local government leaders are also skilled at playing the game. In 1993, municipal leaders negotiated an increase—from one-twelfth to one-tenth—in the share of state income tax revenues automatically distributed to cities and counties, thus reducing the amount available to be spent in the state budget. This game has been aptly labeled the politics of "shift and shaft."

One justification for shifting money from one government to another is that the receiving government can deliver the service more effectively. These monies can also act as a carrot to induce state or local governments to initiate or change programs. Prominent examples of federally supported but state-administered programs include Aid to Families with Dependent Children, Medicaid, and highway construction. In FY 1995, over $7 billion in federal funds was directed to Illinois state government,[16] more than half in grants for social services. This represents more than one-fourth of total state revenues.

Nevertheless, Illinois will continue to receive less from the federal government than do most states because many federal programs allocate funds on the basis of per capita wealth, and poorer states receive more support. Being above average in wealth, Illinois receives less per capita for many programs. Illinois is required to provide 50 percent of the cost of the Medicaid program, for instance, while neighboring Indiana and Iowa each pays only 37 percent. Illinois is also less generous with its own funding for such programs, typically providing payments for health and welfare programs that are below the national average. In 1992 Illinois ranked twenty-fourth among the states with monthly welfare payments of $367 for a family of three, compared to $663 in California and $577 in New York. Among neighboring states, Wisconsin paid $517 and Indiana a much lower $288. Because that state spending is matched on a percentage basis with the federal government, Illinois cannot capture more federal money unless it raises its payment levels.[17]

There is a close working relationship between Illinois and its local governments on matters of finance, with the state government collecting local sales tax revenues and distributing them back to the local governments; the state also shares with local governments part of the income, sales, and motor fuel taxes. Major state appropriations are for education and social services, and about 60 percent of all state expenditures are distributed in grants and awards to local governments, nongovernment agencies, and individuals.[18]

Nevertheless, the single largest source of revenue for Illinois governments continues to be the local property tax. In 1993 the property tax provided $11.1 billion to local governments, more than was generated that year for state government by the personal income tax, the state sales tax, and lottery profits combined.[19] Schools received 59 percent of total property tax revenues; municipalities about 16 percent; special districts, 12 percent; counties, 10 percent; and townships, 3 percent.

The property tax has been a revenue mainstay since the state and its local governments were established, and today Illinois relies more heavily on the property tax to fund local services than do most states. In 1991, Illinois property tax revenues came to $785 per person, while the average was $666 for the nation.

This heavy use of the property tax has caused problems. First, the property tax is consistently considered the least fair tax in Illinois, according to an annual opinion survey by Northern Illinois University.[20] Second, property wealth is not spread evenly across the state. In 1993 total property taxes per person by county ranged from almost $1,400 in Lake and DuPage in the collar counties to less than $200 in Hardin and Pulaski County in deep southern Illinois. Third, during the 1980s, property values were generally climbing in the metropolitan Chicago area while they were declining, often steeply, in rural Illinois. As a result, many urban residents complained bitterly about tax increases and rural local governments were hard-pressed to provide basic services.

The great wealth and property tax differentials across the state have important implications for regional politics. Both income taxes and the residential property tax burden are significantly higher in the collar counties than downstate. For example, per capita income was $26,600 in DuPage County and homeowners paid an average of 3.4 percent of their income in property taxes. Downstate counties had less per capita income, and homeowners also paid much lower percentages of that income in property taxes. If taxes paid as a percentage of income represent a reasonable measure of tax "effort" or burden, these regional differences add fuel to the debate over which regions are paying their fair share for education.

Shifting more of the burden to local governments is not an attractive revenue-raising option in Illinois because it has already been done. In fact, the push is in the other direction, toward the state taking over more of the local burden. According to Douglas L. Whitley, former director of the Illinois Department of Revenue, "The number one issue facing Illinois government finance is how best to deal with the heavy reliance local governments have placed upon the real estate tax base."[21] He says there are two distinct policy questions. What is the appropriate revenue source and tax mix to fund state and local government services? And how does the state assure financial equity and equal educational opportunity when the current education system favors local control and financial independence?

Although the traditional cures for revenue shortages are coming up short, sometimes revenue windfalls can temporarily make up the difference. When the U.S. Tax Reform Act of 1986 eliminated or curtailed several federal income tax deductions, some residents of Illinois had to pay taxes on a higher adjusted gross income on their federal *and* state income tax forms. With deductions down and taxable income up, the following year Illinois reaped $150 million in additional state income tax revenues, without touching the state tax rate.

By the same token, when the federal government increases its tax rates on items such as gasoline, cigarettes, beer, and other alcoholic beverages, as it did in 1990, Illinois's ability to increase its own taxes on these items is diminished because of taxpayer resistance. State officials worry that the federal government will one day impose a tax on sales, thus constraining state and local governments from drawing further on that important source of state revenue.

POLITICAL DYNAMICS OF BUDGETING

In the 1960s, one scholar saw budgeting in Illinois as a ritualized game in which each interested party played its part and, if all went well, everyone came out a winner.[22] The agencies would request more than they needed, and the governor and legislature would each make some cuts. The final budget would provide the agencies what they actually wanted—sometimes even more than expected—and the politicos could claim to have cut the budget.

Players in the budget game still anticipate the actions of others. Since the 1960s, however, the process has been complicated by the addition of the governor's Bureau of the Budget, legislative staffing, the Illinois Board of Higher Education (which recommends university budgets), and the reduction veto provided to the governor by the 1970 Constitution. As a result, the state agencies probably have less influence than in an earlier era, and the legislature has become more involved in the substance of budgeting negotiations.

In simplified form the process is as follows. State agencies make budget requests to the Bureau of the Budget. BOB makes its recommendations for each agency to the governor. If an agency head feels strongly that the budget level recommended by BOB is unreasonably low, the agency head can appeal directly to the governor, who resolves the differences. The final budget document, often running more than a thousand pages, is presented in March via a formal budget address by the governor to the General Assembly.

The budget then is transformed into about one hundred appropriations (spending authority) bills, generally one for each agency. Roughly half these bills are introduced into the senate and half into the house, where they are reviewed in public hearings by appropriations committees. The bills are often amended as they wend their way through the two chambers.

Throughout the process, the interest groups and beneficiaries of state spending press their claims. If budget recommendations are seen as inadequate, there are cries of catastrophe. University presidents cite a brain drain of faculty who are leaving for higher salaries elsewhere. The rhetoric often heats up, as in this 1989 statement in a press release from the state school superintendent: "School districts are going down the financial tube; Chicago school reform is jeopardized before it gets underway. . . . We are in disgraceful condition and it's time for the people of this state to say we've had enough."[23]

The governor generally dominates the budget process because he builds the original budget and later can impose line-item and reduction vetoes. The legislature has, however, shown the capacity to impose its own spending priorities. In FY 1991 the legislature was unwilling to support Thompson's proposals for cigarette and telephone taxes. As a result, over Thompson's protestations, Democrats and Republicans agreed to varying cuts, paring back education 1 percent, major social service agencies by 1.5 percent, and all others 3.2 percent. The legislature also eliminated several of Thompson's initiatives.

In summary, the budget represents accommodation. Seldom does any participant—agency head, BOB analyst, governor, lawmaker, legislative staffer, lobbyist—see his or her budget agenda fully satisfied. Each uses influence and power, whether it is expert information, a key vote in committee, veto action, campaign support, or editorial comment, to pursue budget goals. The final appropriations, after the legislature responds to the governor's vetoes, roughly approximate the will and values of the political society of Illinois.

WORKINGS OF THE BUREAU OF THE BUDGET

After the annual budget process is complete, the chief executive has the responsibility to match spending with revenue. Budgeting at this stage is basically cash management, and it is a challenging task. The monthly balance in the state's general funds "checkbook" has often fallen into the fiscal "danger zone" of less than $200 million, sometimes for a year or more at a time. Management of the budget falls to the governor's Bureau of the Budget, which must ensure that budget promises are being met, and to the state comptroller, who holds the state checkbook and must delay payments of valid claims to avoid overdrawing the accounts. As former BOB division chief Craig Bazzani put it: "The Bureau is also something of an 'efficiency engineer.' As a protagonist in the budgeting process, it is the bureau's job to help departments find a more efficient way to 'build a better mousetrap'— that is, educate more students at less cost, improve management, or save more agricultural land."[24]

A quarterly spending allotment plan is the primary tool that BOB imposes upon the agencies. Each agency under the jurisdiction of the governor is required to identify planned expenditures for each line item for each quarter. This forces an agency to refine its internal budget and gives the BOB program analyst assigned to work with that agency a plan to monitor.

The checkbook balance of cash on hand can give a misleading picture of the state's fiscal situation because the balance is subject to manipulation.[25] The balance can be built up by delaying payments to nursing homes, hospitals, and school districts and by speeding up collections of certain taxes. If a governor wants to help build a case for a tax increase, BOB can plunge the available balance into the fiscal warning zone by speeding up the flow of payment requests to the comptroller and by slowing the processing of collections.

THE POLITICS OF TAXATION

As the old saw goes, "The only good tax is one you pay and I don't." In 1978, James Thompson was running for his second term as governor, shortly after tax limitation Proposition 13 was adopted by California voters. To show his concern about taxes, he led a petition drive to put an advisory referendum on the ballot. This so-called Thompson Proposition asked voters if they favored ceilings on their state and local taxes. As might have been expected, 82 percent favored the idea.

Yet voters can be convinced to support tax increases. In elections between 1972 and 1993, from one-fifth to one-half of all referendums for school tax rate increases were passed by the voters. Many rejected issues went back to the voters time and again until they were ultimately passed.

Illinois state finance is a cyclical affair, according to budget expert Michael D. Klemens: "Spending increases have preceded gubernatorial elections; then tax increases followed elections. Tax increases have prompted spending increases; then revenues have lagged and more tax increases are needed."[26] In a display of candor, Governor Thompson acknowledged in 1987 that he had signed into law dozens of programs without funds to pay for them:

> Many of them I signed against the advice of my director of the Bureau of the Budget [Robert Mandeville], who for 11 years has stood for fiscal integrity and "don't sign a bill unless you can pay for it, regardless of how good it is." And I'd say to him, "Doc, this is a good idea" And he'd say, "You can't pay for good ideas with no money." . . . And I'd sit and say to myself, well, maybe the economy will pick up. Maybe they'll [the legislature] do the right thing next year. Maybe prosperity is around the corner. Maybe, maybe, maybe. . . . I should have listened to Dr. Bob.[27]

In part as a result of his actions, Thompson sought tax increases in 1987 and 1988, each time leading the ritual dance with legislators and interest groups. For two years the legislature rejected the governor's pleas for more revenue, but in 1989, following the lead of Speaker of the house Michael Madigan, lawmakers enacted a temporary 20 percent increase in the state income tax. It was less than Thompson wanted and in a different format, but he signed the bill and moved on, the crisis averted for the time being.

ILLINOIS AS A LOW-TAX STATE

A consistent characteristic of Illinois tax policy is the relatively modest tax burden imposed on residents. State and local taxes in Illinois have consistently represented a smaller percentage of personal income than for the nation as a whole. In 1992, state and local taxes in Illinois represented 10.1 percent of personal income, while the national average was 10.8 percent. In revenues generated per person from state and local sources, at $2,936 per person in 1992, Illinois generated more than its neighbors to the south and east but less than Minnesota, Wisconsin, Iowa, and Michigan[28] and less than the national average of $3,111.

Is the mix of state and local taxes fair? Economist Therese McGuire found the tax mix as of 1992 to be unfair to the poor and unresponsive to state economic growth.[29] She observed that Illinois had a flat-rate income tax with only a $1,000 personal exemption, which means that families with incomes below the poverty line pay income taxes at the same rate as wealthy families.

In a 1991 analysis of comparative state and local tax burdens, the liberal Citizens for Tax Justice named Illinois one of the "Terrible Ten" states with the highest overall taxes on the poor and the lowest taxes on the well-to-do.[30] The study showed that Illinois took a tax bite of 16.5 percent of income from the poorest fifth of the state's population, while extracting an aggregate tax of just 6 percent of income from the state's richest fifth.

There are advocates in Illinois for higher taxes to address education reform and social challenges. There are equally intense opponents to tax boosts. Each side makes its arguments, one on behalf of improving workforce quality and social justice, the other in the interests of enhancing the business climate. The state's leading newspaper, the *Chicago Tribune,* has become a predictable supporter of tax increases, in particular a boost in the income tax to provide school funding and reduce property tax burdens. But by 1994 the editorials had had little effect, and the gubernatorial candidate who championed a tax increase, Dawn Clark Netsch, was soundly beaten by incumbent governor Jim Edgar, who had kept a pledge not to increase taxes during his first term.

For better or worse, the levels of taxation and performance in Illinois are probably reflections not so much of governors and legislators as of the attitudes and values that Illinois citizens bring to government. Good services and good schools everywhere would be nice, the voters and their leaders seem to say, but if it means a consistently higher tax effort, perhaps the current system will be good enough after all.

CHAPTER TWELVE

As Landscape Tilts,
Culture Holds On

As the new century dawns in Illinois, the landscape will have tilted more sharply toward the expanding metropolitan frontier, yet the individualistic government-as-marketplace culture will endure.

Citizens of the megalopolis along Lake Michigan will still seek the wide-open spaces and will motor outward as far as Rockford, enveloping DeKalb and Morris and bringing suburban lifestyles to communities such as Mendota, Rochelle, and Princeton, eighty miles and more from Chicago. DeKalb is only forty minutes along I-88 from the heart of the western suburbs and its mother lode of jobs. Princeton, an attractive town of seven thousand, straddles both I-80 and the Amtrak line that connects to the western suburbs and Chicago. As of 1994, housing values there were escalating rapidly, and other signals were clear enough: early retirees and telecommuters were buying homes, and trendy shops were opening near the Main Street cafes where farmers and townsfolk gather to gossip.

Under this relentless tide, the old downstate region will become physically smaller and politically weaker. As the suburban frontier expands utward, the former downstate residents and their leaders will face new problems. They will build streets, schools, sewers, and waste treatment facilities, cope with an influx of newcomers, and try to hold down property taxes on ever-more-valuable homes.

The media will help them forget about downstate and concentrate on their own issues. Grown bored with Springfield, the Chicago media had gutted their coverage by the mid-1990s.[1] The *Chicago Tribune* and *Sun-Times,* each of which had two permanent reporters in the Capitol pressroom in the 1980s, were down to one apiece by 1994. Chicago television stations never bothered to staff the capital. At the same time, media resources were being poured into the collar counties. By 1994, the *Tribune* had four major suburban bureaus and five satellite bureaus with fifty-one full-time suburban reporters.

The old problems will still be around, of course; they too will ride the wave of suburbanization. As longtime suburbanites move farther out, urban dwellers of lesser means will replace them, especially in the older suburbs, where the problems of urban America were already evident in the 1990s. In a grand and ironic illustration of the urban development cycle, the inner core will continue its rejuvenation as industrial sites and uninhabitable properties are cleared and fenced so that urban homesteaders can create what the ex-urbanites seek: secure and attractive places to live.

In 1993, Chicago Mayor Richard M. Daley created a stir by moving from the family's longtime political base in the working-class neighborhood of Bridgeport into a posh residential complex called Central Station, built on railroad property near downtown. Nearby, former printing and manufacturing plants were transformed into loft apartments for young professionals, and west of the Loop new public facilities, commercial buildings, and residential developments were reclaiming long-dormant vacant lots.

Like a beating heart pumping vitality into the surrounding tissue, the expanding downtown area was creating a new ripple of middle-class expansion into once-struggling neighborhoods, pushing poorer blacks and Hispanics and ethnic whites outward. As the middle-class population grew in the central city, it reinforced the role of Chicago's Loop as a magnet that draws the powerful, including political leaders, into its grasp. When the century turns, the new balance will be clear. As in 1900, two players will dominate, but instead of the city and downstate, they will be uneasy neighbors: the city and its own suburbs.

WINNERS AND LOSERS

Since the origin of Illinois, political leaders have bargained for funding and benefits for their respective regions. In the 1830s, Abraham Lincoln and eight fellow legislators from the Springfield area (they were known as the "Long Nine" because each was over six feet tall) worked as a bloc to move the state capital from Vandalia in southern Illinois to Springfield in rapidly growing central Illinois.

The state's leaders have since distilled the bargaining process into a fine art of regional quid pro quo, taking in everything from school aid and transportation to state university campuses and construction of civic centers. Compromise is the key, as is sharing the wealth. In 1984, the Chicago public school system requested $22 million from the legislature to end a strike.

Leaders for the other two regions stepped forward, stated their price, and upped the tab to $75 million, providing something for everyone.[2] When the Chicago Transit Authority sought an increased state subsidy in 1985, the legislature took care of it after arranging for similar boosts for several downstate transit districts.[3]

As in any negotiation, the uncomfortable question is who gets the better part of the deal. Downstaters have long believed Chicago drains resources from the hinterland, especially for welfare spending. Chicagoans complain that downstaters waste money to build highways in sparsely populated areas. Collar county leaders, citing the tax load, whine that the other regions take advantage of the hard-earned wealth of the suburban middle class.

The Legislative Research Unit found in 1987 that the collar counties paid more proportionally in taxes than either downstate or Chicago and received less back in spending for state programs. That did not surprise political economists James Fossett and Fred Giertz. Governments, after all, are in the business of taking in taxes and redistributing the resources, generally from the more prosperous to those less so. Even greater redistribution might well be in order, say Fossett and Giertz: "Considering the severity of their problems, Chicago and other hard-pressed areas are receiving relatively less state funds from a number of program areas, while the prosperous areas are receiving relatively more. The state appears to be spreading funds more broadly than the distribution of social and governmental problems suggest is desirable."[4]

But that shift will not happen without a fight, in part because suburban legislators, as indeed most lawmakers in Illinois, have come to see political work as lifetime careers. To help their reelection chances, they have become more intent on showing the home folks that they bring in their fair share of money and projects. This tends to perpetuate the status quo and constrain redistribution from one region to another.[5]

JOINING FORCES AGAINST THE SUBURBS

Whatever its faults, the individualistic culture shows a remarkable degree of resilience. The market-driven political culture by its very nature helps strong economic players become stronger and encourages the weaker players to find the right allies and develop the tactics needed to grab a piece of the action. So if the suburbs in the 1990s are climbing to the top of the hill, the careful observer will look at who is being displaced and consider how they might recover lost ground. The inescapable conclusion is that the coming years will see increased use of Chicago-downstate coalitions to confront the richer collar counties.

Downstaters and their city cousins have already begun to realize that they have more in common than previously thought. In 1990, when poor rural school districts were joined by the Chicago Board of Education in a lawsuit over school spending disparities, the Chicago Urban League and the Illinois Farm Bureau were additional unlikely allies. Two years later, when a constitutional amendment proposal sought increased school funding, the chief sponsors were a Chicago Democratic senator and a Republican senator-farmer from central Illinois. The business coalition that opposed the measure targeted its media campaign at the suburbs.

The school aid formula provides a lens that shows where the greatest needs are in Illinois. It bases allocations on property wealth, need, and the numbers of poor children and consistently shows that Chicago and downstate would almost always be the winners in terms of where more resources should be spent. In the 1994 gubernatorial campaign, Democratic candidate Dawn Clark Netsch proposed a state income tax that would be tied to property tax relief and increased state school aid. Confirming the obvious, the Legislative Research Unit showed inquiring legislators that in the aggregate Chicago and downstate would be net beneficiaries, at the expense of the collar counties.

An economic battle between the regions is heating up, in part because the collar counties have their own growing needs for transportation, higher education, and social services. With their budgets tightening and the redistribution of tax dollars continuing to favor the city and downstate, collar county leaders will insist, ever more intently as their power grows, upon accountability from Chicago and downstate on how the suburbanites' tax dollars are being spent. Such demands surfaced in 1993, when senate president James "Pate" Philip of DuPage County insisted that Chicago public schools limit job protection for teachers in exchange for increased school funding. In a 1994 editorial, the *Chicago Tribune* wrote about a metropolitan region at war with itself:

> The fighting shifts across many fronts, no longer confined to city against suburbs. Often it's about taxes and whether affluent communities should share with poorer ones. Sometimes it's about building a third airport instead of expanding O'Hare, or where low-income housing should go, or whether the state should foster business growth on the urban fringe or back in the job-starved city. Granted, our region has never been mistaken for the Love Boat.

In bygone days a mighty Chicago did as it pleased, with little regard for what the late Mayor Daley dismissively termed the country towns. Savvy suburbs took a lesson, annexing tax-rich shopping malls and telling their neighbors to go scratch. Subtle forms of discrimination were perfected to keep minorities in their place, which is to say, in the city, or in a handful of resegregating suburbs. That's the history. Now it may get worse.[6]

TOLERATING THE SEAMY SIDE

The chapters of this book provide plentiful evidence that the individualistic culture of Illinois is deeply ingrained. Illinois has shown generally lax attitudes toward ethics in politics; a tradition of managing government for political ends; and only modest effort to make government perform for the people as opposed to those in power. Government in Illinois, a state with a rich and successful history of commerce, is simply another marketplace. Politics and elective office are just another way of making a good living.

Political corruption in this context has been tolerated, as if reaping the spoils of government is no more shameful than overindulging at the grocery store. "To the victor belongs the spoils" is the enduring value that drives campaigns in Illinois. In 1972, Chicago Mayor Richard J. Daley transferred some of the city's insurance business to a company that his son had just joined. When challenged by the media, an angry Daley retorted: "If I can't help my sons . . . then they can kiss my ass . . . I make no apologies to anyone. There are many men in this room whose fathers helped them and they went on to become fine public officials. . . . If a man can't put his arms around his sons, then what kind of world are we living in?"[7] As a consequence, the mayor's image as a good family man improved.

The awarding of government business on a no-bid basis to lawyers, investment bankers, consultants, and other professionals has been called "pinstripe patronage." Former governor James R. Thompson was a strong believer in the practice. He personally oversaw the awards of millions of dollars of business to friends, former colleagues, and political fund-raisers. "It's a deliberate policy," Thompson said. "If I don't [oversee the awards], somebody else will, and I'll be held responsible. And if I do, then I'm assured that it's being rotated among the firms and among the bond houses."[8] It might be added that these were firms and houses that contributed to his campaigns.

This situation would not be tolerated in moralistic Wisconsin and Minnesota. In Wisconsin it has been considered scandalous for a state legislator to use a state phone to make personal calls home. In Minnesota a legislative candidate was chided for providing free Hostess Twinkies to a meeting of senior citizens. Nor would citizens of those states condone the extensive job patronage awarded by Illinois state government. The three governors who preceded Governor Jim Edgar—Richard Ogilvie, Dan Walker, and James Thompson—all called for patronage reform in their initial campaigns. Once in office, however, each used this tool for dispensing jobs.[9] Under Governor Thompson patronage became progressively stronger until almost every opening—even for temporary clerks and student summer internships—was scrutinized to see if any patron had a candidate for the opening. The practice was bipartisan: a powerful Democratic state senator would take a list of patronage demands to Republican Thompson's office before each legislative session. If the job requests were fulfilled, the senate committee chairman would look more kindly on the governor's legislative program.

A fine line often separates spoils politics from illegal corruption. When, for example, does a major campaign contribution become a bribe, a direct payment for an action the elected official might not have taken otherwise? Many Illinois public officials have crossed that line. In 1956, state auditor Orville Hodge was convicted of writing checks on state government for his own use in amounts totaling $1.5 million and of misusing another $1 million.[10] In the 1950s, Speaker of the house (later Illinois secretary of state) Paul Powell bought stock in a new horse racing association at ten cents a share. He then helped the racing group get prime racing dates; Powell's stock escalated to $17.50 per share. When questioned by reporters about the apparent conflict of interest, Powell said his only mistake was in not buying more stock in the first place.[11] When Powell died unexpectedly in 1970, he left a fortune of $3 million, including $800,000 in small bills stuffed in shoe boxes in his Springfield hotel room.

Since the 1960s, evidence of high-level corruption has been uncovered frequently. Two justices of the Illinois Supreme Court resigned over the appearance of improprieties in stock they held in a bank organized by a state official.[12] Two governors were convicted of felonies—Otto Kerner, for racetrack bribery while in office, and Dan Walker, for financial wrongdoing after leaving office.[13] Since 1970, several state legislators have been convicted of selling votes.

The most spectacular—and disheartening—revelations of official and pervasive corruption came in 1988 with the Operation Greylord investigation of the Cook County court system; sixty-five judges, court officials, and attorneys were convicted for systematic bribery.[14] For scores of participants throughout the court system (and for hundreds, possibly thousands, of knowledgeable bystanders within the system) illegal payoffs at all levels, from a bailiff to a presiding judge, were standard operating procedure. Although the scandal generated headlines for months, the public seemed little surprised, for it was generally understood, in Chicago at least, that this was simply the way one did business in the halls of government. Chicago congressman Dan Rostenkowski, indicted in 1994 on seventeen counts of corruption, behaved just as Chicagoans expect their influential politicians to behave, according to John Gardiner, a specialist in political ethics.[15]

CASH AND POLITICAL CAMPAIGNS

The use of cash contributions to garner business from state government is another practice that would be disdained in moralistic political cultures but is accepted in Illinois as the accepted way of doing business. Gubernatorial candidates talk openly of the need to raise as much as $15 million to fund their campaigns, though it would seem obvious that the people most vulnerable to appeals to generate such amounts are those who do or want to do business with the state. There are no limits on contributions in Illinois, as there are at the national level and in many states, to prevent donors from getting carried away. Construction companies alone contributed half a million dollars to Governor Thompson's 1986 campaign.[16] The list of road builders and engineering companies and the amounts they contributed tend to confirm that these companies make their contributions—of $1,000 to $20,000 and more—on a basis roughly proportionate to their shares of state business. This practice has gone on for decades under both Republican and Democratic administrations.

In the early 1980s, the head of a small engineering firm came to a political consultant.[17] "We don't seem to be able to get any state business, though we have been submitting what we think are good, competitive bids for some time now. Do you have any suggestions?" The consultant responded, "If you make a campaign contribution of $1,000 or $2,000 to the governor's campaign committee and make sure a certain person at the Illinois Department of Transportation is aware of it, I am told it might help." The engineer did so, and he began to win state contracts.

Many law firms and investment banking houses also routinely contribute $5,000 to $20,000 to gubernatorial campaigns. In 1984 and 1985, during a nonelection period, Governor Thompson's political committee raised $1 million, two-thirds of it in amounts of $1,000 or more. A review of the contributors suggests that three-quarters of the total raised in those larger contributions came from people and companies that did business with the state or were affected directly by state regulations. Thompson's personal role in the awarding of pinstripe patronage was a key element in his extraordinary success at fund-raising. Governor Thompson's campaign committee raised $24 million during his fourteen years in office.[18]

INSTEAD OF REFORM, MINOR TUNE-UPS

Illinois has never been a leading reform state and yet, in the early 1900s, it was at the forefront of government reorganization. In the 1960s the legislative and executive branches in Illinois were among the first to modernize their respective operations, and in 1970 the Illinois Constitutional Convention authorized home-rule powers for municipalities and vastly improved upon the 1870 charter. These improvements illustrate one of the strengths of the individualistic culture: it is adept at correcting its own excesses to protect itself from more fundamental change.

There will be opportunities for such corrections as the century plays out, but they will not be engineered without a good deal of effort. Constitutional amendments failed time and again between 1870 and 1970 because the old system was carefully guarded by vested interests and no organization could pull all the players together until Samuel Witwer forged a bipartisan and statewide coalition, which resulted in the 1970 Constitution.

Illinois in the 1990s lacks a good reason to come together. There is little sense of statewide community. Residents of metropolitan Chicago tend to vacation in Wisconsin and Michigan, not downstate. The Cubs and the White Sox draw downstaters, but the visitors seldom venture far from the buses parked near the ballparks. It is not unknown for a newly elected legislator from Chicago to make his first-ever trip downstate on the day he or she is sworn into office in Springfield.

Likewise, suburbanites spend little time in Chicago, and city dwellers tend to disdain the suburbs. In his role as manager for a statewide political campaign in 1978, one of the authors invited the campaign's collar county coordinators to Chicago's Loop for a luncheon meeting in the stately Walnut Room of Marshall Field's department store.[19] "How often do you ladies come into the Loop," he asked. "Oh, I never come in," and "This is the first time I've been in the Loop in years" were typical responses.

Illinois has no unifying themes. There is no "Eyes of Texas" or "My Old Kentucky Home" to arouse sentiment. The fight song of the University of

Illinois is little known outside the campus and alumni community. This helps explain why as of 1994 disparities in per pupil spending between poorest and richest schools were among the greatest among the states.[20] There is almost no emotional connection from region to region, except perhaps distrust.

Chicago is no longer the fourth largest city in the world but the thirty-seventh, just ahead of Yokohama, Japan. Chicago can still boast of the world's tallest office building and the world's busiest airport, but it also has the world's biggest—and one of the nation's most violent—public housing project at the Robert Taylor Homes in Chicago and a public school system that has been labeled the worst in the nation.[21] When former U.S. secretary of education William Bennett made that remark, it was met not with outrage but with hangdog embarassment and a flurry of pronouncements that finally something would have to be done.

What does the future hold? The expansion of the metropolitan frontier will accelerate. Because of the increased work that can be accomplished away from the office, place will become less important to where many people work and more important to where they live. The trend to earlier retirement will fuel the outward wave, and as more jobs are created in the suburbs, more employees can locate farther out on the fringe and commute inward to their jobs, just as the original suburbanites commuted in to the central city.

The Northeastern Illinois Planning Commission will keep up the good fight against the excesses of sprawl. But its efforts probably will be to little avail because the siren call from the frontier is too compelling. As John Herbers notes from a national perspective, "In almost every contest between repairing the old and building anew in undeveloped areas, the new wins."[22] He adds, "We have created a whole new form of the American community, one that is diffused, fragmented, and without a center, but also one that is charged with energy, individual initiative, and the capacity to organize around particular interests."[23]

Consistent with this development, Chicago's lakefront business center and its environs will become even more vibrant. As diffusion increases throughout vast suburbia, the need will intensify for a strong regional center, a marketplace for action, creativity, ideas, and deals. Chicago will also become ever more at the heart of state politics. The major electronic and newspaper media based in the city reach three-quarters of the state's population, and the city is preferred to Springfield as a meeting place by most political, government, and association leaders, primarily because of transportation convenience. The futuristic James R. Thompson Center, adjacent to Chicago's city hall and the Cook County building, now surpasses the Capitol as a place to do state business.

With good location and natural resources and envied networks of rail, air, and interstate highway transportation, the state's diverse economy should chug along, relatively stable, with moderate growth. Illinois and its governments will continue to muddle along, supporting the business community that in turn supports the governments. Public policy responses will be cautious, conventional, and modest, as always. Illinois will someday address the glaring issue of disparities in education resources, probably when new political coalitions, under pressure from the civic and business communities, bargain tough over more state aid in grudging return for stricter accountability in how it is spent. The individualistic culture, after all, does not see government as a primary instrument for solving social problems, and its professional elected officials have found that the politics of caution plays well in Illinois.

Sources for Further Study

The quantity of material available on Illinois politics and government is considerable. The material is also quite good. In addition, much scholarly literature of a more general nature, including histories, has been written about Illinois and its major city, Chicago.

It has been said that Illinois is not a natural community. It is a sharply divided state—politically, economically, and culturally. The major divisions are between Chicago, collar counties, and downstate. To understand this diversity requires a careful reading of both historical materials and contemporary documents. A good start may be made by looking at *Diversity, Conflict, and State Politics: Regionalism in Illinois*, edited by Peter Nardulli (Urbana: University of Illinois Press, 1989). This collection of essays grew out of a 1986 conference ("Illinois: A House Divided?") organized by the Institute of Government and Public Affairs at the University of Illinois. A brief (sixteen-page) synthesis of the background papers for this conference as well as some of the discussions at the conference are contained in the pamphlet, *Regionalism and Political Community in Illinois* by Anna J. Merritt (Urbana: Institute of Government and Public Affairs, 1988).

An earlier work, *Cities of the Prairie Revisited* by Daniel J. Elazar and associates (Lincoln: University of Nebraska Press, 1986), looks at certain communities in Illinois and elsewhere to draw on the varied experience of specific and typical communities to illustrate some of the trends confronting our urban society. Among the Illinois cities discussed are Champaign-Urbana, Peoria, Joliet, and Springfield. Another brief discussion of the political and historical context of this state is contained in the chapter on Illinois in *The Book of America: Inside the Fifty States Today* by Neal Peirce and Jerry Hagstrom (New York: Warner Books, 1984).

GENERAL REFERENCES

The best overall reference for all three branches of state government is the *Illinois Blue Book,* published biennially by the Illinois secretary of state and available free of charge. A shorter version, also published by that office, is the *Handbook of Illinois Government.* The *Blue Book* contains biographies of all Illinois federal and state elected officials; descriptions of all state boards, agencies, and commissions; lists of newspapers and radio and television stations; lists of counties and incorporated cities and villages; lists of past governors and other state officers; the text of the state constitution; and other material. The State Board of Elections also issues *Illinois State Officers,* which contains a section on the judiciary. The Legislative Research Unit (formerly the Illinois Legislative Council) of the General Assembly has published *State Board and Commission Descriptions* (1991). This volume lists all committees, commissions, task forces, advisory boards, and so on created by state statute or executive order, or by federal law, to which persons may be appointed. The research unit also publishes the *Directory of Illinois State Officials* after each statewide election. A similar directory, the "Roster of State Government Officials," is published by *Illinois Issues* annually.

The Illinois Legislative Research Unit publishes the *Directory of Registered Lobbyists in Illinois* (most recently revised in 1992). It is organized by categories, has an index, and contains useful information in a brief introduction. Another list of lobbyists is distributed by the secretary of state's office; this list appears fairly frequently and is in alphabetical order by lobbyist, with a cross-reference section organized by subject.

The Illinois Municipal League puts out a detailed directory of municipal officials every other year. County officials are included in the *Blue Book* and in a directory published by the State Board of Elections. The State Board of Elections publishes lists of municipal, township (road district), school and community college officials; the State Board of Education lists appointed school officials in its publications.

The Illinois State Library, located in Springfield and under the jurisdiction of the secretary of state, is another excellent resource. Its charge is to maintain a library for state officials and employees, operate a government research service, secure and distribute documents and materials, and provide research services to all state agencies and their staffs.

Most of the materials and documents mentioned here are available through large university libraries or through local libraries that are part of

ILLINET (Illinois Library and Information Network). ILLINET provides access for all Illinois residents to the specialized collection of the state library. Library development is carried on in conjunction with the eighteen state-supported library systems and their member libraries.

ILLINET includes four reference and research centers—the Chicago Public Library, the University of Illinois at Urbana-Champaign, Illinois State University, and Southern Illinois University at Carbondale. These centers can provide access—via fax, telephone, Statewide Online Catalog (ILLINET ONLINE) and mail—to a vast array of specialized collections and reference services. ILLINET makes statewide library resources available to all public library cardholders. It is augmented by a referral system to other major libraries in the nation. In addition to the research and reference centers, there are three other valuable special resource centers—the John Crerar Library in Chicago, the Northwestern University Library in Evanston, and the University of Chicago Library.

There are several bibliographies on Illinois government. The Institute of Government and Public Affairs published two, one in 1953 and another in 1965. Neal Peirce, in his *The Megastates Of America: People, Politics, and Power in the Ten Great American States* (New York: Norton, 1972), lists significant references at the end of the chapter on Illinois. An updated bibliography is contained in a later study, *The Great Lakes States of America: People, Politics, and Power in the Five Great Lakes States* done by Peirce and John Keefe (New York: Norton, 1980). In 1972 the Center for Governmental Studies at Northern Illinois University published *Chicago's Politics and Society: A Selected Bibliography* (DeKalb: Northern Illinois University Press).

A number of general academic studies and textbooks on Illinois government are in print. *Illinois: Political Processes and Governmental Performance,* edited by Edgar Crane (Dubuque IA: Kendall-Hunt, 1980), contains chapters contributed by Illinois political scientists and others.

A new textbook by David Kenney and Barbara L. Brown is *Basic Illinois Government* (3d ed., Carbondale: Southern Illinois University Press, 1993). Neil Garvey's *The Government and Administration of Illinois* is quite dated (New York: Thomas Y. Crowell, 1958) but good for historical purposes. There are also some textbooks specifically prepared for high school classes, as well as handbooks put out by the League of Women Voters on various aspects of state and local government. A new high school text, *Governing Illinois: Of the People, by the People, and for the People* (Springfield: *Illinois*

Issues, 1991), was written by high school teachers and edited by James M. Banovetz and Caroline A. Gherardini.

The Institute of Government and Public Affairs at the University of Illinois has prepared several excellent books and monographs on state affairs. The institute's Assembly papers (final reports and background papers of its almost biennial assemblies which were held between 1957 and 1982, each on a specific policy issue confronting state decision makers), *Illinois Government Research* (a series of short research reports that appeared between 1959 and 1985) and *Occasional Papers in Illinois Politics* (1981–84) all contain frequently cited material. The institute also issues a newsletter, *Policy Forum,* modeled after the earlier IGR.

Several other university-based research centers include the Social Science Research Institute and the Center for Governmental Studies at Northern Illinois University in DeKalb; the Legislative Studies Center at the University of Illinois at Springfield (now part of the Institute for Public Affairs); the Rural Studies Center at Western Illinois University in Macomb; the Institute for Public Policy and Administration at Governors State University in University Park; and the Bureau of Business and Economic Research at the University of Illinois at Urbana-Champaign.

Public opinion polls are another good source of information. The Public Opinion Lab at Northern Illinois University at DeKalb has conducted statewide polls since 1984. Topics range from science and technology to citizenship and political views. Public opinion polls include surveys of the general public and special surveys of policymakers such as state legislators and science policy leaders. Sangamon State's Institute of Public Affairs conducted political polls during the 1992 election for *Illinois Issues.*

The Survey Research Laboratory at the University of Illinois and other polling organizations from time to time take statewide surveys on specific topics.

Illinois Issues, which began publishing in 1975, plays an important role in discussions of state public affairs. It is published by the University of Illinois at Springfield and is patterned after the *National Journal.* From time to time, the magazine also prepares a special monograph on a particular topic, such as *Home Rule in Illinois* by Banovetz and Thomas W. Kelty, which appeared in 1987.

Newspapers are a good source for material on state government and politics. The two major papers in Chicago are the *Chicago Tribune* and *Sun-Times.* There are also the *Chicago Defender,* devoted primarily to black community interests; the *Chicago Reporter,* a monthly newsletter on racial issues in metropolitan Chicago; and two suburban dailies, the *Daily Southtown* and the *Daily Herald*. The weekly *Crain's Chicago Business* regularly runs stories and OpEd pieces about Chicago and Illinois government policies and administration. *Chicago Enterprise,* in a magazine format, contained in-depth analyses of Chicago's economy and other policy issues before ceasing publication in 1994.

Downstate Illinois has a large number of dailies and weeklies. The 1993–94 *Blue Book* lists all the dailies and weeklies in Illinois plus radio, TV, and cable stations. The listing takes fourteen single-spaced pages. The St. Louis paper, the *Post-Dispatch,* has considerable Illinois government coverage. Several years ago, the State Historical Library microfilmed all the files of at least one newspaper in every county. The collection provides a wealth of historical information from every section of the state.

Of particular value to researchers is the *Illinois Daily Press Summary* published by the Illinois Information Service for use by officials of Illinois state government and the state university system. There is a subscription fee. Unfortunately, it is not indexed.

Surprisingly, the only newspaper in Illinois that has been indexed over time is the *Chicago Tribune,* and that only since 1972. An index for the *Sun-Times* has been provided since July 1985 by DataTimes, located in Oklahoma City. DataTimes has also issued the Chicago Newspaper Index since January 1976.

HISTORIES

The literature on Illinois history is a rich source of information for students of Illinois government and politics. Among general histories, Robert P. Howard's *Illinois: A History of the Prairie State* (Grand Rapids MI: William B. Eerdmans, 1972) is the most comprehensive recent study. Richard J. Jensen's *Illinois: A Bicentennial History* (New York: Norton, 1978) is newer but less complete. A two-volume reader edited by Robert P. Sutton, *The Prairie State—A Documentary History of Illinois* (Grand Rapids MI: William B. Eerdmans, 1976), also provides helpful background. An in-depth examination of Chicago's importance in the nineteenth-century growth of the West and Midwest is William Cronon's *Nature's Metropolis: Chicago and the Great West* (New York: Norton, 1991). An earlier standard work is Theodore C. Pease's *The Story of Illinois,* 3d ed., rev. and enlarged by Marguerita Jenison Pease (Chicago: University of Chicago Press, 1965). Another classic is Thomas Ford's volume, *A History of Illinois, from Its Commencement as a State in 1818 to 1847,* published in 1854 and reprinted in

1945 and 1946 (Chicago: Lakeside Press, R. R. Donnelly and Sons). Milton Derber's *Labor in Illinois: The Affluent Years, 1945–80* (Urbana: University of Illinois Press, 1989) is rather specialized.

The definitive resource work on Illinois history is John Hoffman, ed., *A Guide to the History of Illinois* (Westport CT: Greenwood Press, 1991). It is divided into bibliographic essays and archival and manuscript collections.

In 1929 Illinois became the first state to establish a state archive, a separate administrative unit under the secretary of state. The State Archives building in Springfield was constructed in 1938. The archives staff maintains state records of permanent, legal, administrative, or historical value; arranges them in the order of their creation; and prepares them for public use. The archives are a very valuable resource. In 1978 the archives published in loose-leaf form "A Descriptive Inventory of the Archives of the State of Illinois," with a separate 131-page index. In 1983 the archives published *A Guide to County Records in the Illinois Regional Archives,* a descriptive guide to the Illinois Regional Archives Depository System, which collects local government records at regional depositories at six university campuses.

Another excellent source of historical information is the *Illinois Historical Journal,* published quarterly by the Illinois Historic Preservation Agency for the Illinois State Historical Society.

ILLINOIS CONSTITUTION

Illinois adopted a new constitution in 1970, following a year-long effort by the Sixth Illinois Constitutional Convention (1969–70). One side benefit was the creation of a body of exceptional literature on Illinois constitutional developments.

Earlier constitutional conventions had been held in 1818, 1848, 1862, 1870, and 1922. All have been extensively documented and analyzed in Janet Cornelius's comprehensive study, *Constitution Making in Illinois, 1818–1970* (Urbana: University of Illinois Press, 1972).

Much preparatory work went into the 1969 convention. Two works about it are notable—George D. Braden and Rubin G. Cohn, *The Illinois Constitution: An Annotated and Comparative Analysis* (Urbana: Institute of Government and Public Affairs, 1969), and *Con-Con: Issues for the Illinois Constitutional Convention* (Urbana: University of Illinois Press, 1970), prepared by the Governor's Constitution Research Group and edited by Samuel Gove and Victoria Ranney. The former work is a most careful analysis of all aspects of the 1870 Constitution. The latter is a collection of papers on public issues that the delegates were expected to face.

The official documents from the 1969–70 convention are excellent sources of information. Most valuable is the seven-volume *Record of Proceedings, Sixth Illinois Constitutional Convention, December 8, 1969–September 3, 1970* (Springfield: John W. Lewis, Secretary of State, in cooperation with the Sixth Illinois Constitutional Convention, 1969–70, 1972). These include the daily journals with floor roll-call votes, the transcript of all floor debates, and committee reports. Some contain valuable lists of references. Volume 5 contains a subject index of the transcripts. In 1988 the Illinois State Library issued an index organized by articles and section number of the constitution.

An overview analysis of the convention is *The Sixth Illinois Constitutional Convention* by Gove and Thomas Kitsos (New York: National Municipal League, 1974). A more in-depth analysis may be found in a ten-volume series edited by Joseph Pisciotte and published by the University of Illinois Press for the Institute of Government and Public Affairs. In addition to the Cornelius work already cited, the series includes *For the First Hours of Tomorrow: The New Illinois Bill of Rights* (1972) by Elmer Gertz; *Lobbying at the Illinois Constitutional Convention* (1973) by Ian D. Burman; *To Judge with Justice: History and Politics of Illinois Judicial Reform* (1973) by Rubin G. Cohn; *Ballots for Change: New Suffrage and Amending Articles for Illinois* (1973) by Alan S. Gratch and Virginia H. Ubik; *Politics of the Purse: Revenue and Finance in the Sixth Illinois Constitutional Convention* (1974) by Joyce D. Fishbane and Glenn W. Fisher; *A Fundamental Goal: Education for the People of Illinois* (1975) by Jane G. Buresh; *Roll Call! Patterns of Voting in the Sixth Illinois Constitutional Convention* (1975) by David Kenney, Jack R. Van Der Slik, and Samuel J. Pernacciaro; and *Electing a Constitution: The Illinois Citizen and the 1970 Constitution* (1979) by JoAnna Watson. The capstone volume, *Charter for a New Age: An Inside View of the Sixth Illinois Constitutional Convention* (1980) is by Elmer Gertz and Joseph P. Pisciotte.

Samuel W. Witwer, considered by many to be the "father" of constitutional reform and who served in 1969–70 as convention president, is the subject of a political biography, *Quest for a Constitution: A Man Who Wouldn't Quit*, by Elmer Gertz and Ed Gilbreth (Lanham MD: University Press of America, 1984).

Illinois constitutional conventions, especially the 1970 meeting, have generated many doctoral dissertations. Many of these are listed in the August 1977 issue of the *Journal of the Illinois State Historical Society,* now the *Illinois Historical Journal.* Many law review articles have also been published on specific issues raised by the 1970 Constitution.

Persons interested in studying the results of the Constitutional Convention would do well to look at *1970 Illinois Constitution Annotated for Legislators,* published by the Legislative Research Unit; the third edition came out in 1987. In anticipation of the November 1988 referendum on whether another constitutional convention should be called, a Committee of 50 was formed to look at various aspects of the 1970 Constitution. In addition to holding meetings and hearings, it commissioned ten background papers that serve as a further source of information and analysis: "Constitutional Developments in Illinois" by Gove; "The Bill of Rights of the 1970 Constitution" by John Garvey; "The Suffrage, Elections and Constitutional Revision Articles" by John Jackson; "The Executive Article" by William Monat; "The Judicial Article" by Nancy Ford; "The Local Government Article" by Banovetz and Ann Elder; "The Public Finance Article" by Giertz; "The Education Article" by Donald Sevener; "Legislative Redistricting" by Paul Green, and "The Legislative Article" by Van Der Slik. The series was published by the Illinois Commission on Intergovernmental Cooperation.

For the November 1988 referendum, the *Northern Illinois University Law Review* devoted its fall 1988 issue to the Illinois Constitution. It contains an introduction by Witwer, nine articles (some by authors who also wrote background papers for the Committee of 50), and a lengthy bibliography.

THE EXECUTIVE BRANCH

Much has been written about the executive branch of state government, its organizations, and its functions and powers. Several gubernatorial biographies have been published.

John Peter Altgeld, who served as governor between 1893 and 1897, was the subject of at least two biographies; the best known is Harry Barnard's *"Eagle Forgotten": The Life of John Peter Altgeld* (Indianapolis: Bobbs-Merrill, 1938). Another governor with national visibility was Frank O. Lowden (1917–21), the subject of a two-volume biography, *Lowden of Illinois,* by William T. Hutchinson of the University of Chicago (Chicago: University of Chicago Press, 1957). Newsman Thomas B. Littlewood wrote *Horner of Illinois* (Evanston: Northwestern University Press, 1969) about Henry Horner, who was governor from 1933 to 1940. Horner was best known for his successful challenge to the Chicago organization in the 1936 gubernatorial primary. Adlai E. Stevenson is the subject of many studies. Most highlight his activities after he left the governorship to seek the presidency in 1952. In addition, historian Walter Johnson has published a monumental eight-volume collection of Stevenson's papers. Volume 3 contains the papers for the period when he was governor, 1949–53. Governor William G. Stratton's biography is by David Kenney and is titled *A Political Passage: The Career of Stratton of Illinois* (Carbondale: Southern Illinois University Press, 1990). Controversial Governor Dan Walker's biography is *Dan Walker: The Glory and the Tragedy* by Taylor Pensoneau and Bob Ellis (Evansville IN: Smith Collins, 1993).

The immediate past governor, James Thompson, is the subject of a good 1979 midterm biography by Robert E. Hartley, *Big Jim Thompson of Illinois* (Chicago: Rand McNally, 1979). For Thompson's version of his years in office see *Illinois, State of the State: 1977–1991, the Thompson Administration* (Springfield: State of Illinois, 1991).

A volume that looks at the state's governors is Robert P. Howard's *Mostly Good and Competent Men: Illinois Governors, 1818 to 1988* (Springfield: *Illinois Issues*, Sangamon State University, and the Illinois State Historical Society, 1988). Separate chapters are devoted to each governor since Illinois became a state. Daniel J. Elazar wrote an analysis, "The Office of Governor in Illinois, 1818–1933," for a 1962 Illinois assembly on that topic by the University of Illinois, Institute of Government and Public Affairs.

Except for the very early governors, the papers of Illinois governors are generally not available in published form. They may be found in the state archives and the State Library. One governor who did make an effort to have his papers published was Richard G. Ogilvie (1969–73). He published his executive papers in Illinois General Assembly, *Major Legislation, 1969–72* (Springfield: Illinois General Assembly, 1973). The Bureau of the Budget (an agency created by Ogilvie) published *Papers in Public Finance—The Ogilvie Years/Bureau of the Budget* (Springfield: Bureau of the Budget, 1973).

Interesting material on the executive branch can be found in the oral histories published by the Oral History Office at Sangamon State University. Between 1977 and 1985, the office put out eleven volumes in this series, one of them on Dan Walker; the others are interviews with people who have served in the executive branch as appointed officials.

During his term of office, Governor Ogilvie called for a change in the traditional biennial executive budget. The 1970 Constitution instituted such a change, and today the budget is prepared annually and delivered to the General Assembly around March 1. It is a good resource document on the agencies of the state government and their finances and functions. The comptroller's office also publishes a valuable overall fiscal document, *Illinois Comprehensive Annual Financial report*. A very good fiscal analysis for a specific period is the Taxpayers' Federation of Illinois report *Illinois State Spending: The Thompson Years, 1978–88* (Springfield: Taxpayers' Federation of Illinois, 1988).

Two guides to state agency services are also available; though quite different, both are useful. In 1982 the Department of Commerce and Community Affairs published a *Guide to Illinois State Services*. It describes all elected executive offices as well as departments, agencies, boards, and commissions; it also indicates what services are provided. The guide has not been updated. More recently (1992) the Legislative Research Unit published a *Constituent Services Guide* that lists most state departments and agencies, some of the typical questions asked about each, the answers to those questions, and persons to contact for more information.

Legislators devote a good deal of their attention to taxes. To facilitate their understanding of the issues, the Legislative Research Unit published in 1994 the *Illinois Tax Handbook for Legislators* (10th ed.). Another valuable resource, *Illinois Tax Climate,* is published biennially by the Taxpayers' Federation of Illinois. It compares six of this state's taxes (corporate income, corporate license, personal income, general sales, property, and utility) to the same taxes in Illinois's neighbors (Indiana, Iowa, Kentucky, Michigan, Minnesota, Missouri, Ohio, and Wisconsin) as well as the other nine leading industrial states (California, New York, Texas, Ohio, Pennsylvania, Michigan, New Jersey, North Carolina, and Massachusetts). For an insight into how one particular tax issue was resolved in the political arena, an interesting study was done by Joan Parker, *Summit and Resolution: The Illinois Tax Increase of 1983* (Springfield: Sangamon State University, 1984).

The executive branch of Illinois state government has been reorganized several times since the turn of the century. In fact, Illinois was a leader in executive reorganization with the Lowden reorganization of 1917 and the enactment of the Civil Administrative Code. The reorganization was a result of the book-length report published by the Efficiency and Economy Committee in 1915 during Governor Dunn's term. Another reorganization report was by the Commission to Study State Government (Little Hoover Commission), which reported during Governor Stevenson's term. The Commission on State Government—Illinois reported to Governor Kerner in 1967. In 1976, gubernatorial candidates Thompson and Howlett created a bipartisan reorganization committee that prepared a report, *Orderly Government*. A more recent survey and analysis of the state's personnel system is the Governor's Human Resources Advisory Council report *Recommendations for Change in Illinois* (1993). There have also been other reports over the years, which frequently offer valuable insights into the structure and function of state government.

THE LEGISLATIVE BRANCH

Documentation on the Illinois General Assembly is good, and persons interested in information on legislators and legislation have easy access.

A valuable contribution to information about the legislature is a series of memoirs published by the Oral History Program at Sangamon State University. Begun in 1980 and concluded in 1988, the series includes more than two dozen titles, which provide unique insights into the General Assembly. Each volume includes a carefully crafted conversation with an individual who played an important role in the state's legislative history.

An earlier source on the workings of the General Assembly is *The Illinois Legislature: Structure and Process,* by Samuel K. Gove, Richard W. Carlson, and Richard J. Carlson (Urbana: University of Illinois Press, 1976). Of particular value is the ten-page bibliographic essay that makes up Chapter 8. An earlier, more academic look at the legislature is contained in *Legislative Politics in Illinois* by Gilbert Y. Steiner and Gove (Urbana: University of Illinois Press, 1960). A good addition to the collection of books on the General Assembly is *Lawmaking in Illinois* (1986, rev. ed. Springfield: Sangamon State University, 1989) by Jack R. Van Der Slik and Kent Redfield of Sangamon State University's Legislative Studies Center. It contains a good list of references.

Among official legislative documents, the most valuable is the *Legislative Synopsis and Digest,* published weekly by the Legislative Reference Bureau when the legislature is in session. It provides considerable information on the status of pending legislation, amendments, and committee and floor actions. Information on the status of bills is on computer. The floor debates of the General Assembly are not published, but they are transcribed. Debates on microfiche may be obtained from the index department of the Office of the Secretary of State. The tapes for the debates are located in the archives. House committee debates are taped but not routinely transcribed.

Several thousand bills are introduced each session of the legislature. These bills are generally available in the bill rooms of the two legislative chambers.

Each house publishes a daily journal that records all floor actions and roll calls. The house alone includes committee votes in its journal. No charge is made when the journals are picked up at the bill room, but they should also be available in most libraries. Several months after the session concludes, the journals are bound and indexed by each house.

The Legislative Information System publishes *Weekly Report 10*, giving the status of bills at the end of each week. At the end of each session, it publishes *Final Report 10*. These are sent to state agencies and are available free of charge to the general public from the LIS office in Springfield. The LIS also offers a computer-based Bill Status System that subscribers can access by telephone for display on their terminals. The status of bills is updated approximately every fifteen minutes during legislative sessions. There is an annual fee for the service.

A calendar for each house is prepared each day the legislature is in session. These are designed to fit in coat pockets or purses. They list all bills, resolutions, and motions that are before each house on the floor. The calendars are available each day from the bill room of each house at no charge.

A private organization, the State Capital Information Service, provides the best summary of the previous day's legislative action in committees and on the floor. There is a substantial charge for this service.

For a monthly rundown of General Assembly activities, a good source is the newsletter *First Reading,* put out by the Legislative Research Unit. After the session—in fact several months later—the bills and resolutions adopted by that General Assembly are published by the secretary of state.

The comptroller annually publishes in a separate volume all the appropriations bills approved by the General Assembly.

The continuing legislation is codified and published by West Publishing Company for the State Bar Association. A major recodification took place in 1992 and the statutes are now cited as *Illinois Compiled Statutes*. There is a transition period as the statutes are adopted by the courts. The previous codification was referred to as the *Illinois Revised Statutes*. The new compiled statutes are in seven volumes with a separate index.

Every ten years, the apportionment of legislative districts is a big issue for state legislatures. Until the 1991 General Assembly session, the secretary of state put out a volume, *Apportionment Maps and Descriptions—Congressional, Legislative, and Judicial*. After the 1991–92 redistricting, the state Board of Elections published an updated version. Another source is *Redistricting: An Exercise in Prophecy,* published by the Institute of Government and Public Affairs in 1982. A more recent and extremely interesting publication is the *Political Atlas of Illinois,* published by Northern Illinois University Press in 1988. It provides maps as well as statistical snapshots of each state senate and house district.

A most valuable new *Illinois Issues* publication is the *Almanac of Illinois Politics—1994* edited by Jack R. Van Der Slik. It has detailed political and economic data for each legislative district, including a biography of each legislator. Roll-call votes on major issues are included, as are data on elections as well as on the executive and judicial branches.

The legislature has recently taken a greater interest in the administrative rules adopted by state agencies. The Joint Committee on Administrative Rules reviews proposed rules and comments on them. The proposed and adopted rules are published in the *Illinois Register* by the secretary of state. In 1985 the secretary of state's office published the Administrative Code in nine volumes; supplements appear annually. More on this general topic is contained in *Legislative Oversight: A Final Report and Background Papers of the Illinois Assembly on Legislative Oversight* published in 1982 by the Institute of Government and Public Affairs.

THE COURTS

Court decisions are important in determining the course of state government and politics. Understanding the decisions is not always easy for the non-lawyer.

The state's court decisions are published in the *Illinois Supreme Court Reports* and the *Illinois Appellate Court Reports.* Because the publication of these volumes takes some time, the reporter of decisions prepares combined advance sheets that come out biweekly. From time to time, the advance sheets list relevant law review articles and opinions of the attorney general. The decisions of the circuit courts generally are not available and are not published.

The Administrative Office of the Illinois Courts issues an annual report that contains much administrative and statistical data pertaining to the state's courts.

The opinions of the attorney general, although not binding as are court opinions, have considerable impact in legal circles. A selection of opinions is published in an annual volume by the attorney general.

There are many law reviews in the state: ten are published by university law schools. In addition there is the *Chicago Bar Record, Illinois Bar Journal, Illinois State Bar Association Quarterly,* and *Chicago Daily Law Bulle-*

tin. None of the university law reviews is devoted solely to Illinois legal affairs. The *University of Illinois Law Forum* does have an annual article reviewing decisions of the Illinois Supreme Court.

For the more political side of the judiciary, one should look at the publications stemming from the federal investigation of the Cook County courts— Operation Greylord. The best summary of the investigation is James Tuohy and Rob Warden's *Greylord: Justice, Chicago Style* (New York: G. P. Putnam's Sons, 1989). A more personal account is Brocton Lockwood, *Operation Greylord: Brocton Lockwood's Story* (Carbondale: Southern Illinois University Press, 1989).

After the Greylord and Gambat federal investigations, the state supreme court created a Special Commission on the Administration of Justice. The commission's two-volume report, The Illinois Supreme Court Special Commission on the Administration of Justice, *Final Report, Part I and II,* chairman Jerold S. Solovy (Chicago: N.p., December 1993) contains an in-depth analysis of the problems of the Illinois judicial system.

LOCAL GOVERNMENT

Local governments play an important role in Illinois, especially because there are more of them (more than sixty-eight hundred) than in any other state. Readers interested in the financial aspects of local government should refer to the annual reports put out by the state comptroller's office. Those interested in other aspects of these governments should contact the local officials of these government units, their statewide organizations, or, in some cases, the state agency responsible for them (for instance, the State Board of Education, which has jurisdiction over much of what local public school districts may and may not do). A useful general guide to local government is the *1985 Local Government Handbook* put out by the League of Women Voters of Illinois. It is clearly written and contains basic information.

A good local government reference is James F. Keane and Gary Koch, eds., *Illinois Local Government: A Handbook* (Carbondale: Southern Illinois University Press, 1990). It contains essays on various aspects of local government.

A somewhat different purpose is fulfilled by the *Catalog of State Assistance to Local Governments,* published by the Illinois Commission on Intergovernmental Cooperation; the sixth edition was dated June 1995. It summarizes state programs that provide financial and technical assistance to counties, municipalities, townships, and special districts (except school districts). The commission also publishes a newsletter, *Intergovernmental Issues,* which has material on local government but also intergovernmental affairs involving the state and federal governments.

One local government issue of great significance to state government is the very liberal home-rule power granted to cities and counties by the 1970 Constitution. Cities over twenty-five thousand population and counties with a chief executive officer (i.e., Cook County) automatically receive home-rule powers. This has had an important impact on state-local relations. A valuable contribution to the study of home rule and its impact on the state's cities and counties is *Home Rule in Illinois: Image and Reality* (Springfield: *Illinois Issues,* Sangamon State University, 1987) by James M. Banovetz and Thomas W. Kelty.

For students of home rule and municipal government in general, a valuable reference is the two-volume loose-leaf "Illinois Municipal Law and Practice in Illinois" (1994) edited by Stewart Diamond. It contains twenty-five chapters, each on a different topic and by a different author. For downstate cities, a good overview is contained in *The Middle-Size Cities of Illinois: Their People, Politics, and Quality of Life,* edited by Donald M. Johnson and Rebecca M. Veach (Springfield: Sangamon State University, 1980). Separate chapters are devoted to Bloomington-Normal, Champaign-Urbana, Decatur, East St. Louis, Peoria, Rockford, Rock Island–Moline, and Springfield.

Among the state's many local governments, one stands out as the most intriguing: Chicago. Because the literature on the Windy City is so voluminous, a separate section is devoted to it here.

CHICAGO GOVERNMENT AND POLITICS

One of the classics on Chicago's politics is still in print, *Machine Politics, Chicago Model* (Chicago: University of Chicago Press, 1937) by Harold F. Gosnell, reissued in 1967. The studies done in the late 1930s at the University of Chicago by Charles E. Merriam and his associates on metropolitan problems of the city were—and continue to be—impressive.

Two good sources on government problems in Chicago are the book-length reports of two Chicago Home Rule Commissions. The 1954 report, *Chicago's Government,* was published by the University of Chicago Press; in 1972, *The Chicago Home Rule Commission Report and Recommendations* was published by the University of Illinois at Chicago Circle.

On the administrative side, Dick Simpson of the University of Illinois–

Chicago has prepared several reports, including *Chicago's Future: In a Time of Change* (Champaign: Stipes, 1988), a series of short articles on various problems of Chicago; *Blueprint of the Chicago Government 1989* (Chicago: University of Illinois at Chicago, 1989), a report describing the many functions of Chicago and other governments in Cook County; and *The City Council's Role in Chicago Budget Making* (Chicago: University of Illinois at Chicago, 1990). In cooperation with the City Club of Chicago, Simpson also published *Chicago City Council Reform* (Chicago: University of Illinois at Chicago, 1988).

To help people understand the workings of the Chicago City Council and the Cook County Board, the Citizens Information Service of Illinois since 1980 has published the *City Council/County Board Report*. These useful newsletters include directories of city/county officials, roll-call votes in the city council and county board, and other information.

The many ethnic, religious, and racial groups that make up Chicago have served as a theme for a number of books. To list just a few that have appeared in recent years: *The Irish in Chicago* (Urbana: University of Illinois Press, 1987) by Lawrence McCaffrey, Ellen Skerrett, Michael Funchion, and Charles Fanning; *Hispanics in Chicago* (Chicago: Chicago Reporter and the Center for Community Research and Assistance of the Community Renewal Society, 1985) by Jorge Casuso and Eduardo Camacho; *Race and Politics in Chicago* (Chicago: Community Renewal Society, 1987) by Ben Joravsky and Eduardo Camacho; and *Race and Ethnicity in Chicago Politics* (Urbana: University of Illinois Press, 1987) by Dianne M. Pinderhughes.

Of endless fascination to students of Chicago politics have been the men (and briefly, one woman) who have served as mayor. Among the recent titles on this subject: *The Mayors: The Chicago Political Tradition* (Carbondale: Southern Illinois University Press, 1987) edited by Paul M. Green and Melvin G. Holli; *Fighting Jane: Mayor Jane Byrne and The Chicago Machine* (New York: Dial Press, 1980) by Bill Granger and Lori Granger; and *Big City Boss in Depression and War: Mayor Edward J. Kelly of Chicago* (DeKalb: Northern Illinois University Press, 1984) by Roger Biles.

Mayor Richard J. Daley has been the subject of numerous studies. A sampling of the better books are Mike Royko's *Boss: Richard J. Daley of Chicago* (New York: E. P. Dutton, 1971); Len O'Connor's *Clout: Mayor Daley and His City* (Chicago: Henry Reagnery, 1975), and *Requiem: The Decline of Mayor Daley and His Era* (Chicago: Contemporary Books, 1977); Eugene Kennedy's *Himself: The Life and Times of Mayor Richard J. Daley* (New York: Viking Press, 1978); and Milton Rakove's *Don't Make No Waves:*

Don't Back No Losers (Bloomington: Indiana University Press, 1975), and *We Don't Want Nobody Nobody Sent: An Oral History of the Daley Years* (Bloomington: Indiana University Press, 1979). After Daley's death in 1976, Northwestern University's Center for Urban Affairs and the University of Illinois Institute of Government and Public Affairs jointly published a series of monographs (primarily by academicians) on the post-Daley era titled *Chicago Politics Papers*. These papers were published by the University of Illinois Press in a single volume titled *After Daley: Chicago Politics in Transition* (1982) edited by Samuel K. Gove and Louis H. Masotti.

The last dozen years in Chicago politics have been tumultuous and will doubtless produce a large number of books. Among the volumes that have already appeared are Paul Kleppner's *Chicago Divided: The Making of a Black Mayor* (DeKalb: Northern Illinois Press, 1985); *The Making of the Mayor: Chicago 1983* (Grand Rapids MI: William B. Eerdmans, 1984), edited by Paul M. Green and Melvin G. Holli; Green's *Paul Green's Chicago* (Springfield: *Illinois Issues,* Sangamon State University, 1988), a collection of the author's columns and articles from *Illinois Issues; Courthouse over White House: Chicago and the Presidential Election of 1960* (Orlando: University Presses of Florida, 1988) by Edmund F. Kallina, Jr.; and *Bitter Fruit: Black Politics and the Chicago Machine, 1931–1991* (Chicago: University of Chicago Press, 1992) by William Grimshaw.

ILLINOIS ELECTIONS

Statewide data on election returns are readily available. *America Votes* (Election Research Center), which has been appearing regularly since 1956, contains a county-by-county and Chicago ward breakdown of the contests for president, U.S. senator, and governor. More detailed data for the same elections, as well as the primaries for each year, may be found in the biennial *Official Vote* now published by the state Board of Elections. A historical compilation of county election data is found in *Illinois Votes, 1900–1958*, edited by Samuel K. Gove (Urbana: Institute of Government and Public Affairs, 1959). The foreword describes sources of earlier election data. The institute also published two companion compilations, *Illinois Major Party Platforms, 1900–1964* (1966) and *Illinois Major Party Platforms II, 1966–1980* (1980) compiled by James D. Nowlan. A new contribution to this literature is Paul Kleppner's *Political Atlas of Illinois, 1988* (DeKalb: Northern Illinois University Press, 1988), as well as Craig A. Roberts and Kleppner's *Illinois Issues Almanac of Illinois Politics—1994*, ed. Jack R. Van Der Slik

(Springfield: Institute of Public Affairs, Sangamon State University, 1994) and James H. Lewis, D. Garth Taylor, and Paul Kleppner, *Metro-Chicago Political Atlas* (Institute for Public Affairs, Sangamon State University, 1994).

Numerous academic studies analyzing Illinois elections have been referred to throughout this essay. The best and most recent analysis of trends is the *Illinois Issues* monograph *Illinois Elections,* revised in 1986. A new single-party study is by Mildred A. Schwartz: *The Party Network: The Robust Organization of Illinois Republicans* (Madison: University of Wisconsin Press, 1990).

GENERAL BACKGROUND AND DATA

Trying to find data on certain aspects of Illinois government is difficult. One document that makes the task less onerous is Mary Redmond, comp., *Guide to Statistics in Illinois State Documents* (Springfield: Illinois State Library, 1979) published by the secretary of state. The two-hundred-page supplement is well indexed and well referenced. Included in the supplement are references to official state publications, department and agency reports, monthly and annual reports required of various agencies, and a wealth of other statistical material.

A good source for historical data is *The Illinois Fact Book and Historical Almanac, 1673–1968,* published by the Southern Illinois University Press in 1970 as a sesquicentennial document. It was prepared by John Clayton and contains a wealth of government data. Another good data source is the *State and Regional Economic Data Book,* published by the Department of Commerce and Community Affairs; the latest edition, the eighth, appeared in 1985. An up-to-date collection is the Legislative Research Unit's *Illinois County Data Book* (1989), which has population, economic, and political information by county.

ADDITIONAL SOURCES

Biles, Roger. *Richard J. Daley: Politics, Race, and the Governing of Chicago.* DeKalb: Northern Illinois University Press, 1995.

Freedman, Anne. *Patronage: An American Tradition.* Chicago: Nelson-Hall Publishers, 1994.

Fremon, David. *Chicago: Ward by Ward.* Bloomington: Indiana University Press, 1988.

Green, Paul M., and Melvin G. Holli, eds. *Restoration 1989: Chicago Elects a New Daley.* Chicago: Lyceum Books, 1991.

Hall, William K. *Illinois Government and Politics: A Reader*. Dubuque IA: Kendall-Hunt, 1975.

Illinois Statecraft. Springfield: Oral History Office, Sangamon State University, various dates. A collection of oral history memoirs on modern Illinois government and politics.

Illinois Statistical Abstract, 1994. Urbana: Bureau of Economic and Business Research, University of Illinois.

Johnson, Walter. *The Papers of Adlai E. Stevenson, Governor of Illinois 1949–1953*. Vol. 3. Boston: Little, Brown, 1973.

Matsler, Franklin G., and Edward R. Hines. *State Policy Formation in Illinois Higher Education*. Normal: Center for Higher Education, Illinois State University, 1987.

"The 1970 Illinois Constitution in Review: A Symposium for Change." *NIU Law Review* 8, no. 3 (1988).

Nowlan, James D., and Anna J. Merritt, eds. *Legislative Oversight: A Final Report and Background Papers of the Illinois Assembly on Legislative Oversight*. Urbana: Institute of Government and Public Affairs, 1982.

Van Der Slik, Jack R. *One for All and All for Illinois: Representing the Land of Lincoln in Congress*. Springfield: Institute of Public Affairs, Sangamon State University, 1995.

Notes

CHAPTER ONE

1 Michael Martinez, "Motorola's Move Signals that Exurbia Isn't so Far Away," *Chicago Tribune*, April 24, 1994, sec.2, p.3.

2 Robert M. Sutton, "The Politics of Regionalism Nineteenth Century Style," in *Diversity, Conflict, and State Politics: Regionalism in Illinois,* ed. Peter F. Nardulli (Urbana: University of Illinois Press, 1989), 97.

3 Cullom Davis, "Illinois: Crossroads and Cross Section," in *Heartland: Comparative Histories of the Midwestern States*, ed. James H. Madison (Bloomington: Indiana University Press, 1988), 133.

4 For a good discussion of the internal improvements effort, see Robert P. Howard, *Illinois: A History of the Prairie State* (Grand Rapids MI: William B. Eerdmans, 1972), chap.9.

5 Richard J. Jensen, *Illinois: A Bicentennial History* (New York: Norton, 1978), chap.2.

6 Jensen, *Illinois: A Bicentennial History*, 86.

7 For excellent discussions of the settlement of Illinois, see Frederick M. Wirt, "The Changing Social Bases of Regionalism: People, Cultures, and Politics in Illinois," in *Diversity, Conflict,* ed. Nardulli, 31, and Davis, "Illinois: Crossroads."

8 Jensen, *Illinois: A Bicentennial History*, throughout.

9 Jensen, *Illinois: A Bicentennial History*, 53–54.

10 Jensen, *Illinois: A Bicentennial History*, 48–49.

11 For a superb analysis of the interdependence of city and country in development of wealth, see William Cronon, *Nature's Metropolis: Chicago and the Great West* (New York: Norton, 1991). This section draws heavily on Cronon, especially chap.8.

12 Kristina Valaitis, "Understanding Illinois," *Texas Journal,* 14 (fall/winter 1992): 20–22.

13 Cronon, *Nature's Metropolis,* 208–9.

14 Cronon, *Nature's Metropolis,* chap.7, "The Busy Hive," provides an assessment of the business dynamics of Chicago and the Midwest.

15 As cited in Cronon, *Nature's Metropolis,* 3, from Frank Norris, *The Pit,* 1903.

16 Howard, *Illinois: A History,* chap.21.

17 Cronon, *Nature's Metropolis,* 347.

18 Jensen, *Illinois: A Bicentennial History,* 162.

19 Nelson Algren, *Chicago: City on the Make* (New York: McGraw Hill Book Company, 1951), 56.

20 Daniel J. Elazar, *Cities of the Prairie* (New York: Basic Books, 1970), 282. As if to confirm this observation, in 1991, *American Demographics* named three Illinois cities (Springfield, Bloomington, and Rockford) in the top ten list of "Perfectly Ordinary Places" among 555 cities evaluated (*Chicago Tribune,* January 2, 1992).

21 Quoted in James D. Nowlan, *A New Game Plan for Illinois* (Chicago: Neltnor House, 1989), 5–6.

22 Elazar, *Cities of the Prairie,* 282–316.

23 See Elazar, *American Federalism: A View from the States* (New York: Crowell, 1966), generally, and Wirt, "The Changing Social Bases of Regionalism." Wirt provides an excellent essay on the topic as applied to early Illinois.

24 Elazar, *Cities of the Prairie,* p.286.

25 See map in Robert P. Sutton, ed., *The Prairie State: A Documentary History of Illinois,* 2 vols. (Grand Rapids MI: William B. Eerdmans, 1976), 1:369.

26 Davis, "Illinois: Crossroads," 147–8.

27 For a lyrical essay on diversity of people in Illinois, see Paul Gapp, "Chicagoans All—Our 'Melting Pot' Is Really a Savory Stew," *Chicago Tribune Sunday Magazine,* September 25, 1988.

28 Elazar, *Cities of the Prairie,* 181.

29 Davis, "Illinois: Crossroads," 147.

30 St. Clair Drake and Horace R. Cayton, *Black Metropolis: A Study of Negro Life in a Northern City* (Chicago: University of Chicago Press, 1993), 47. The material that follows is based in part on chapters 2 through 5 of this book.

31 This subsection is drawn largely from John Chiang and Jim Nowlan, "Demographics Pressure the State Budget," *Tax Facts* (Springfield: Taxpayers' Federation of Illinois, May 1992), 1–8.

32 Extrapolation by the authors from Cheng H. Chiang and Richard Kolhauser,

"Who Are We? Illinois' Changing Population," *Illinois Issues*, December 1982, 6–8.

33 *Illinois State Budget, 1990* (Springfield: Illinois Bureau of the Budget, Office of the Governor, 1989), xii.

34 "Gimme Land, Lots of Land," *Chicago Tribune*, January 7, 1995, sec.4, p.1.

35 Everett G. Smith, Jr., "Population Changes in Illinois during the 1980s," *Policy Forum* 6, no.1 (1992): 1–8.

36 Cheng H. Chiang and Ann Geraci, "Regional Demographic Trends in Illinois, 1950–85," in *Diversity, Conflict*, ed. Nardulli, 143.

37 Chiang and Geraci, "Regional Demographic Trends," 120, 137.

38 John Gruidl and Norman Walzer, *A Profile of Conditions and Trends in Rural Illinois* (Macomb: Illinois Institute for Rural Affairs, Western Illinois University, 1990), 70.

39 Chiang and Geraci, "Regional Demographic Trends," 141–42.

40 As recalled by coauthor Nowlan, who represented Bureau, Carroll, Henry, Stark, and Whiteside counties in the Illinois House of Representatives from 1969 to 1972.

41 *Bocce ball* is a lawn game enjoyed by many Italian Americans. Bud Billiken is a mythical hero of blacks on the south side of Chicago who is celebrated each year in a parade that is obligatory for local and some statewide politicians.

42 Gapp, "Chicagoans All."

43 Extrapolated by the authors from *Illinois State Budget, 1990*.

44 Gapp, "Chicagoans All."

45 *Chicago Tribune*, June 14, 1992.

46 Gregory D. Squires, Larry Bennett, and Philip Ryder, *Chicago: Race, Class, and the Response to Urban Decline* (Philadelphia: Temple University Press, 1987), 98, 106.

47 *Ten Latino Nationalities Have 1,000+ Persons in Chicago* (Chicago: Latino Institute, 1992).

48 1990 U.S. Census, as quoted in *Chicago Sun-Times*, October 2, 1994.

49 See Lawrence J. McCaffrey, Ellen Skerrett, Michael F. Funchion, and Charles Fanning, *The Irish in Chicago* (Urbana: University of Illinois Press, 1987), 90.

50 Edward R. Kantowicz, *Polish-American Politics in Chicago* (Chicago: University of Chicago Press, 1975), 41–42.

51 *Illinois Economic Bulletin* (Springfield: Illinois Department of Commerce and Community Affairs, February 1994).

52 *Railway Age*, April 1993.

53 These figures are taken from William R. Bryan and Lori Williamson, eds., *1992*

Illinois Economic Outlook (Urbana: Bureau of Business and Economic Research, University of Illinois, 1992), 6.

54 *Facts & Figures on Government Finance* (Washington: Tax Foundation, Inc., 1979, 1991), and *States in Profile: The State Policy Reference Book, 1992* (McConnellsburg PA: 1992).

55 *Economic Leadership in Illinois* (Springfield: Illinois Department of Commerce and Community Affairs, n.d. [ca. 1990]), II-5.

56 Bryan and Williamson, eds., *1992 Illinois Economic Outlook*, 10.

57 "Chicago's Economic Transformation from 1970 to 2000," *Chicago Fed Letter*, Federal Reserve Bank of Chicago, no.60, August 1992.

58 This discussion of economic distress in parts of downstate is drawn from Nowlan, *New Game Plan for Illinois*, 11–1.

59 Squires, Bennett and Ryder, *Chicago: Race, Class*, 24.

60 William Julius Wilson, *The Truly Disadvantaged: The Inner City, the Underclass, and Public Policy* (Chicago: University of Chicago Press, 1987), 49–52.

61 *1989 Illinois Statistical Abstract* (Urbana: Bureau of Economic and Business Research at the University of Illinois, 1990).

CHAPTER TWO

1 "Suburbs: Huntley Strives for Guilt-Free Growth," *Chicago Enterprise*, January 1994, 13–15.

2 John Herbers, *The New Heartland* (New York: Time Books, 1986), and "Look Out, Wasco, Here Comes Suburban Sprawl," *Chicago Tribune*, March 18, 1994.

3 *Illinois Statistical Abstract, 1993* (Urbana: Bureau of Economic and Business Research, University of Illinois, 1994).

4 Joel Garreau, *Edge City: Life on the New Frontier* (New York: Doubleday, 1991).

5 Ann Durkin Keating, *Building Chicago: Suburban Developers and the Creation of a Divided Metropolis* (Columbus: Ohio State University Press, 1988), chap. 1.

6 U.S. Bureau of the Census, *Census of Population (1990): Social and Economic Characteristics* (Washington DC: U.S. Department of Commerce, Bureau of the Census, 1993).

7 Janita Poe, "Blacks Finding Places to Call Their Own in the Suburbs," *Chicago Tribune*, September 29, 1992.

8 Interview, April 4, 1994.

9 *1993 Metro Survey Report* (Chicago: Metro Information Center, 1993).

10 Patrick Reardon and Laurie Goering, "North Suburbs Pulling Away in Personal Income," *Chicago Tribune*, June 2, 1992.

11 Quoted by Laurie Goering, "Inner-Ring Losing Its Glow," *Chicago Tribune*, September 4, 1994, 1.

12 *Crain's Chicago Business*, January 31, 1994, R1.

13 *Strategic Plan for Land Resource Management* (Chicago: Northeastern Illinois Planning Commission, June 18, 1992), 27.

14 *Strategic Plan*, 23.

15 *Strategic Plan*, 4. See also Robert Heuer, "NIPC Speaks on Growth and Decline Trends, Taxes and Land Management," *Illinois Issues*, June 1992, 17–19.

16 *Strategic Plan*, 17.

17 *Illinois Voter Project Survey* (Chicago: University of Illinois at Chicago, January 1994).

18 Interview, January 15, 1994.

19 *The* 1991 Chicago Collar County Survey, Charles Cappell, study director (DeKalb: Department of Sociology, Northern Illinois University, August 1991). There were 340 completed surveys, proportional to population in the five-and-one-half-county region, from 1,124 households contacted.

20 Tom Andreoli, "Missing in Action: Suburban Leaders," *Crain's Chicago Business*, September 23–29, 1991.

21 Andreoli, "Missing in Action."

22 This section draws heavily on the excellent series "Moving Out," from the *Chicago Tribune*, November 28–December 4, 1993.

23 "Moving Out," *Chicago Tribune*, November 28, 1993.

24 "Moving Out," *Chicago Tribune*, November 28, 1993.

25 *A Profile of Chicago's Poverty and Related Conditions* (Evanston: Center for Urban Affairs and Policy Research, Northwestern University, 1993).

26 Patrick Barry, "Boom," *Chicago Times Magazine*, September/October 1987.

27 Milton Rakove, *We Don't Want Nobody Nobody Sent: An Oral History of the Daley Years* (Bloomington: Indiana University Press, 1979), 318.

28 Howard, *Illinois: A History*, 459–83.

29 Michael B. Preston, "Political Change in the City: Black Politics in Chicago, 1871–1987," in *Diversity, Conflict*, ed. Nardulli, 180–87.

30 Paul Kleppner, *Chicago Divided: The Making of a Black Mayor* (DeKalb: Northern Illinois University Press, 1985), 67.

31 Preston, "Political Change in the City," 179–80. Preston draws on Charles Branham, "Accommodation Politics before the Great Migration," in *Ethnic Chicago*, ed. Melvin G. Holli and Peter d'A. Jones (Grand Rapids MI: William B. Eerdmans, 1984).

32 David K. Fremon, "Chicago's Spanish-American Politics in the '80s," *Illinois Issues*, January 1990, 17.

33 Len O'Connor, *Requiem: The Decline and Demise of Mayor Daley and His Era* (Chicago: Contemporary Books, 1977), 35.

34 Norm Walzer et al., *Rural Economic Indicators*, (Macomb: Rural Affairs Institute, Western Illinois University, 1990), 100–101.

35 *Diversity, Conflict*, ed. Nardulli, especially chaps. 10 and 11.

36 *Diversity, Conflicts*, ed. Nardulli; for a full discussion of the survey findings, see chapter 10.

37 *Diversity, Conflict*, ed. Nardulli, 271.

38 *The Illinois Survey, 1993* (DeKalb: Center for Study of Government, 1993). Ellen Dran, director of the survey, and Debra Krankavitch provided the regional cross-tabulations.

39 *Illinois Survey, 1993*, 299 and 289–91.

40 *Illinois Survey, 1993*, 298.

41 Mildred A. Schwartz, *The Party Network: The Robust Organization of Illinois Republicans* (Madison: University of Wisconsin Press, 1990), 178–80.

42 Patrick D. O'Grady, *Taxes and Distribution by Region of the State* (Springfield: Legislative Research Unit, Illinois General Assembly, March 9, 1989).

43 From notes of Nowlan, taken during speech by Sanders in 1987, undated.

44 *Chicago Tribune*, November 3, 1989.

45 Robert M. Sutton, "The Politics of Regionalism, Nineteenth Century Style," in *Diversity, Conflict*, ed. Nardulli, 113.

CHAPTER THREE

1 Quoted in Peter J. Wilson, *The Domestication of the Human Species* (New Haven: Yale University Press, 1988), 117.

2 For discussions of power and influence in politics, see Roger Scruton, *A Dictionary of Political Thought* (London: Macmillan, 1982), 224, and Dennis Wrong, *Power: Its Forms, Bases, and Uses* (Oxford: Oxford University Press, 1979).

3 This profile is based in large part on an interview with John P. Dailey, who was the top aide to Arrington during the 1965–68 sessions of the Illinois General Assembly, August 8, 1990.

4 This profile is drawn largely from recollections of coauthor Nowlan, who was a member of the Illinois House of Representatives from 1969 to 1972.

5 The figures are taken from the *Journal of the House*, Illinois General Assembly, Springfield, June 30, 1969. The analysis is by coauthor Nowlan, who was one of the Republican members who voted that day in support of the income tax bill. The final tally was ninety-one votes in favor, seventy-three against, with three voting present.

6 John Camper and Daniel Egler, "Democrats Find It Pays to Be on Madigan Team," *Chicago Tribune*, April 16, 1989. Much of the discussion on Madigan is drawn from this lengthy profile.

7 Camper and Egler, "Democrats Find It Pays to Be on Madigan Team."

8 Camper and Egler, "Democrats Find It Pays to Be on Madigan Team." This paragraph and the quotations from Philip H. Corboy that follow are taken directly from the *Tribune* profile of Madigan.

9 For an illuminating brief history of parties in Illinois, see Paul M. Green, "History of Political Parties in Illinois," in *Illinois: Political Processes and Governmental Performance*, ed. Edgar Crane (Dubuque IA: Kendall/Hunt, 1980), 167–176. The discussion that follows is drawn primarily from this article.

10 Kent Redfield, "Limited Role of State Political Parties in Financing Illinois Campaigns," *Illinois Issues*, November 1992, 16–19.

11 llustration provided by Edwin Dale of Champaign, former member of the Illinois House of Representatives, July 15, 1990.

12 Redfield, "Limited Role of State Political Parties," 17.

13 Thomas Hardy, "Political Slatemaking Not What It Used to Be," *Chicago Tribune*, December 26, 1993, sec.4, p.8.

14 Redfield, "Limited Role of State Political Parties," 18–19.

15 Redfield, "Limited Role of State Political Parties," 19.

16 *Dubious Disclosure* (Chicago: Common Cause/Illinois, October 1989).

17 David H. Everson and Samuel K. Gove, "Interest Groups in Illinois: The Political Microcosm of the Nation," in *Interest Group Politics in the Midwestern States*, ed. Ronald J. Hrebenar and Clive S. Thomas (Ames: Iowa State University Press, 1993).

18 Everson and Gove, "Interest Groups in Illinois."

19 *Money and Elections in Illinois, 1992* (Springfield: State Board of Elections, September 1993).

20 *Money and Elections in Illinois, 1992*, 20–23.

21 Jack R. Van Der Slik, ed., *Almanac of Illinois Politics—1994* (Springfield: *Illinois Issues*, Sangamon State University, 1994), 408.

22 Van Der Slik, ed., *Almanac of Illinois Politics—1994*, table 19.1, p.408, and Everson and Gove, "Interest Groups in Illinois."

23 Kent D. Redfield, "Investing in the General Assembly," in *Almanac of Illinois Politics—1994*, ed. Van der Slik, 1–26.

24 Redfield, "Investing in the General Assembly," 16.

25 Redfield, "Investing in the General Assembly," 17.

26 Toby Eckert, "Legislative Lawyer: Burying Stereotypes While Building a Repu-

tation," *Weekend Journal, the State Journal-Register*, August 21, 1987, 11a, as reported by Everson and Gove in "Interest Groups in Illinois."

27 Sarah McCally Morehouse, *State Politics: Parties and Policy* (New York: Holt, Rinehart, and Winston, 1981), 10.

28 Everson and Gove, "Interest Groups in Illinois."

29 Redfield, "Investing in the General Assembly," 4.

30 Jane Addams, *Twenty Years at Hull-House* (1910; rpt. New York: New American Library, 1960).

31 Saul Alinsky, *Reveille for Radicals* (Chicago: University of Chicago Press, 1947).

32 Patrick Barry, "Organized Chicago: Community Groups Start to Guide Development," *Chicago Sun-Times*, April 19, 1985, Neighbors section, p. 1.

33 John McCarron, "Chicago on Hold," *Chicago Tribune*, August 28, 1988, sec. 1, p. 12.

34 Wilfredo Cruz, "UNO: Organizing at the Grass Roots," in *After Alinsky: Community Organizing in Illinois*, ed. Peg Knoepfle (Springfield: *Illinois Issues*, Sangamon State University, 1990), 11–21.

35 Cruz, "UNO," 12.

36 Unpublished memo from Dobmeyer, September 24, 1994; additional material from interview with Dobmeyer.

37 As reported in Green, "History of Political Parties in Illinois," 170.

38 Morehouse, *State Politics*, 110.

39 Observations of coauthor Nowlan, who was Percy's campaign manager in 1978.

40 The series ran between September 19 and December 1, 1985, and was collected into a book: *The American Millstone: An Examination of the Nation's Permanent Underclass* (Chicago: Contemporary Books, 1986).

41 The following discussion is drawn from James D. Nowlan, "Television Charts a New Campaign Map for Illinois," in *Occasional Papers in Illinois Politics, Number 2*, ed. Anna Merritt (Urbana: Institute of Government and Public Affairs, University of Illinois, December 1981).

42 This case study is taken from James D. Nowlan and Mary Jo Moutray Stroud, "Broadcasting Advertising and Party Endorsement in a Statewide Primary: An Illinois Case Study," in *Occasional Papers in Illinois Politics, Number 4*, ed. Anna Merritt (Urbana: Institute of Government and Public Affairs, University of Illinois, November 1983).

CHAPTER FOUR

1 Janet Cornelius, *Constitution Making in Illinois, 1818–1970*, (Urbana: University of Illinois Press, 1972), 34. The sections on early constitutions rely heavily on the Cornelius work.

2 Illinois does allow for public initiative only on matters pertaining to the legislative article of the constitution. This petitioning process was used in the successful 1980 amendment that reduced the size of the house and eliminated cumulative voting in Illinois. Later, state treasurer Patrick Quinn initiated a successful petition to require term limits on Illinois legislators, but the Illinois Supreme Court in 1994 ruled that the petition was invalid because it did not address structural or procedural subject matter required by the constitution.

3 For further discussion on the slavery issue, see Cornelius, *Constitution Making*, 15–24.

4 Cornelius, *Constitution Making*, 13–14.

5 Cornelius, *Constitution Making*, 42. Cornelius quotes from the *Debates and Proceedings of the Constitutional Convention of the State of Illinois Convened at the City of Springfield, Tuesday, December 13, 1869*, 2 vols. (Springfield, 1870), 2:1316.

6 Howard, *Illinois: A History*, 333.

7 Daniel J. Elazar, "Constitutional Design in the U.S. and Other Federal Systems," *Publius, The Journal of Federalism*, (1982): 19.

8 Elazar "Constitutional Design," 20.

9 Cornelius, *Constitution Making*, 110–15.

10 Elmer Gertz and Joseph P. Pisciotte, *Charter for a New Age: An Inside View of the Sixth Illinois Constitutional Convention* (Urbana: University of Illinois Press, 1980), 6. This book provides a detailed and readable summary of the workings of the convention.

11 Elmer Gertz and Edward S. Gilbreth, *Quest for a Constitution: A Man Who Wouldn't Quit, a Political Biography of Samuel W. Witwer* (Lanham MD: University Press of America, 1984), 76–77.

12 Cornelius, Constitution Making, 124.

13 Quoted in Samuel K. Gove and Thomas R. Kitser, *Revision Success: The Sixth Illinois Constitutional Convention* (New York: National Municipal League, 1974), 15.

14 *Thorpe v. Mahin* (43 Ill. 2d 36 [1969]). In this decision the Illinois Supreme Court overturned the 1932 *Bachrach v. Nelson* (349 Ill. 579 [1932]) decision that stated the legislature was limited to enacting property taxes, occupation taxes, and franchise taxes.

15 Elazar, "Constitutional Design," 20.

16 Elazar, Introduction to this book.

17 Illinois Constitution, 1970, art.1, sect.8.1.

18 Neil R. Peirce, *The Megastates of America: People, Politics, and Power in the Ten Great American States* (New York: Norton, 1972), 393–94.

CHAPTER FIVE

1 For a thorough assessment of the Illinois General Assembly, see Jack R. Van Der Slik and Kent D. Redfield, *Lawmaking in Illinois* (Springfield: Sangamon State University, 1986). An earlier yet still useful work is Samuel K. Gove, Richard W. Carlson, and Richard J. Carlson, *The Illinois Legislature: Structure and Process* (Urbana: University of Illinois Press, 1976).

2 Howard, *Illinois: A History*, 425–27.

3 Citizens Conference on State Legislatures, *The Sometime Governments: A Critical Study of the Fifty American Legislatures* (New York: Bantam Books, 1973), chap.4.

4 Burdett A. Loomis, "Political Careers and American State Legislatures," paper presented at the Eagleton Institute of Politics Symposium "The Legislature in the Twenty-First Century," April 27–29, 1990, Williamsburg, Virginia.

5 For extensive data on the makeup of the membership of the legislature, see Jack R. Van Der Slik, ed., *Almanac of Illinois Politics—1990* (Springfield: Sangamon State University, 1990), esp. tables 17.1 through 17.6.

6 Van Der Slik and Redfield, *Lawmaking in Illinois*, 64, and Van Der Slik, ed., *Almanac of Illinois Politics—1990*, 362.

7 Debra M. Beck, "Gender and the Legislative Process: A Case Study of the Illinois General Assembly" (honors' thesis, Knox College, 1992), 19.

8 Kent D. Redfield, "Candidates, Campaigns and Cash," *Illinois Issues*, July 1993, 17–21.

9 Figures from *Money and Elections in Illinois, 1992* (Springfield: State Board of Elections, 1993), various pages; *Money and elections in Illinois, 1994* (Springfield: State Board of Elections, 1995), 36, 41.

10 For a detailed explanation of the intricacies of lawmaking and how a bill becomes a law, see *Preface to Lawmaking 1990* (Springfield: Legislative Research Unit, Illinois General Assembly, November 1990).

11 See Gove, Carlson, and Carlson, *The Illinois Legislature*, chap.4, for a thorough discussion of lawmaking and legislative action on vetoes.

12 Gilbert Y. Steiner and Samuel K. Gove, *Legislative Politics in Illinois* (Urbana: University of Illinois Press, 1960), 82.

13 Van Der Slik and Redfield, *Lawmaking in Illinois*, 144.

14 *Galesburg Register-Mail*, July 3, 1989.

15 Van Der Slik and Redfield, *Lawmaking in Illinois*, 139, and the *Cook-Witter Report*, 9, no.5 (May 26, 1993): 1.

16 Interview with Michael E. Pollack, June 5, 1989.

17 Van Der Slik, *Almanac of Illinois Politics—1992*, table 25, pp.398–99.

18 Gove, Carlson, and Carlson, *Illinois Legislature*, 97.

19 *Money and Elections in Illinois, 1994.*

20 Richard R. Johnson, "Partisan Legislative Campaign Committees: New Power, New Problems," *Illinois Issues*, July 1987, 16–18, and Redfield, "Candidates, Campaigns and Cash."

21 This illustration is drawn from James D. Nowlan and Joan Agrella Parker, "Notes from the Inside," *Tax Facts* (Springfield: Taxpayers' Federation of Illinois, August 1993).

22 Gertz and Pisciotte, *Charter for a New Age*, 230.

23 Charles N. Wheeler III, "'Great Compromiser' World Legislature," *Chicago Sun-Times*, October 13, 1990.

24 Alan Rosenthal, *Governors and Legislatures* (Washington DC: CQ Press, 1990), 205.

25 Rosenthal, *Governors and Legislature*, 15.

26 Van Der Slik, ed., *Almanac of Illinois Politics—1990*, table 14, pp.346–52.

27 Bernard Schoenburg and John Dowling of the Associated Press, "Four Leaders at Top of Lobbyists' Lists," as reported in the *Galesburg Register-Mail*, June 26, 1990.

28 Observations of coauthor Nowlan, who served in the House of Representatives from 1969 to 1972.

29 Michael D. Klemens, "Lawmakers' Class of '88: One Bona Fide Surprise," *Illinois Issues*, January 1989, 19–21.

30 Alan Rosenthal, *Legislative Life* (New York: Harper & Row, 1981), 19.

31 Mark Brown, "How Legislators Pump Up Pensions," *Chicago Sun-Times*, September 12, 1994, 1.

32 Schwartz, *Party Network*, 174–79. The survey was conducted before cumulative voting was eliminated.

33 David Moberg, "Where's the Party," *Reader* (Chicago), November 2, 1990, 24–25.

34 This section is drawn largely from James D. Nowlan, "Redistricting: The Politics," in *A Media Guide to Illinois REMAP '91*, No.5 (Urbana: Institute of Government and Public Affairs, March 1991).

35 Rick Pearson, "Once Again, Philip's Blunt Talk Ignites a Firestorm," *Chicago Tribune*, October 7, 1994, 1.

CHAPTER SIX

1 For Thompson's version of his years in office, see James R. Thompson, *Illinois, State of the State, 1977–1991: The Thompson Administration* (Springfield: State of Illinois, 1991).

2 "Political Hiring Out, Court Rules," *Chicago Tribune*, June 22, 1990.

3 *Rutan v. Republican Party of Illinois*, 110 U.S. S. Court, 2729, 1990.

4 Chris Gaudet, "Financing Gubernatorial Campaigns," *Illinois Issues*, May 1987, 13–14.

5 This section draws heavily on the highly readable profiles of Illinois governors by Robert P. Howard, *Mostly Good and Competent Men: Illinois Governors, 1818–1988* (Springfield: *Illinois Issues*, Sangamon State University, and Illinois State Historical Society, 1988).

6 Howard, *Mostly Good and Competent Men,* 79.

7 Howard, *Mostly Good and Competent Men,* 21.

8 Howard, *Mostly Good and Competent Men,* 188.

9 Howard, *Mostly Good and Competent Men,* 340.

10 Samuel K. Gove, "Illinois: Jim Edgar, the New Governor from the Old Party," in *Governing and Hard Times*, ed. Thad Beyle (Washington DC: CQ Press, 1992), 107.

11 "For Governor: Jim Edgar," *Chicago Tribune*, October 23, 1994, sec.4, p.1.

12 As of July 1, 1995, the salaries for these elected officers were as follows: governor, $105,778; lieutenant governor, $74,667; secretary of state and attorney general, both $93,333; comptroller and treasurer, both $80,889. State law enacted in 1990 will increase these salaries at a rate tied to inflation, with a maximum increase of 5 percent annually.

13 For more complete descriptions of the duties of the executive officers, see the *Illinois Blue Book*, published every two years by the Illinois secretary of state. This is a comprehensive, though sometimes self-serving, guide to state government. For more balanced articles about the offices and the personalities and politics therein, see the annual index to *Illinois Issues*, a monthly magazine of public affairs published by Sangamon State University in Springfield in cooperation with the University of Illinois.

14 *Illinois Blue Book, 1989–90* (Springfield: Illinois Secretary of State, 1991).

15 Joseph A. Schlesinger, "The Politics of the Executive," in *Politics in the American States*, ed. Herbert Jacob and Kenneth N. Vines, 2d ed. (Boston: Little, Brown, 1971), 232.

16 Here is more detail on the veto powers, taken from "Governor's Action on Bills: A Primer," pages 23 and 24 in *First Reading*, a publication of the Legislative Research Unit of the Illinois General Assembly, October 1987.

　　"*Total veto*: The Governor may reject an entire bill and send it back with a statement of objections. The house where the bill started enters the objections on its journal. Then, within 15 calendar days after receipt of the bill, that house votes on overriding the veto. If, by at least three-fifths of the members elected to it (71 in the House, 36 in the Senate), the first house repasses the bill over the veto, the bill is sent to the second house. If that house within 15 calendar days repasses the bill by vote of at least three-fifths of the members elected to it, the bill enacts a law. Otherwise the total veto stands and the bill is dead.

"*Amendatory Veto*: A Governor who approves the general purpose of a bill but finds fault with some of its details can return the bill "with specific recommendations for change" to the originating house. In practice, Governors have returned these bills with the exact wording of suggested changes.

"An amendatorily vetoed bill is considered the same way as a vetoed bill, except that each house may, instead of overriding the veto, accept the recommendations by a majority of the members elected to it. Thus two responses are possible: override the veto by three-fifths vote of each house and enact the bill into law, or accept the Governor's recommendations by a majority of the members elected in each house. In the latter case, the bill is returned to the Governor, and if he certifies that it conforms to his recommendations, this enacts a law. The constitution does not say how long a Governor has to certify a bill or return it as a vetoed bill. If the General Assembly refuses to accept the proposed changes and also fails to override the veto, the veto stands and the bill is dead.

"*Item and Reduction Vetoes*: Item and reduction vetoes allow a Governor to cut parts (line items) of an appropriation bill without vetoing the whole bill. In an "item" veto, the Governor eliminates an entire line item; in a "reduction" veto, he merely reduces an amount in a line item. In either case, the amounts remaining in the bill are enacted immediately upon the Governor's transmission of his veto message. However, the majorities needed to restore amounts cut are different. A line item that has been vetoed is treated like a totally vetoed bill—that is, a three-fifths majority in each house is needed to restore the item. An item reduced, however, can be restored to its original amount by a majority of the members elected to each house."

17 *First Reading* (Legislative Research Unit, Illinois General Assembly), 4, no.9 (October 1989): 11.

18 *First Reading* 4, no.9 (October 1989): 11.

19 Rosenthal, *Governors and Legislatures*, 11.

20 Rosenthal, *Governors and Legislatures*, 15.

21 Recalled by coauthor Nowlan, who was a Republican house member in that 1969 conference.

22 Rosenthal, *Governors and Legislatures*, 75–79.

23 Rosenthal, *Governors and Legislatures*, 113.

24 "State's Prison Population Surges," *First Reading* (Legislative Research Unit, Illinois General Assembly), 5, no.3 (March 1990): 1–6.

25 110 S. Court 2729 (1990).

26 Rosenthal, *Governors and Legislatures*, 170.

27 Rosenthal, *Governors and Legislatures*, chap.1.

28 Ronald D. Michaelson, "An Analysis of the Chief Executive: How the Governor Uses His Time," *Public Affairs Bulletin*, 4, no.4 (Carbondale: Public Affairs Research Bureau, Southern Illinois University) (September–October 1971): 1–8.

29 Tom Berkshire and Richard J. Carlson, "The Office of the Governor," in *Inside State Government in Illinois*, ed. James D. Nowlan (Chicago: Neltnor House, 1991).

30 For a full discussion of patronage, see James D. Nowlan, William S. Hanley, and Donald Udstuen, "Personnel and Patronage," in *Inside State Government in Illinois*, ed. Nowlan.

31 *Rutan v. Republican Party of Illinois*.

32 Van Der Slik, ed., *Almanac of Illinois Politics—1992*, 401.

33 Berkshire and Carlson, "Office of the Governor."

34 James D. Nowlan, "An Introduction to State Government," in *Inside State Government: A Primer for State Managers*, ed. James D. Nowlan (Urbana: Institute of Government of the University of Illinois, 1983), 5.

35 This discussion of management is taken from Nowlan, *New Game Plan for Illinois*, chap.9, pp.127–44.

36 "The Department of Corrections," *State of Illinois Fiscal Condition Report* (Springfield: Office of the Comptroller, May 31, 1989), 1–6.

37 "State's Prison Population Surges," *First Reading*, 5, no.3 (March 1990).

38 This sketch of the Department of Mental Health and Developmental Disabilities is taken from two excellent articles, both from *Illinois Issues:* Judy Emerson, "Serving the Mentally Ill," November 1985, and Michael D. Klemens, "Ann Kiley of DMHDD," March 1988.

39 Klemens, "Ann Kiley of DMHDD," p.8.

CHAPTER SEVEN

1 Howard, *Illinois: A History*, 212.

2 James Touhy and Rob Warden, *Greylord: Justice, Chicago Style* (New York: G. P. Putnam's Sons, 1989), 45–46.

3 Cornelius, *Constitution Making*, 131–32.

4 Administrative Office of the Illinois Courts, *1991 Annual Report to the Supreme Court of Illinois*, 19.

5 Cornelius, *Constitution Making*, 26–33.

6 Cornelius, *Constitution Making*, 26–33.

7 1970 Illinois Constitution, art. VI, sec.16.

8 "1990 Annual Report of the Supreme Court to the General Assembly," in *1990 Annual Report of the Supreme Court of Illinois* (Springfield: Administrative Office of the Illinois Courts, 1990), 14.

9 *1993 Annual Report of the Supreme Court to the General Assembly,* 1.

10 *Chicago Tribune,* February 3, 1994.

11 Howard, *Illinois: A History,* 559.

12 This issue has been carefully analyzed by legal scholars. See Pinky Wassenberg, "A Search for Accountability: Judicial Discipline under the Judicial Article of the 1970 Illinois State Constitution," *Northern Illinois University Law Review,* 8, no.3 (1988): 781–800.

13 Touhy and Warden, *Greylord,* Appendix 2, p.262, and The Illinois Supreme Court Special Commission on the Administration of Justice, *Final Report, Part I and II,* chairman Jerold S. Solovy (Chicago: N.P., December 1993) Part II 54–68; cited here as *Solovy Report.*

14 Much of the detail recounted here is from Touhy and Warden, *Greylord.*

15 Anne Keegan, "Inside Greylord," *Chicago Tribune Magazine,* December 17, 1989, 16.

16 Touhy and Warden, *Greylord,* 26.

17 Touhy and Warden, *Greylord,* 207–13.

18 The Gambat illustrations are from the *Solovy Report,* 7–43.

19 Touhy and Warden, *Greylord.*

20 Brocton Lockwood, *Operation Greylord: Brocton Lockwood's Story* (Carbondale: Southern Illinois University Press, 1989), 156.

21 Nancy Ford, "From Judicial to Merit Selection: A Time for Change in Illinois," *Northern Illinois University Law Review* 8, no.3 (1988): 665–707.

22 This and the material that follows is from the *Solovy Report, Part I,* 73–74.

23 *Solovy Report, Part I,* 69–75, quote on 75.

24 *Solovy Report, Part I,* 75.

25 Lawyers are encouraged to participate by canon eight of the American Bar Association code: "Generally, lawyers are qualified by personal observation and investigation to evaluate the qualifications of persons seeking or being considered for such public offices, and for this reason they have a special responsibility to aid in the selection of those who are qualified."

26 "Our Picks for Subcircuit Judges," *Chicago Sun-Times,* October 18, 1994, 27.

27 Ford, "From Judicial to Merit Selection," 685.

28 *People of the State of Illinois ex rel. Chicago Bar Association v. The Illinois State Board of Elections,* 138 Ill. 2nd 513 (1990). The supreme court ruled that appel-

late districts could not be sub-districted as the basis for finding the 1989 legislation unconstitutional.

29 *Chicago Reporter*, March 1994, 5.

30 Jim Bray, "Campaigning for a Supreme Court Seat," *Illinois Issues*, October 1984, 27–30.

31 Marlene Arnold Nickolson and Bradley Scott Weiss, "Funding Judicial Campaigns in the Circuit Court of Cook County," *Judicature*, 70, no. 1 (1986): 17–25.

32 Nickolson and Weiss, "Funding Judicial Campaigns in the Circuit Court of Cook County," 25.

33 The delegates who drafted the 1970 Illinois Constitution expected the legal profession to be directly involved in the selection and retention processes. The role of the bar in the retention process was specifically referred to in the report of the majority of the committee on judiciary: "The 60 percent factor may serve to remove a judge in whom the Bar and the public has lost confidence" (Ford, "From Judicial to Merit Selection," 6).

34 William K. Hall, *Judicial Retention Elections: Do Bar Association Polls Increase Voter Awareness?* (Urbana: Institute of Government and Public Affairs, University of Illinois, 1985), 3.

35 Editorial, *Chicago Tribune*, November 4, 1986.

36 More attention was given to the bar association recommendations in 1990 when ten judges (seven in Cook County and three downstate) were not retained. In 1992 bar association recommendations did not determine the electoral outcome.

37 Hall, *Judicial Retention Elections*, 19.

38 *Solovy Report, Part I*, 51.

39 Supreme Court of Illinois, "Amended Responses to the Financial and Compliance Audit Report" (State of Illinois, Springfield, October 4, 1989).

40 *Chicago Sun Times*, March 6, 1990.

41 *Chicago Sun-Times*, July 15, 1990.

42 *Rock v. Burris* 139 Ill. S.C. 494 (1990).

43 Thompson, *Illinois, State of the State*, 855–56.

44 Beverley Scobell, "Adult Probation: Alternatives to Prison Exist Already, But the System in Illinois Operated under the Courts Is Overburdened," *Illinois Issues*, June 1993, 29–33.

45 *Solovy Report, Part II*, 1–15.

46 *Solovy Report, Part II*, 20–24.

47 John Kincaid, "State Court Protections of Individual Rights under State Constitutions: The New Judicial Federalism," *Journal of State Government*, September/October 1988, 163–69. Also Ronald K. L. Collins, Peter J. Galie, and John Kincaid, "State High Courts, State Constitutions, and Individual Rights Litiga-

tion since 1980: A Judicial Survey," *Publius, The Journal of Federalism*, 16 (Fall 1986): 155–72.

48 Lou Ortiz, "Poor Schools Not Necessarily Bad, Court Rules," *Chicago Sun-Times*, September 30, 1994, 15.

49 *In re. Contest of the Election for Governor and Lieutenant Governor*, 93 Ill. 2d 463–507 (1983).

50 On October 12, 1990, the Illinois Supreme Court issued an order in *Norman v. Reed* 112 U.S. 698 (1992). Later that same month U.S. Supreme Court justice John Paul Stevens issued an order staying or recalling the Illinois Supreme Court's mandate, pending further orders from the U.S. Court. The Illinois court recalled its mandate. Then on October 25, 1990 (just eleven days before the November 6 election), the U.S. Supreme Court affirmed the Cook County Officers Electoral Board's decision that the party's candidates should remain on the ballot.

CHAPTER EIGHT

1 Regional Revenue and Spending Project, *Seeking a New Balance: Paying for Government in Metropolitan Chicago* (Chicago: Regional Partnership, 1991), Executive Summary, 2.

2 Van Der Slik, ed., *Almanac of Illinois Politics—1994*, table 37, p.452. The overall figure is for 1987; types of districts were counted in 1990.

3 James F. Keane and Gary Koch, eds., *Illinois Local Government: A Handbook* (Carbondale: Southern Illinois University Press, 1990), ix. Another estimate in the same book puts the figure at one hundred thousand.

4 Howard, *Illinois: A History*, 479.

5 Daniel J. Lehmann, "Payroll 'Ghost' Admits Scheme," *Chicago Sun-Times*, October 13, 1994, 1.

6 Phillip Bloomer, *Champaign-Urbana News Gazette*, March 2, 1990.

7 Samuel K. Gove, *The Illinois Municipal Electoral Process* (Urbana: Institute of Government and Public Affairs, 1964).

8 Illinois Commission on Intergovernmental Cooperation, *Catalog of State Assistance to Local Governments*, 6th ed. (Springfield: Illinois Commission on Intergovernmental Cooperation, June 1995), xix.

9 Advisory Commission on Intergovernmental Relations, *State and Local Roles in the Federal System* (Washington DC: GPO, 1982), table 106, p.262.

10 Illinois Constitution, art. VII, sec.6.

11 A debate went on in the state's second largest county, DuPage, on whether the county qualifies for home rule. The full-time chairman of the DuPage County board is elected on an at-large basis. The issue is whether he is a chief executive

officer as mentioned in the constitution. The *Chicago Tribune*, June 17, 1990, said editorially: "Jack Knuepfer [the board chairman] committed political suicide when he insisted on the eve of the March [1990] primary that the county, like Cook, had 'home rule' power—the right to govern itself." The editorial concluded, "With home rule authority, DuPage would have the power to manage its own affairs and chart its own future. Knuepfer understands that. Someday, the voters of DuPage County may understand that, too. For now, they at least should appreciate that someone with nothing more to lose is trying to point the way for a county with a lot to gain." Knuepfer was defeated in the March 1990 primary.

12 James Banovetz and Thomas W. Kelty, *Home Rule in Illinois* (Springfield: *Illinois Issues*, Sangamon State University, 1987).

13 Illinois Commission on Intergovernmental Cooperation, *A Review of the Illinois State Mandates Act, 1981–1985* (Springfield: Illinois Commission on Intergovernmental Cooperation, 1986), 6. Also see Kathy Hanger, "State Mandates Act Revisited," *Illinois Municipal Review*, September 1990, 15–16.

14 "Annual Financial Reports: Unused and Unusable," *Tax Facts*, October 1990, 7.

15 Regional Revenue and Spending Project, *Seeking a New Balance*, Executive Summary, 25.

16 Regional Revenue and Spending Project, *Seeking a New Balance*, 27.

17 An exception to this statement is Samuel K. Gove, "State Impact: The Daley Legacy," in *After Daley: Chicago Politics in Transition*, ed. Gove and Louis H. Masotti (Urbana: University of Illinois Press, 1982), 203–16. The Chicago political organization has been much analyzed by scholars and journalists. The literature on Chicago politics is voluminous, but little attention is given to the city's relationship with the state because the authors do not believe that the relationship is important for an understanding of Chicago politics.

18 Charles E. Merriam, Spencer D. Parratt, and Albert Lepawsky, *The Government of the Metropolitan Region of Chicago* (Chicago: University of Chicago Press, 1933), 179.

19 The recent black/white political conflict in the city led to various proposals for a nonpartisan election of the mayor by those who thought it would help their side win the office, and this was accomplished in 1995.

20 In the suburbs of Cook County, township committeemen are elected to serve on the county central committee. Outside Cook County, precinct committeemen are elected and they then select the county chairmen.

21 Zay N. Smith and Pamela Zekman, *The Mirage* (New York: Random House, 1979), 39–40.

22 John Gardiner and Theodore R. Lyman, *Decisions for Sale* (New York: Praeger,

1978), 80–83. Gardiner and Lyman document other examples of corruption in land-use and building regulation in Illinois and elsewhere.

23 Malcolm Galdwell, "Paring the Big Apple," *Washington Post National Weekly Edition*, March 21–27, 1994, 33. The author relied heavily on the study by Ester R. Fuchs, *Mayors and Money* (Chicago: University of Chicago Press, 1992).

24 *Crain's Chicago Business*, March 5–11, 1990, 57.

25 *Crain's Chicago Business*, March 5–11, 1990, 64.

26 Phelan was an unsuccessful candidate for governor in the 1994 Democratic primary.

27 Dick Simpson, ed., *Blueprint of Chicago Government, 1989* (Chicago: University of Illinois at Chicago, 1989), 6.

28 James D. Nowlan, "Hope Still Blooms in East St. Louis," *St. Louis Post-Dispatch*, September 3, 1989.

29 *Report of the East St. Louis Financial Advisory Board to Governor James R. Thompson* (Springfield: East St. Louis Advisory Board, May 9, 1990). See also "Bailout Plan Proposed," *St. Louis Post-Dispatch*, Illinois Edition, May 10, 1990, 1 and 20.

30 Staci D. Kramer, "State Takes over E. St. Louis School Finances," *Chicago Tribune*, October 21, 1994.

CHAPTER NINE

1 *Chicago Enterprise*, January–February 1994.

2 Governor's 1994 budget document.

3 In the 1988 Democratic primaries, Illinois had two candidates who received serious consideration—Rev. Jesse Jackson and Senator Paul Simon. President Ronald Reagan was the only Illinois-born president. President U. S. Grant spent much of his adult life in the state. Galena has built a thriving tourism enterprise based on Grant's residence there for a year. Adlai E. Stevenson (*D*) and Charles G. Dawes (*R*) were vice-presidents.

4 Len O'Connor, *Clout: Mayor Daley and His City* (Chicago: Henry Regnery, 1975), 156–57.

5 Mitchell Locin, "Michel's 19 Terms Loom over 18th District Race," *Chicago Tribune*, October 22, 1994.

6 William Barry Furlong, "The Marvelous Double Life of Dan Rostenkowski," *Chicago Magazine*, June 1981, 152–59.

7 Steve Neal, "Despite Trouble, Rosty Still Delivers," *Chicago Sun-Times*, October 14, 1994, 39.

8 Michael Arndt, "EPA to Give Big Push to Ethanol," *Chicago Tribune*, June 30, 1994, 1.

9 Arndt, "EPA to Give Big Push."

10 Lynn Sweet and Basil Talbott, "Decatur Exec Becomes White House Regular," *Chicago Sun-Times*, October 3, 1994, 12.

11 Patrick Barry, "Gale Cincotta and Heather Booth," in *After Alinsky*, ed. Knoepfle, 54–60.

12 Lloyd Wendt and Herman Kogan, *Big Bill of Chicago* (Indianapolis: Bobbs-Merrill, 1953), 248.

13 Thompson, *Illinois, State of the State*, 119.

14 Illinois Department of Commerce and Community Affairs, International Business Division, quoted in *Chicago Enterprise*, January 1991, 21.

15 Karl Bishop, "Illinois and the World: Globetrotting Is Not Enough," in *Illinois: Problems and Promise*, ed. James D. Nowlan (Galesburg: Illinois Public Policy Press, 1986), 24.

16 Liane Clorfene-Casten, "Institute for Illinois Launches Campaign for More Federal Contracts and Grants," *Chicago Enterprise*, October 1986, 1.

17 Kathleen O'Leary Morgan, Scott Morgan, and Neal Quitno, eds., *State Rankings 1994: A Statistical View of the 50 United States* (Lawrence KS: Morgan Quitno Press, 1994), 252.

18 City of Chicago in Conjunction with Roosevelt University, Institute for Metropolitan Affairs, "Putting Federalism to Work for America: Tackling the Problems of Unfunded Mandates and Burdensome Regulations," mimeo, November 19, 1992.

19 *State Legislatures*, May 1994, 31.

CHAPTER TEN

1 Illinois Constitution, art. X.

2 For more detail see *State, Local and Federal Financing for Illinois Public Schools, 1992–93* (Springfield: Illinois State Board of Education, 1994), and *Illinois Nonpublic School Statistics, 1988–89* (Springfield: Illinois State Board of Education, 1990).

3 U.S. Department of Commerce, Bureau of the Census, *Government Finances: 1990–91* (Washington DC: GPO, 1992).

4 The enrollment figures are drawn from the annual reports of the Illinois State Board of Education. See also Michael J. Bakalis and C. Arthur Safer, "Education: State of the Region," in *The State of the Region* (Chicago: Metropolitan Planning Council, December 1988), 5-1–5-33.

5 *Chicago Tribune*, January 7, 1990.

6 For an excellent discussion of education in Illinois before 1975, see Martin Bur-

lingame, "Politics and Policies of Elementary and Secondary Education," in *Illinois*, ed. Crane, 370–89. See also Cullom Davis, "Illinois: Crossroads and Cross Section," in *Heartland*, ed. Madison, 154.

7 For more detail on school finance, see *State, Local, and Federal Financing for Illinois Public Schools, 1992–93*, and the annual reports of the Illinois State Board of Education.

8 See *The State's Role in Regulating Education—1990 Report and Recommendations* (Springfield: Illinois State Board of Education, January 1990). For an excellent discussion of values in education, including local control, see Frederick Wirt and Samuel K. Gove, "Education," in *Politics in the American States*, ed. Virginia Gray et al. (Glenview IL: Scott, Foresman, 1990), 447–78.

9 *Illinois Revised Statutes, 1990* (St. Paul: West, 1990), chap.122, art.27.

10 *Illinois Revised Statutes, 1990*, chap.122, art.27.

11 News release, Illinois State Board of Education, Springfield, June 29, 1990. See also Illinois Commission on Intergovernmental Relations, *Intergovernmental Issues* (Springfield: Illinois Commission on Intergovernmental Relations, November 1991).

12 Fred Coombs, "The Effects of Increased State Control on Local School District Governance," paper presented at the annual meeting of the American Educational Research Association, Washington, 1987, and reported in Wirt and Gove, "Education," 466–67.

13 Martin Hepner, Illinois Association of School Boards Workshop, Lombard IL, undated.

14 Coombs, "The Effects of Increased State Control."

15 Wirt and Gove, "Education," especially the section "Political Culture and Policy Choices."

16 As reported in *First Reading* (Legislative Research Unit, Illinois General Assembly, Springfield), December 1989.

17 "Education Choice Policy Recommendations" (Illinois State Board of Education, Springfield, January 10, 1990).

18 Burlingame, "Politics and Policies in Elementary and Secondary Education," 370–89, provides a thorough discussion of the development and central role played by the School Problems Commission from about 1950 up to the creation of the Illinois State Board of Education in 1971.

19 Interview with Ken Bruce, February 1, 1990, Springfield.

20 Reflection of chapter author Nowlan, who was special assistant to the governor in 1977.

21 Van Der Slik, ed., *Almanac of Illinois Politics—1994*, table 19.1, p.408.

22 Kent D. Redfield, "Investing in the General Assembly," in *Almanac of Illinois Politics—1994*, ed. Van Der Slik, 8.

23 Paul C. Bishop, "Making the Grade," *Illinois Business Review* (Bureau of Economic and Business Research, University of Illinois, Urbana), 47, no.1 (Spring 1990): 10. See also the *Comptroller's Monthly Fiscal Report* (Springfield, October 1991).

24 *State, Local and Federal Financing for Illinois Public Schools, 1988–89* (Springfield: Illinois State Board of Education, 1990).

25 Remarks before a meeting of the Voice of the Prairie, Galesburg, Illinois, October 28, 1989.

26 This section is drawn largely from Nowlan, *New Game Plan for Illinois*, 47–54, and the series in the *Chicago Tribune* in May 1988.

27 From *Chicago Schools: Worst in America* (Chicago: *Chicago Tribune*, 1988) as quoted in "A View from the Elementary Schools: The State of Reform in Chicago" (Consortium on Chicago School Research, Chicago, July 1993), 1.

28 Mary O'Connell, *School Reform Chicago Style: How Citizens Organized to Change Public Policy* (Chicago: Neighborhood Works and Center for Neighborhood Technology, 1991), 21.

29 O'Connell, *School Reform Chicago Style*, 22.

30 According to David Nasaw, big city schools were centralized in the early years of the century, when a progressive reform aimed at taking control from ethnic politicians. This was achieved in Chicago at the time of World War I. See Nasaw, *Schooled to Order: A Social History of Public Schooling in the United States* (New York: Oxford University Press, 1979), chap.7.

31 O'Connell, *School Reform Chicago Style*, 28.

32 John Camper, "Chicago School Reform Defies the Conventional Wisdom," *Illinois Issues*, January 1990, 36.

33 "A View from the Elementary Schools," 37.

34 Harold L. Hodgkinson, *Illinois: The State and Its Educational System* (Washington DC: Institute for Educational Leadership, 1989), 7.

35 From Illinois Board of Higher Education reports.

36 This background is taken from James D. Nowlan, *The Politics of Higher Education: Lawmakers and the Academy in Illinois* (Urbana: University of Illinois Press, 1976), chap.1.

37 Personal observation in private conversation with James Nowlan, undated.

38 Commission to Study Non-Public Higher Education in Illinois, *Strengthening Private Higher Education in Illinois* (Springfield: Commission to Study Non-Public Higher Education in Illinois, 1969), 5.

39 From an Ameritech Foundation study, as reported in the *Bloomington* (IL) *Pantagraph*, January 18, 1990.

CHAPTER ELEVEN

1 For a discussion of the politics of budgeting, see the chapter "Budgeting and Taxing for a New Game Plan," in Nowlan, *New Game Plan for Illinois,* 111–26.

2 For a delightful, highly instructive essay on budgeting, see Robert Mandeville, "It's the Same Old Song," in *Illinois State Budget, Fiscal Year 1991* (Springfield: Illinois Bureau of the Budget, March 1990), 1–14.

3 Illinois Constitution, 1970, art. VIII, sec. 2(a).

4 As observed by coauthor Nowlan, who was a member of the 1976 transition team.

5 Mandeville, "It's the Same Old Song," 5.

6 As reported in Nowlan, *New Game Plan for Illinois,* 113.

7 Raymond F. Coyne, "The Legislative Appropriations Process: Selective Use of Authority and Tools," in *Illinois*, ed. Crane, 287–305. A former staff member of the Illinois Economic and Fiscal Commission of the Illinois General Assembly, Coyne provides an excellent analysis of the legislature's role in budgeting.

8 Illinois Bureau of the Budget, Springfield, 1990.

9 *An Assessment of Build Illinois* (Springfield: Taxpayers' Federation of Illinois, 1987), 28.

10 Press release, "Nearly $43 Million Diverted from General Revenue Fund in FY89" (Office of the Comptroller, Springfield, May 24, 1990).

11 *Illinois Tax Handbook for Legislators* (Springfield: Illinois General Assembly Legislative Research Unit, 1994).

12 *Illinois Tax Handbook for Legislators,* 77–81.

13 From Illinois Bureau of the Budget sources as reported in "Non-Tax Revenue Raising: A Survey of Illinois' User Charges and Fees" (Taxpayers' Federation of Illinois, Springfield, 1990, draft manuscript).

14 "The Illinois Highway Program," in *State of Illinois Fiscal Condition Report* (Springfield: Office of the Comptroller, March 28, 1990).

15 Jack R. Van Der Slik, "Legalized Gamblers: Predatory Policy," *Illinois Issues*, March 1990, 30.

16 *Illinois State Budget Book, FY 1995* (Springfield: Office of the Governor, 1995), chap. 2–14.

17 "A Look at Public Aid in Illinois," in *State of Illinois Fiscal Condition Report* (Springfield: Office of the Comptroller of Illinois, October 30, 1990), 7.

18 Randy Erford, *Illinois State Spending: The Thompson Years* (Springfield: Taxpayers' Federation of Illinois, 1988), 9.

19 For an exhaustive study of property taxes in Illinois, see Ronald J. Picur and Rowan Miranda, *Taxation without Explanation* (Springfield: Taxpayers' Federation of Illinois, 1993). See also the *1994 Practical Guide to Illinois Real Estate Taxation* (Springfield: Taxpayers' Federation of Illinois, 1994), and the *Comptroller's Annual Report, 1994.*

20 Center for Governmental Studies, *The Illinois Poll* (DeKalb: Northern Illinois University, 1991).

21 Douglas L. Whitley, *Tax Facts* (Taxpayers' Federation of Illinois, Springfield) 42, no.9 (November–December 1989).

22 Thomas J. Anton, *The Politics of State Expenditure in Illinois* (Urbana: University of Illinois Press, 1966).

23 Press release, Illinois State Board of Education, Springfield, January 19, 1989.

24 For an informative look at the Bureau of the Budget, see Craig S. Bazzani, "The Executive Budget Process," in *Inside State Government in Illinois*, ed. Nowlan, 42.

25 Coyne, "Legislative Appropriations Process," 144.

26 Michael D. Klemens, "An Overture to Overcome Overspending," *Budget Watch Reporter* (Illinois Tax Foundation, Springfield), no.5 (June 1990): 1–8.

27 Michael D. Klemens, "Budget Crisis: The Seeds and the Harvest," *Illinois Issues*, August–September 1987, 46.

28 U.S. Department of Commerce, *Government Finances, 1991–92* (Washington DC: GPO, 1994).

29 Therese J. McGuire, "Illinois' State and Local Revenue System: What It Is and What It Could Be," unpublished paper for the Illinois Tax Foundation, Springfield, 1992.

30 Citizens for Tax Justice, *Far Cry from Fair: CTJ's Guide to State Tax Reform* (Washington DC: Citizens for Tax Justice, April 1991).

CHAPTER TWELVE

1 "Capital Punishment," *Chicago Magazine*, January 1994.

2 Nowlan, *New Game Plan for Illinois*, 7.

3 James W. Fossett and J. Fred Giertz, "Money, Politics, and Regionalism: Allocating State Funds in Illinois," in *Diversity, Conflict*, ed. Nardulli, 244.

4 Fossett and Giertz, "Money, Politics, and Regionalism," 237.

5 Fossett and Giertz, "Money, Politics, and Regionalism," 244–45.

6 Editorial, *Chicago Tribune*, May 29, 1994.

7 Squires, Bennett, and Ryder, *Chicago: Race, Class*, 6–7.

8 Mark Brown and Chuck Neubauer, "The Thompson Legacy: Real Insiders Reap Rewards," *Chicago Sun-Times*, October 11, 1990.

9 For an expanded discussion of patronage practices in Illinois, see James D. Nowlan, William Hanley, and Donald Udstuen, "Patronage and Personnel," in *Inside State Government in Illinois*, ed. Nowlan.

10 Howard, *Illinois: A History*, 549–50.

11 From notes taken by Nowlan in 1963–64, when he worked in Springfield, from conversations with former statehouse journalists who covered state government when Powell was Speaker of the house and later secretary of state.

12 Howard, *Illinois: A History*, 559.

13 Howard, *Illinois: A History*, 563.

14 Tuohy and Warden, *Greylord*.

15 As reported in the *Peoria Journal-Star* by Associated Press reporter Paul Driscoll, June 1, 1994.

16 This discussion is taken from Nowlan, *New Game Plan for Illinois*, 140–42.

17 The recollection of coauthor Nowlan, who operated a small political consulting firm in the 1980s.

18 Brown and Neubauer, "Thompson Legacy."

19 Recounted by coauthor Nowlan, who served as campaign manager for former U.S. senator Charles H. Percy in 1978.

20 U.S. Department of Commerce, Bureau of the Census, *Government Finances: 1990–91* (Washington DC: GPO, 1992).

21 Patrick T. Reardon, "City Can Boast the Best and the Blightest," *Chicago Tribune*, December 21, 1992.

22 Herbers, *New Heartland*, 168.

23 Herbers, *New Heartland*, p.17.

About the Authors

Samuel K. Gove is director emeritus, Institute of Government and Public Affairs, and professor of political science, emeritus, University of Illinois. He has been a student of Illinois politics throughout his career and served on many boards and commissions concerned with Illinois public policy issues. Gove was the founding chairman of *Illinois Issues* and for ten years was director of the Legislative Staff Internship Program.

Among his honors is the Samuel K. Gove Illinois Legislative Intern Hall of Fame instituted in November 1990. The plaza at the entrance to the new Institute of Government and Public Affairs building on the Urbana campus is named the Gove Plaza and was dedicated by Governor Jim Edgar in a September 1992 ceremony.

Gove has written extensively on state and local government and politics and on the politics of higher education. Among his authored and coauthored books are *Legislative Politics in Illinois* (1960); *Con-Con: Issues for the Illinois Constitutional Convention* (1970); *Revision Success: The Sixth Illinois Constitutional Convention* (1974); *Political Science and School Politics: The Prince and the Pundits* (1976); *After Daley, Chicago Politics in Transition* (1982); *Political Controversies in Higher Education* (1986); and *Governors and Higher Education* (1988).

James D. Nowlan has been an Illinois legislator, state agency director, statewide candidate, and campaign manager for U.S. senatorial and presidential candidates.

Nowlan was elected to the Illinois House of Representatives in 1968, at age twenty-six. Four years later he was the Republican candidate for lieutenant governor, running mate of Governor Richard B. Ogilvie, in an election in which they were narrowly defeated. In 1978 he managed the successful reelection campaign of U.S. senator Charles H. Percy and the following year organized the national presidential campaign of U.S. representative John B. Anderson. During the governorship of James R. Thompson (1977–90), Nowlan served in eight different capacities, including trouble shooting state agency director (three times), special assistant for education, and executive director of a special transition team that bridged the governor's third and fourth terms.

Nowlan received his Ph.D. in political science from the University of Illinois at Urbana. His books include *The Politics of Higher Education in Illinois* (1976), *Inside State Government in Illinois* (1982), and *A New Game Plan for Illinois* (1989).

A former community newspaper owner and publisher, Nowlan served as president of the Taxpayers' Federation of Illinois from 1991 to 1994. He is an adjunct professor of public policy at Knox College and a Senior Fellow with the University of Illinois Institute of Government and Public Affairs.

Index

Addams, Jane, 57

African Americans: constitution (1848) on, 69; entrance into Chicago politics by, 31–33; within General Assembly, 81; settlement of Illinois by, 11; steady in-migration of, 12–13. *See also* ethnic groups

agencies: administrative rules adopted by, 241; authorized to issue bonds, 208–9; executive branch links to, 121–23; listed, 112; of local governments, 154–55; management of, 125–28

agreed bills, 57, 91, 92

Aid to Families with Dependent Children, 212

Aleman, Harry, 135

Algren, Nelson, 9

Alinsky, Saul, 57

Almanac of Illinois Politics, 241

Altgeld, John Peter, 108

amendatory veto, 75, 114, 261 n.16

Andreas, Dwayne, 171

Andreoli, Tom, 26

antidiscrimination constitution provisions, 75

appellate courts, 131

appointive system, 137

appropriated funds: budgeting process for, 205–8; for capital projects, 208–9; priorities/needs for, 204–5; shift and shaft game for, 212–14; state budget and, 202–4; using no-pain revenues for, 209–12. *See also* government budgeting; taxes

appropriations bills, 91

Archer Daniels Midland Company (ADM), 171

Armour, Gustavus, 8

Arrington, W. Russell, 41, 79

Asian Americans, 12. *See also* ethnic groups

attorney general, 111

Attorney Registration and Disciplinary Commission, 144

auditor general, 144

Australian secret ballot, 48

Back of the Yards neighborhood, 57

Banovetz, James, 156

Bauler, "Paddy," 161

Bennett, William, 191

In the Politics and Governments of the American States series

Alabama Government and Politics
By James D. Thomas and William H. Stewart

Alaska Politics and Government
By Gerald A. McBeath and Thomas A. Morehouse

Arkansas Politics and Government: Do the People Rule?
By Diane D. Blair

Colorado Politics and Government: Governing the Centennial State
By Thomas E. Cronin and Robert D. Loevy

Illinois Politics and Government: The Expanding Metropolitan Frontier
By Samuel K. Gove and James D. Nowlan

Kentucky Politics and Government: Do We Stand United?
By Penny M. Miller

Maine Politics and Government
By Kenneth T. Palmer, G. Thomas Taylor, and Marcus A. LiBrizzi

Michigan Politics and Government: Facing Change in a Complex State
By William P. Browne and Kenneth VerBurg

Mississippi Government and Politics: Modernizers versus Traditionalists
By Dale Krane and Stephen D. Shaffer

Nebraska Government and Politics
Edited by Robert D. Miewald

Nevada Politics and Government: Conservatism in an Open Society
By Don W. Driggs and Leonard E. Goodall

New Jersey Politics and Government: Suburban Politics Comes of Age
By Barbara G. Salmore and Stephen A. Salmore

North Carolina Government and Politics
By Jack D. Fleer

Oklahoma Politics and Policies: Governing the Sooner State
By David R. Morgan, Robert E. England, and George G. Humphreys

South Carolina Politics and Government
By Cole Blease Graham Jr. and William V. Moore